PUGLIA TRAVEL GUIDE

Your Ultimate Companion to Italy's Enchanting South –
Unveiling Secret Spots, Timeless Traditions, and Breathtaking
Landscapes for an Unforgettable Adventure of a Lifetime

Nicholas Ingram

Copyright © 2024 Nicholas Ingram

This travel guide is protected by copyright law. Reproduction, distribution, or transmission in any form without the author's prior written permission is prohibited, except for brief quotations in critical reviews and certain noncommercial uses allowed by copyright law. Unauthorized reproduction or distribution may result in civil and criminal penalties, including fines and imprisonment. Readers have a limited license for personal, non-commercial use; any other use requires explicit written permission. By accessing and using this guide, readers agree to respect the outlined copyright and disclaimer provisions.

The information in this guide is based on the author's experiences, research, and knowledge up to the publication date. While efforts have been made to ensure accuracy, the author and publisher are not liable for changes, inaccuracies, or omissions after this date. Travel conditions may change, and readers should independently verify details before making arrangements. The author and publisher do not assume responsibility for readers' actions following the guide, as travel involves inherent risks. Readers are advised to exercise caution and make informed decisions based on their individual circumstances.

For permissions requests or complaints, please contact: *theworldexplorergs@gmail.com*

Vieste

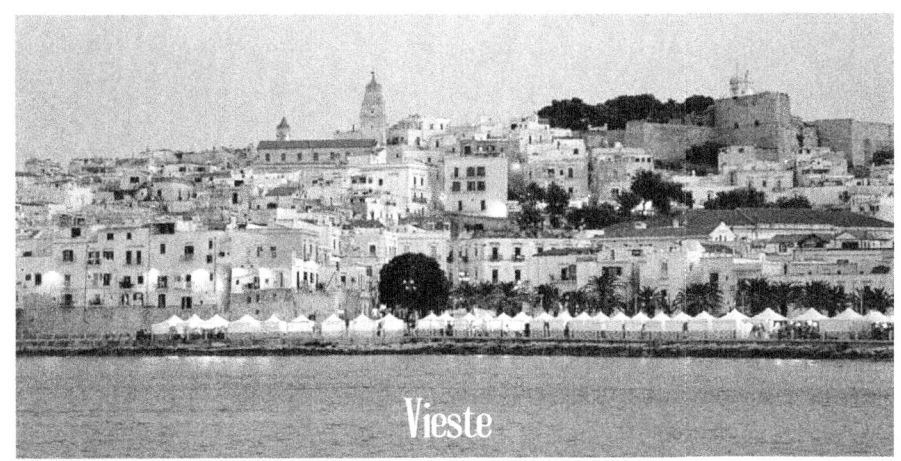

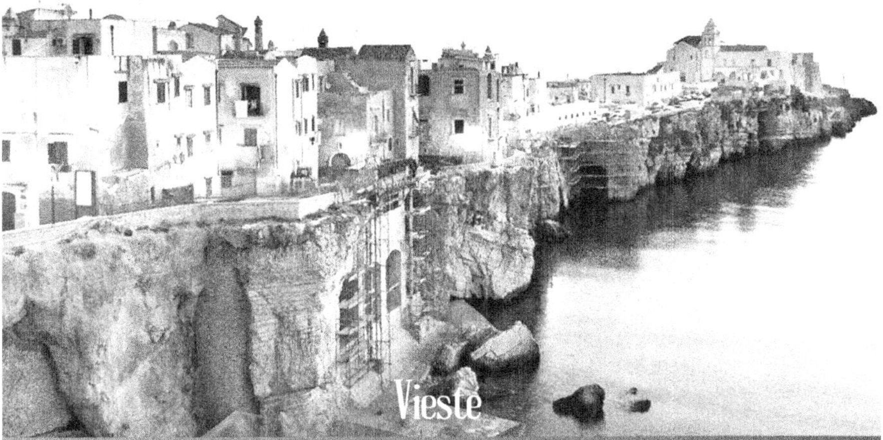
Vieste

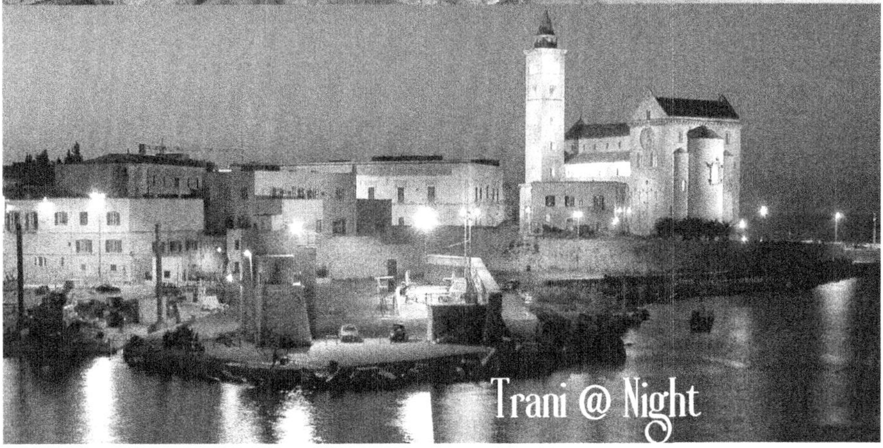
Trani @ Night

Ostuni

Monopoli

Coast of Otranto

Locorotondo

Castello di Monte Sant'Angelo

Trani

Ceglie Messapica, Puglia,

The Trulli of Alberobello

Piazza Del Duomo - Lecce

HOW TO USE THIS GUIDE

This extensive guide endeavors to serve as your ultimate resource for orchestrating a memorable excursion to Puglia. Whether you're a seasoned explorer or setting foot in the region for the first time, this guide offers invaluable insights, suggestions, and advice to personalize your experience in Puglia.

Introduction: Read through the introduction to gain insights into the history and allure of Puglia, as well as essential tips and considerations before embarking on your journey.

Familiarizing Yourself with Puglia: Explore Chapter 1 to understand Puglia's geographical location, climate, and top destinations, providing a solid foundation for your travel plans.

Planning Your Puglian Adventure: Dive into Chapter 2 for guidance on the best time to visit Puglia, how to reach the region, and transportation options within Puglia, ensuring a smooth and efficient travel experience.

Exploring Puglia: Navigate through Chapter 3 to discover the diverse regions of Puglia, including the Gargano Peninsula, Terra di Bari, the Itria Valley, and Salento, with detailed insights into each area's highlights and attractions.

Puglia's Finest Beaches: Refer to Chapter 4 for recommendations on experiencing the coastal splendor of Puglia, including top beaches near major cities and insider tips for beach exploration.

Indulging in Puglia's Culinary Wonders: Delve into Chapter 5 for a mouthwatering journey through Puglia's culinary scene, featuring must-try dishes, top dining spots, and opportunities for culinary experiences.

Immersive Puglian Experiences: Explore Chapter 6 to discover unique and immersive activities in Puglia, from wine tasting and olive oil tours to cycling adventures and traditional music and dance performances.

Shopping and Souvenirs: Browse Chapter 7 for guidance on purchasing souvenirs and exploring the vibrant shopping scene in Puglia, ensuring you bring home cherished mementos of your journey.

Practical Information: Consult Chapter 8 for practical tips and resources, including essential Italian phrases, packing advice, recommended reading and films, useful websites and apps, and tourist information centers.

Detailed 8-Day Itinerary: Plan your Puglian adventure with precision using the detailed 8-day itinerary provided in Chapter 9, offering day-by-day exploration plans for discovering the highlights of the region.

Bonus Chapter: Explore the Bonus Chapter for hidden gems, family-friendly activities, romantic experiences, and recommended romantic hotels, adding extra depth and excitement to your Puglia adventure.

Additional Recommendations:
⇾ Employ the Table of Contents for swift access to particular sections.
⇾ Take advantage of the "Explore Puglia" segments to craft a bespoke itinerary aligning with your preferences and schedule.
⇾ Ensure not to overlook the bonus chapter, unveiling concealed gems and distinctive adventures.
⇾ Throughout the guide, embedded hyperlinks lead to supplementary websites, maps, and materials for deeper investigation.
⇾ Keep in mind: This guide serves as a launchpad. Allow your inquisitiveness to lead the way as you uncover the enchantment of Puglia, forging enduring memories.

By following this guide step-by-step, you'll be equipped to embark on a memorable journey through Puglia, immersing yourself in its rich culture, breathtaking landscapes, and unforgettable experiences.

Bon voyage!

CONTENTS

HOW TO USE THIS GUIDE
INTRODUCTION
A Brief History of Puglia
Why Puglia Should Top Your Travel Bucket List
Recommended Duration for a Visit to Puglia
Cost of Visiting Puglia
27 Things to Know Before You Go to puglia

CHAPTER 1: GETTING ACQUAINTED WITH PUGLIA	1
Location of Puglia	2
Geography, Climate & Weather of Puglia	3
The Provinces of Puglia	4
Best Places to Visit in Puglia	6
CHAPTER 2: PLANNING YOUR PUGLIAN ADVENTURE	9
Best Time to Visit Puglia	10
How to Get to Puglia	11
Getting Around Puglia	13
CHAPTER 3: EXPLORING PUGLIA	14
PART 1: THE GARGANO PENINSULA	15
Vieste	16
Monte Sant'Angelo	21
Foresta Umbra	25
Peschici	28
Tremiti Islands	32
Other Towns Worth Exploring in the Gargano Peninsula	38
PART 2: TERRA DI BARI	40
Bari	41

Trani	48
Polignano a Mare	52
Monopoli	58
Castel del Monte	62
Other Terra Di Bari Towns Worth Exploring	65
PART 3: THE ITRIA VALLEY	67
Alberobello	68
Locorotondo	73
Cisternino	77
Ostuni	81
Martina Franca	86
Other Itira Valley Towns Worth Exploring	91
PART 4: SALENTO	92
Lecce	93
Otranto	101
Gallipoli	107
Santa Maria di Leuca	112
Other Salento Towns Worth Exploring	118
CHAPTER 4: THE BEST BEACHES OF PUGLIA	119
LIDOS: Italian Beach Clubs	120
Top Beaches Near Bari and Ostuni	121
Top Beaches in Salento	122
Best Beaches in Gargano	123
Tips for Exploring Puglia's Beaches	124
CHAPTER 5: SAVORING PUGLIA CULINARY DELIGHTS	125
20 Must-Eat Puglian Cuisine	126
Best Places to Dine & Wine in Puglia	130
Top Seafood Dining Spots in Puglia	133

Puglia's Food Festival	135
Cooking Classes: Mastering Puglian Cuisine	137
CHAPTER 6: PUGLIAN IMMERSIVE EXEEPRIENCES	138
Wine Tasting & Tours	139
Olive Oil Tours and Tastings	142
Cycling	143
Hiking	145
Watersports	146
Horseback Riding	147
Puglian Folk Music and Dance	148
Puglia Festivals and Events Calendar	150
CHAPTER 7: SHOPPING & SOUVENIRS	153
Top 5 Souvenirs to Take Home From Puglia	154
Best Places for Shopping in Puglia	156
CHAPTER 8: PRACTICAL INFORMATION	158
60 Basic Useful Italian Phrases and Vocabulary	160
Packing Tips	162
Useful Contacts	163
Books To Read Before Visiting Puglia	164
Movies to Watch Before Exploring Apulia	165
Useful Websites for Visiting Puglia	166
Useful Apps To Explore Puglia	167
Puglian Tourist Information Centers	168
CHAPTER 9: DETAILED ITINERARY FOR EXPLORING PUGLIA IN 8-DAYS	169
Day 1 - Discovering Bari & Authentic Puglia Vibes	170
Day 2: Bari to Matera	171
Day 3: Nature Trekking & Rupestrian Churches in Matera	173

Day 4: Matera to Lecce via the Valle d'Itria	174
Day 5: Discovering Baroque Lecce	176
Day 6: Traveling from Leuca to Otranto	178
Day 7: Coastal Relaxation in Savelletri	180
Day 8: Beachside Leisure, Culinary Delights & Polignano a Mare	181
EXPLORE THE GARGANO PENINSULA & THE COAST OF PUGLIA IN 8 DAYS	182
BONUS CHAPTER	184
Off the Beaten Path: Secret Gems & Hidden Treasures	185
Top 10 Family-Friendly Activities in Puglia	189
Top Puglian Romantic Experiences	191
Romantic Hotels in Puglia (Recommendation)	193
CONCLUSION	194

INTRODUCTION

Welcome, wanderers, to the sun-kissed haven of Puglia, where time dances in harmony with ancient olive groves and whispers of a captivating past echo through its limestone streets. Nestled in the heel of Italy's boot, this enchanting region awaits those seeking a symphony of cultural richness, pristine coastlines, and a tapestry of flavors that tell the tale of centuries gone by.

As dawn breaks over the Adriatic Sea, painting the sky with hues of coral and gold, you'll find yourself drawn to the rugged beauty of Puglia's coastline. Here, hidden sea caves and secret coves beckon, inviting intrepid souls to explore the mysterious allure of the Grotte di Castellana. Venture beneath the earth's surface and marvel at the intricate stalactite formations, a silent witness to the passage of time.

Puglia's landscape is an artist's palette, where rolling hills adorned with silvery olive trees stretch as far as the eye can see. Trulli, the iconic conical dwellings with whitewashed walls, stand like ancient sentinels, guarding the stories of generations past. Explore the UNESCO-listed town of Alberobello, where these whimsical structures transport you to a fairytale realm, their limestone domes adorned with symbols of ancient folklore. As you meander through the narrow, winding streets of Ostuni, the "White City," feel the history beneath your fingertips. Whitewashed buildings, perched high on a hill, offer panoramic views of the Adriatic Sea, while the scent of citrus and jasmine fills the air. Lose yourself in the labyrinth of alleys, discovering hidden chapels and vibrant piazzas where locals gather to share laughter and espresso.

Puglia's gastronomic scene is a celebration of simplicity and tradition. Indulge in the robust flavors of local cuisine, where orecchiette pasta dances with fresh tomato sauce, and the earthy aroma of olive oil infuses every dish. Savor the fruits of the sea at seaside trattorias, where the catch of the day is transformed into culinary masterpieces that linger on the palate.

Step back in time as you explore the ancient city of Matera, with its sassi, cave dwellings carved into the limestone cliffs. The haunting beauty of Matera's historic center, a UNESCO World Heritage site, tells a story of resilience and rebirth. Wander through narrow alleys that wind between ancient churches and cavernous homes, transporting you to a bygone era.

Puglia is a captivating symphony of contrasts and invites you to explore its tranquil countryside and lively coastal rhythms. Immerse yourself in the seamless blend of history and vibrancy, where sun-drenched landscapes and ageless charm converge.

A BRIEF HISTORY OF PUGLIA

Puglia, nestled like the sun's embrace at the heel of Italy's boot, harbors an illustrious past steeped in antiquity. Its fertile soil has borne witness to the ebb and flow of civilizations, the blossoming of cultures, and the genesis of enduring customs that continue to enchant travelers to this day. Join us on a journey across the ages as we unveil the layers of Puglia's captivating history:

GENESIS IN PREHISTORY: The tale of Puglia unfolds amidst the mists of time, where traces of Paleolithic settlements scattered across the land whisper of the earliest inhabitants who once traversed these ancient grounds. | **HELLENIC FOOTPRINTS:** In the 8th century BC, Greek settlers, drawn by Puglia's fecund plains and strategic position, established thriving city-states such as Taranto and Brindisi, laying the cornerstone for what would evolve into the renowned Magna Graecia (Greater greece). | **ROMAN LEGACY:** By the 3rd century BC, the insatiable expansion of Rome cast its shadow over Puglia, leaving an indelible imprint on the region. The Romans forged roads like the legendary Appian Way and bestowed upon Puglia architectural marvels such as the amphitheater in Lecce during their over 700 years reign over Puglia. | **BYZANTINE EPOCH:** Following the decline of Rome, Puglia became a bastion of the Byzantine Empire for centuries. This era witnessed the efflorescence of Christianity, epitomized by the construction of grand basilicas like the resplendent one in Trani. | **NORMAN CONQUEST:** The 11th century heralded the arrival of the Normans, a stalwart people who carved out their dominion in southern Italy. Their legacy endures in the form of majestic castles like the UNESCO-acclaimed Castel del Monte. | **HOHENSTAUFEN RENAISSANCE:** The ascendancy of the formidable Hohenstaufen dynasty ushered in a golden age for Puglia. Emperor Frederick II, renowned for his patronage of the arts and sciences, left an indelible mark on the region's cultural landscape. | **ANGEVIN INFLUENCE:** The 13th century saw Puglia under the sway of the Angevins, whose artistic legacy adorns the region in the form of Gothic cathedrals and adorned churches. | **SPANISH DOMINION:** In subsequent centuries, Puglia fell under the dominion of the Spanish Habsburgs and later the Bourbons. This era of relative stability fostered agricultural prosperity and the nurturing of distinctive local customs. | **UNIFICATION AND PROGRESS:** In the 19th century, Puglia became an integral part of unified Italy. Today, it stands as a vibrant testament to its storied past, blending cherished traditions with modern advancements.

Puglia's history is an intricate tapestry woven with threads of ancient civilizations, medieval kingdoms, and artistic renaissances. Each era has left an indelible mark on the landscape, the architecture, and the spirit of its people. As you traverse Puglia, remember that you tread upon ground once trodden by emperors, philosophers, and ordinary folk who collectively shaped this captivating region into the veritable gem it is today.

WHY PUGLIA SHOULD TOP YOUR TRAVEL BUCKET LIST

<u>Enchantment at Every Turn</u>
<u>Scenic Marvels:</u> Immerse yourself in a tapestry of landscapes featuring undulating olive groves stretching as far as the eye can see, glistening coastlines adorned with secluded coves inviting quiet contemplation, quaint whitewashed towns perched atop rugged cliffs offering breathtaking vistas of the azure sea, and trulli houses—charming structures crowned with iconic conical roofs that seem straight out of a storybook.

<u>Rich Historical Tapestry:</u> Embark on a journey through time as you traverse ancient Greek and Roman ruins, where echoes of civilizations past linger amidst weathered stones and crumbling columns. Explore medieval fortresses that once stood as bastions of power and prestige, and stroll through baroque townscapes adorned with ornate facades and grandiose palaces, each bearing witness to Puglia's storied past.

<u>Artistic Splendor:</u> Delight in the vibrant canvases of street art that adorn urban alleys, telling tales of contemporary life and cultural fusion. Lose yourself in the hypnotic rhythms of traditional pizzica dance performances, where swirling skirts and tambourines create an electrifying atmosphere. And marvel at the intricate craftsmanship of local ceramic artisans, whose masterpieces reflect centuries of tradition and ingenuity.

A Gastronomic Delight

Culinary Paradise: Treat your taste buds to the freshest seafood imaginable, plucked straight from the crystalline waters of the Adriatic and transformed into culinary masterpieces bursting with flavor. Sample handmade orecchiette pasta, lovingly crafted by skilled hands and bathed in fragrant olive oil sourced from ancient groves that dot the landscape. And savor the creamy decadence of burrata cheese, a delicacy so divine it practically melts on your tongue. And of course, no culinary journey through Puglia would be complete without indulging in the region's internationally renowned Primitivo wines, whose bold flavors and rich history reflect the very essence of Puglian terroir.

Laid-Back Lifestyle: Embrace the unhurried rhythm of Puglian life, where time seems to slow to a leisurely pace and every moment is savored with effortless grace. Spend lazy afternoons basking in the golden glow of the sun, sipping espresso at bustling cafes, or simply strolling through labyrinthine alleyways steeped in history and charm. And as evening falls, join locals for leisurely dinners at cozy trattorias, where laughter rings out amidst the

clinking of glasses and the aroma of freshly cooked pasta fills the air.
Heartfelt Hospitality: Experience the genuine warmth and hospitality of Puglia's inhabitants, whose open-hearted welcome makes you feel like family from the moment you arrive. Engage in lively conversations with locals eager to share their stories and traditions, and immerse yourself in the rich tapestry of Puglian culture through authentic experiences that celebrate the land's bounty and the spirit of community.

Beyond the Ordinary

Unspoiled Wilderness: Embark on thrilling adventures in Gargano National Park, where hidden beaches await discovery amidst towering cliffs and rugged coastline.

Hike through the majestic peaks and verdant valleys of the Apulian Dolomites, where panoramic vistas and pristine wilderness beckon to intrepid explorers. Or pedal your way through serene olive groves bathed in the golden light of the Mediterranean sun, where the scent of wildflowers fills the air and the sound of cicadas serenades you along the way.
Authentic Encounters: Dive deep into the heart of Puglia's culinary traditions with immersive olive oil tastings that reveal the secrets of the region's liquid gold. Roll up your sleeves and master the art of pasta-making alongside local artisans, whose time-honored techniques have been passed down through generations. Or immerse yourself in the age-old tradition of the harvest season, where families and communities come together to celebrate the abundance of the land with music, dance, and feasting.

Hidden Charms: Escape the tourist crowds and uncover secret treasures tucked away in Puglia's hidden corners. Explore the enchanting trulli valley of Alberobello, where rows of whimsical cone-shaped dwellings transport you to another time and place. Or wander through the picturesque cliffside town of Polignano a Mare, where whitewashed buildings cling to the rugged coastline, offering breathtaking views of the turquoise sea below.

Seaside serenity, cultural immersion, or gastronomic delights, Puglia offers an unforgettable odyssey that tantalizes the senses and nourishes the soul. It's a realm where time seems to stand still, where landscapes inspire wonder, and where every corner whispers tales of heritage and passion. So, pack your bags, secure your flight, and allow Puglia to captivate your senses!

Puglia isn't just a destination—it's an immersion in the art of living, a celebration of life's simple pleasures and timeless treasures.

RECOMMENDED DURATION FOR A VISIT TO PUGLIA

Determining the ideal duration for exploring Puglia can be quite a task. Puglia is vast, and while some guides suggest that a comprehensive tour can be completed in just 5 days, the reality is far from it. To truly experience Puglia, a minimum of 7 days is necessary. However, for a more relaxed and immersive journey, spanning 7 to 14 days is recommended.

With a week at your disposal, it's advisable to concentrate on two specific areas & establish a base in each. Consider spending 3 to 4 days exploring the regions around Ostuni, Savelletri, and the Valle d'Itria, followed by another 3 days in Salento, opting for a base in Lecce or a charming coastal town like Otranto or Gallipoli. This strategic approach ensures that each base offers convenient access to the main attractions & beaches in its respective region, eliminating the need for frequent packing & unpacking throughout the week.

Should your itinerary include Matera, the surroundings of Bari, or the Gargano Peninsula, extending your stay beyond a week becomes imperative. Attempting to cover the entirety of Puglia in just 7 days is impractical and likely to result in excessive time spent in transit.

COST OF VISITING PUGLIA

A decade ago, the response to this inquiry would have been a resounding "no." However, times have changed. Puglia is no longer considered a budget-friendly destination. You should anticipate prices to be relatively on par with other regions in Italy, particularly during the summer months when cities and towns are bustling, accommodations are fully booked, and restaurants require advance reservations. With Puglia emerging as a prominent tourist hotspot, pricing has adjusted accordingly.

Nevertheless, there are still opportunities to find excellent bargains in Puglia, though it may require some effort. Opting to stay in the countryside outside of main urban centers or booking accommodations directly through methods other than major booking platforms like Booking, Expedia, and Airbnb can yield significant savings, sometimes up to 30% or more. Additionally, negotiating discounts for cash payments is common practice.

Another effective cost-saving strategy is to avoid visiting during peak seasons. Hotel rates can skyrocket during the summer months of June, July, and August (with early September still considered high season), but prices drop considerably during the spring or fall. Despite the overall increase in prices, dining expenses in Puglia remain relatively reasonable compared to major cities and tourist hubs such as Rome, Florence, Venice, and the Amalfi Coast. Enjoying a satisfying meal at local restaurants, without indulging excessively in wine, typically costs around 50 euros for two people. Of course, there are opportunities to spend more if desired.

Here's a brief breakdown of expenses:

LODGING: Hostels and B&Bs are available for less than €50 per night, while mid-range hotels typically range between €50 and €100. Luxury accommodations and Masserias (traditional farmhouses) may exceed €200 per night. | **DINING:** Puglia is renowned for its delectable and fresh cuisine. Street food, pizza, and pasta dishes are quite economical, priced at approximately €5-€10. Sit-down meals at restaurants can vary from €15 to €50, depending on the location and culinary offerings. | **TRANSPORTATION:** Public transportation is relatively inexpensive, with bus fares typically ranging from €2 to €5. Renting a car provides more freedom to explore the region but comes at a higher cost, starting at around €30 per day.
ACTIVITIES: Admission fees to attractions vary, but are generally reasonable. For instance, entrance to Castel del Monte is €6, while boat excursions along the coast begin at around €20. | **CAR RENTALS:** The prices for renting have surged notably, now reaching over 80 euros per day. | **OFF-SEASON PRICES:** During off-season and shoulder seasons, prices vary greatly from those during peak season. Expect hotel rates to be roughly half of what they are during high season, and anticipate significant drops in prices for various amenities and services, particularly for car rentals.

27 THINGS TO KNOW BEFORE YOU GO TO PUGLIA

Puglia has emerged as a prominent destination on Italy's travel map. However, its rise to prominence is relatively recent, spanning the last 15 years. This newfound attention has uncovered much of the region's authenticity, yet navigating Puglia's travel landscape isn't as straightforward as in more established tourist hubs in Italy. Below a list of 27 essential insights to equip you with a holistic understanding of what to expect in Puglia. Let's start with some general pointers and then delve into specific tips, advice, and intriguing details to ensuring your Puglia experience is enriching and unforgettable!

1. PUGLIA IS LOCATED IN SOUTHERN ITALY

Situated in the southern region of Italy, Puglia forms the "heel of the boot" and lies in the far southeast. Southern Italy, often referred to as "mezzogiorno" in Italian, extends from south of Rome. Culturally and geographically distinct from the north, Southern Italy has a rich history shaped by various empires and civilizations, including the Greeks, Swabians, Normans, and Spanish. Puglia, with its unique heritage, reflects this rich tapestry of influences, setting it apart from the northern regions.

2. PUGLIA'S EXTENSIVE GEOGRAPHY

Puglia stretches across a long, slender peninsula, making travel times considerable. For instance, a journey from Vieste in the north to Otranto in the south takes approximately 4.5 hours by car, highlighting the region's vast expanse.

3. DUAL COASTLINES

As a peninsula, Puglia boasts two distinct coastlines: the Adriatic and Ionian. The Adriatic coast, characterized by destinations like Gargano and Otranto, contrasts with the sandy shores of the Ionian coast, featuring gems like Gallipoli and Porto Cesareo.

4. PRIME BEACH LOCATIONS

The most pristine beaches in Puglia are found in the northern Gargano and southern Salento regions, along with Ostuni. While the Gargano peninsula offers picturesque spots like Vieste and Peschici, Salento's coastline boasts crystal-clear waters, especially north of Otranto and around Gallipoli.

5. PRIVATE BEACH AREAS

Beaches in Puglia often feature private sections, known as "lidi," typically equipped with loungers and umbrellas for a fee. While technically illegal to privatize beaches, access to certain stretches may require payment, limiting public access. Visitors should inquire beforehand to ensure a hassle-free beach experience.

6. DUAL AIRPORTS

Puglia is served by two international airports: Karol Wojtyla Airport in Bari and Papola Casale (Salento Airport) in Brindisi. While both offer convenient access, choosing the nearest airport depends on your specific destination within Puglia.

7. TRAIN TRAVEL OPTIONS

Traveling to Puglia by train, though slower, is feasible with high-speed connections from Rome and Naples to Bari and Brindisi. However, train services beyond these cities are limited, necessitating alternative modes of transportation for exploring remote areas.

8. LIMITED PUBLIC TRANSPORT

Public transportation in Puglia is relatively inadequate compared to other regions in Italy. While train services are reliable within urban areas, rural connectivity is scarce, often requiring multiple connections and offering limited access to beaches and countryside.

9. CAR RENTAL ESSENTIAL

Given Puglia's vast landscape and limited public transport, renting a car is indispensable for exploring the region comprehensively. A car offers flexibility and convenience, allowing access to remote areas and scenic coastal drives.

10. LANGUAGE CONSIDERATIONS

While English is widely spoken in urban centers, rural areas may have limited English proficiency. Learning basic Italian phrases can facilitate communication and enhance cultural immersion during your Puglia experience.

11. IDEAL DURATION

To fully appreciate Puglia's diverse offerings, a minimum week-long stay is recommended. With shorter stays, you may only scratch the surface of prominent destinations, whereas longer durations allow for in-depth exploration across various regions.

12. OPTIMAL TRAVEL SEASONS

To avoid crowds and scorching temperatures, consider visiting Puglia during shoulder seasons, such as late Spring or early Fall. These periods offer pleasant weather, fewer tourists, and more affordable prices compared to peak summer months.

13. KEY REGIONS TO EXPLORE

When planning your itinerary, focus on four main areas: the Gargano Peninsula, Salento Peninsula, Terra di Bari, and the Itria Valley. Each region offers unique attractions, from coastal retreats to historic towns and lush countryside.

14. MULTI-BASE ITINERARY

Given Puglia's expansive geography, opting for multiple bases ensures efficient exploration without excessive travel times. Strategically selecting bases near key attractions facilitates convenient day trips and maximizes sightseeing opportunities.

15. RELAXED PACE

Embrace the leisurely pace of life in Puglia, where everything, from transportation to restaurant service, operates at a slower rhythm. Cultivate patience and immerse yourself in the region's laid-back charm for a truly authentic experience.

16. CASH CONVENIENCE

While credit cards are widely accepted, carrying cash is advisable, especially for transactions at smaller establishments. Cash payments often yield better deals and ensure smooth transactions, particularly in rural areas.

17. MODERATE EXPENSES

Despite being more affordable than popular tourist hubs, Puglia's rising popularity has led to increased prices. Budget-conscious travelers can still find bargains, especially during shoulder seasons, offering excellent value for money.

18. MATERA EXPLORATION

Though technically not part of Puglia, Matera in Basilicata is easily accessible and worth a visit. Renowned for its ancient cave dwellings, Matera offers a fascinating contrast to Puglia's coastal landscapes.

19. ALBEROBELLO CAUTION

While Alberobello's iconic trulli houses attract visitors, the town's tourist-centric atmosphere can detract from its authenticity. Visit early in the morning or late in the evening to avoid crowds and fully appreciate its charm.

20. LECCE'S ALLURE

Lecce, Puglia's crown jewel, boasts stunning Baroque architecture and a relaxed ambiance. Explore its historic core, savor local delicacies, and indulge in the city's timeless charm for an unforgettable experience.

21. BARI'S RENAISSANCE

Despite past perceptions, Bari offers a vibrant culinary scene, historic landmarks, and captivating coastal views. Spend a day exploring its diverse attractions, dispelling outdated notions and discovering its hidden gems.

22. GASTRONOMIC DELIGHTS

Puglia's culinary heritage is celebrated for its simplicity and freshness, with locally sourced ingredients taking center stage. Indulge in regional specialties like orecchiette pasta, burrata cheese, and frisella bread for a true taste of Puglia.

23. PRISTINE OLIVE GROVES

Puglia is renowned for its olive oil production, boasting vast groves dotted across its landscape. Visit local farms and olive mills to learn about traditional production methods and sample high-quality olive oil straight from the source.

24. WINE TASTING EXPERIENCES

Puglia's wine industry is flourishing, with indigenous grape varieties yielding unique and flavorful wines. Embark on wine tasting tours in regions like Salento and the Itria Valley to discover Puglia's diverse viticultural landscape.

25. FESTIVE TRADITIONS

Immerse yourself in Puglia's vibrant cultural heritage by participating in traditional festivals and events. From religious processions to folkloric celebrations, these gatherings offer insight into the region's rich traditions and community spirit.

26. HOSPITALITY AND WARMTH

Experience Puglia's renowned hospitality firsthand through interactions with locals, who exude warmth and generosity. Embrace their welcoming nature, engage in conversations, and forge meaningful connections for an authentic travel experience.

27. SUSTAINABLE TRAVEL PRACTICES

Respect Puglia's natural and cultural heritage by practicing sustainable travel habits. Minimize environmental impact, support local communities, and contribute positively to the region's preservation for future generations to enjoy.

Embarking on a journey to Puglia promises a captivating blend of history, culture, and natural beauty. By heeding these essential insights and embracing the region's unique character, you'll embark on a transformative travel experience that transcends mere sightseeing.

CHAPTER 1: GETTING ACQUAINTED WITH PUGLIA

Scan this QR Code to explore the full Map of Puglia

Puglia, the enchanting heel of Italy's boot, promises an unforgettable journey filled with sensory delights and cultural treasures. Ancient olive groves dot the landscape, while hilltop towns like Alberobello and Ostuni radiate with Mediterranean charm. Indulge in culinary bliss with warm bread, flavorful orecchiette pasta, and creamy burrata, accompanied by local wines like Primitivo and Negroamaro. Discover hidden coves along the coastline, from the turquoise waters of Salento to the grottoes of Polignano a Mare. Immerse yourself in Puglia's rich history, exploring Baroque cathedrals, ancient castles, and UNESCO-listed trulli houses. Whether by car, train, or foot, Puglia invites you to explore, savor, and fall in love with its captivating beauty.

LOCATION OF PUGLIA

Position of Puglia on the Italian Map

Puglia, situated in southeastern Italy, forms the distinctive "heel" of the Italian boot and encompasses Italy's easternmost point. The region's capital, Bari, _lies approximately 455 km (252 miles) from Rome by road_, while _Naples, the largest city in southern Italy, is around 259 km (160 miles) from Bari_. Traveling from Rome to Bari typically takes just under 5 hours, whereas the journey from Naples to Bari spans approximately 3 hours. On its eastern flank, Puglia is bordered by the Adriatic Sea, directly opposite the Balkan nation of Albania, while its western boundary meets the Ionian Sea and shares borders with the Italian regions of Basilicata and Campania.

The proximity of Greece is notable, evident in the convenient ferry connections available from the ports of Brindisi and Bari to Greek islands like Corfu. These connections underscore the region's accessibility to neighboring countries and destinations.

GEOGRAPHY, CLIMATE & WEATHER OF PUGLIA

GEOGRAPHY: Puglia is a region graced with breathtaking geography and a pleasant Mediterranean climate that welcomes visitors throughout the year. Its landscape presents a captivating blend of features: from undulating hills covered in olive orchards to rugged coastlines caressed by the Adriatic and Ionian Seas. The Gargano Peninsula extends northward, adorned with forests and picturesque hillside villages. In the central region, the Murge plateau rises, while the southern Salento peninsula boasts endless beaches and secluded coves. With an impressive 800 kilometers of coastline, Puglia offers a diverse range of seaside experiences. Sandy expanses such as Salento's Marina Serra and Torre Canne beckon for sunbathing and swimming, while rocky inlets near Polignano a Mare and Monopoli offer striking vistas and pristine waters for diving and snorkeling.

CLIMATE AND WEATHER: Puglia enjoys a classic Mediterranean climate, characterized by hot, dry summers and mild, wet winters, boasting approximately 300 sunny days annually. During the peak *summer months of June to August*, temperatures often soar into the mid-30s Celsius (high 80s Fahrenheit), prompting sun-seekers and beach enthusiasts to flock to the shores of the Adriatic and Ionian Seas for relief. *Spring (April-May) and autumn (September-October)* present milder temperatures, perfect for exploring Puglia's quaint towns and villages amidst blooming wildflowers in spring and the vibrant harvest season in autumn. Even in *winter*, Puglia maintains relatively mild temperatures, rarely dropping below freezing. This season offers opportunities for leisurely strolls through historic sites, indulging in local cuisine, and immersing oneself in the festive ambiance of Christmas and New Year.

THE PROVINCES OF PUGLIA

Puglia is administratively divided into six provinces: Bari (serving as the regional capital), Brindisi, Foggia, Lecce, Taranto, and the newly established province of Barletta-Andria-Trani.

1. BARI: Serving as the regional hub, Bari is a bustling port city characterized by its picturesque historic center and dynamic waterfront. Notably, the province is renowned for its Trulli houses, distinctive cone-shaped stone residences prevalent in the Itria Valley.

2. BARLETTA-ANDRIA-TRANI: This province embodies a fusion of ancient heritage, medieval towns, & breathtaking coastal landscapes. **Barletta** boasts a majestic castle, while **Andria** is celebrated for its Romanesque cathedral. Trani, overlooking the Adriatic Sea, charms with its whitewashed buildings & scenic harbor.

3. BRINDISI: Dubbed the "Gateway to the East," Brindisi has served as a pivotal port city for centuries. The province is peppered with archaeological sites, including the Roman remnants of Egnatia and the Messapian tombs of Torre Guaceto.

4. LECCE: Revered as the "Florence of the South," Lecce dazzles with its wealth of Baroque architecture. The city's historic center showcases ornate churches and palaces, while the surrounding countryside is adorned with quaint villages and olive groves.

5. FOGGIA: Serving as the agricultural nucleus of Puglia, this province is famed for its fertile plains and bountiful production of wheat, tomatoes, and olives. Foggia itself exudes vitality and boasts a rich historical legacy, while the scenic Gargano Peninsula to the north offers spectacular coastline and national parks.

6. TARANTO: Situated on a natural harbor, Taranto is a major industrial center steeped in captivating Greek and Roman history. The province also encompasses the Terra delle Gravine, a network of canyons and caves that showcase breathtaking natural scenery.

Each province encapsulates its own distinct character and allure, providing a diverse array of experiences for visitors to Puglia.

BEST PLACES TO VISIT IN PUGLIA

Apulian Territories

Geographically and culturally, Puglia can be delineated into six distinct areas: **_Gargano and Daunia_**, situated at the northernmost tip of the region. | **_Imperial Puglia_**, located just below Gargano and Daunia.
| **_Magna Graecia, Murgia, and Gravine_**, featuring Taranto along the Ionian Sea.
| **_Bari and the coastal areas_**, positioned along the Adriatic Sea. | **_Valle d'Itria_**, renowned as the land of trulli. | **Salento**, representing the southernmost extremity of Italy's heel. Spanning from the Gargano region in the north to the southern city of Salento, Puglia showcases a myriad of distinctive treasures and architectural marvels.

1. GARGANO & DAUNIA: To one side lies the captivating coastline, adorned with stunning coves, sea caves, pristine golden beaches, & crystalline waters. On the other side, stretches the verdant expanse of the **Gargano National Park**, characterized by lush woods & forests waiting to be explored on horseback, on foot, or by bicycle. Along the coastal stretch between **_Peschici_** and **_Vieste_**, you'll encounter intriguing wooden structures suspended above the water. These are *trabucchi*, ancient fishing contraptions now repurposed into charming seaside restaurants. The silhouette of the ***Tremiti Islands*** graces the horizon, boasting an incredible seabed ideal for diving enthusiasts.

2. IMPERIAL PUGLIA: This region of Puglia is rich in historical landmarks, boasting an array of castles, cathedrals, and magnificent art cities. Notably, it is home to the enigmatic ***Castel del Monte***, a UNESCO World Heritage Site constructed by Frederick II. Additionally, the area encompasses the breathtaking ***Alta Murgia National Park***, a captivating natural reserve that extends into the province of Bari, offering a wealth of scenic wonders and cultural attractions well worth exploring.

3. MAGNA GRAECIA, MURGIA, AND GRAVINE: In this region, the predominant feature is the striking rock formations, which are a must-see for any traveler visiting the area. Characterized by deep crevasses, underground ravines, caves, and steep cliffs, it also encompasses the ***Alta Murgia National Park***. Within this vicinity lies the charming town of ***Altamura***, renowned for its distinctive "Dop" bread, a culinary gem unique to Europe. Nearby, you'll find ***Taranto***, the ancient capital of the Greek Empire. Here, a swing bridge divides the Old Town from the New Town, and owing to its illustrious Greek and Roman heritage, it houses one of Italy's finest museums dedicated to Magna Graecia. This historical significance alone warrants a stopover in Taranto.

4. BARI AND THE COASTAL AREA: Bari boasts one of the most expansive and breathtaking coastlines in Italy, adorned with stretches of golden sand, picturesque fishing ports, and towns nestled atop steep cliffs. ***Exploring the historic heart of Bari***, from the Basilica to the Cathedral of San Sabino, unveils a captivating array of cloisters, convents, churches, artisan workshops, and bakeries. ***Polignano a Mare,*** nestled along the coast, enchants visitors with its remarkable caves, secluded coves, crystal-clear waters, and imposing cliffs. Revered as the "Pearl of the Adriatic," it bears traces of its diverse Arab, Byzantine, Spanish, and Norman heritage, including remnants of the four watchtowers that once safeguarded its ancient settlement. While in Bari, a visit to the nearby town of ***Monopoli*** is highly recommended. Its historic center entices with a labyrinth of narrow alleyways winding between historic buildings and tower houses. Explore the Castle of Carlo V, where exhibitions, concerts, and shows are held, and unwind along its expansive Capitolo beach.

5. THE ITRIA VALLEY: This picturesque region of Puglia is distinguished by its iconic "trulli" and dry stone walls enclosing vineyards and olive groves as far as the eye can see. The landscape is enchanting, inviting travelers to explore towns such as **Alberobello**, a UNESCO World Heritage Site boasting 1400 trulli, or Locorotondo. **Locorotondo** derives its name from the circular layout of the town, dominated by "cummerse," ancient buildings featuring sloping roofs. **Martina Franca** is another historic city worth exploring, especially during the summer months when the *Festival della Valle d'Itria* offers captivating opera performances. Nearby lies **Ostun**i, renowned as Puglia's "white city." This fascinating town unfolds with a maze of arches, towers, palaces, courtyards, terraces, noble residences, and artisanal shops.

6. SALENTO: Transitioning from the verdant landscapes of Valle d'Itria, Salento unfolds with expansive flat fields adorned with endless olive groves, hinting at its Greek heritage. Along the Ionian coast, from **Marina di Pulsano** to **Santa Maria di Leuca**, lies a captivating stretch of golden sandy beaches, adorned with stunning marine protected areas, charming villas, and picturesque waterfront restaurants. Traveling along the Adriatic coastal road towards **Brindisi**, one encounters breathtaking vistas, passing through the historic town of **Otranto.** Otranto's captivating narrative is best experienced within its remarkable cathedral, housing the bones of 813 martyrs displayed in a glass case behind the altar. | An other captivating aspect of the region is the cluster of cities known as the "minor-Baroque," including **Nardo**, **Galatone**, and **Galatina**, where the **Basilica di Santa Caterina d'Alessandria** stands as a testament to exquisite architectural marvels. | Journeying further leads to the ineffable realm of Baroque elegance in ancient **Lecce**. Here, historic cloisters, majestic palaces, papier-mâché workshops, and the exquisite **Santa Croce basilica** await exploration. | **Gallipoli** emerges as arguably the most enchanting town in Salento, adorned with serene Baroque architecture rivaling that of Lecce. Encircled by remnants of its 14th-century walls, the old town of Gallipoli beckons visitors to linger and immerse themselves in its timeless allure, akin to Taranto. | Lastly, **Ceglie Messapica**, along with **Carovigno**, is a culinary haven not to be missed by food enthusiasts. It boasts internationally acclaimed restaurants and award-winning chefs.

CHAPTER 2: PLANNING YOUR PUGLIAN ADVENTURE

BEST TIME TO VISIT PUGLIA

SPRING (MARCH-MAY): *Pros:* Enjoy agreeable temperatures (18-20°C), relish in fewer crowds, witness the blooming wildflowers, ideal for hiking and discovering, and benefit from lower prices. | *Cons:* Possibility of occasional rainy days, beaches may not yet offer optimal swimming conditions. | **EARLY SUMMER (JUNE-AUGUST):** *Pros:* Bask in hot, sunny weather (25-30°C), perfect for indulging in beach activities, swimming, and water sports, immerse yourself in a vibrant atmosphere with numerous festivals and events. | *Cons:* Peak tourist season translates to crowded locales and inflated prices, accommodation fills up swiftly, and the heat may be overwhelming for some travelers. | **AUTUMN (SEPTEMBER-OCTOBER):** *Pros:* Experience lingering warm weather (20-25°C), conducive for swimming and sightseeing, encounter fewer crowds compared to summer, embrace the grape harvest season, and marvel at the picturesque fall foliage. | *Cons:* Occasional rainy days may occur, and beach amenities may begin to wind down as the season progresses. | **WINTER (NOVEMBER-FEBRUARY):** *Pros:* Benefit from the lowest prices, revel in the tranquility of the off-season, explore charming Christmas markets, and potentially witness snow-capped mountains. | *Cons:* Endure the coldest temperatures (5-12°C), contend with many closed restaurants and shops, and beach activities are not viable during this period.

Opt For Early Summer (June-August) if you prioritize beach vacations and don't mind the bustling crowds. | *Choose Spring (March-May) Or Autumn (September-October)* for more temperate conditions and a quieter atmosphere. | *Consider Winter (November-February)* if you're seeking budget-friendly options and are content with cooler weather.

HOW TO GET TO PUGLIA

Traveling to Puglia from within Italy has become significantly more convenient in recent years, with various transportation options available including plane, train, bus, or car. ***For international arrivals***, flying is typically the primary mode of transportation. If arriving from outside of Europe, connecting flights through major European cities such as Rome, Milan, London, Paris, or Zurich are common.

BY AIR: Puglia boasts two international airports, situated in Bari and Brindisi, respectively. Bari's airport is known as Bari International Airport-Karol Wojtyla (BRI), while Brindisi's airport goes by the name Papola Casale Airport (BDS), sometimes referred to as Salento Airport. Both airports provide direct links to various destinations within Italy and across many European capitals. Bari airport additionally offers non-stop flights to Egypt and Israel. However, neither airport in Puglia offers direct connections to the United States or Canada. Therefore, most flights originating from North America typically make a stopover in Rome or Milan. Airlines servicing these airports include national carriers like Alitalia, AirFrance, and Lufthansa, as well as budget airlines such as RyanAir, WizzAir, and EasyJet.

There are frequent direct flights from various Italian cities including Milan, Rome, Venice, Bologna, and Pisa to both Bari and Brindisi airports. Milan particularly stands out with over 20 daily direct flights to Puglia. Flights from Milan to Bari and Brindisi typically last around 1.5 hours, with ticket prices ranging from 20 to 150 euros. Most flights from Milan are operated by low-cost carriers and depart from all three of the city's airports: *Linate*, *Malpensa*, and *Orio al Serio*. From Rome, there are between 5 to 8 direct flights daily to Brindisi or Bari, with a flight duration of about 1 hour. Ticket prices vary between 25 euros to 150 euros, depending on factors such as the time of booking and the airline chosen. Given that Bari and Brindisi are only an hour apart, the choice of airport for your journey doesn't significantly impact your trip.

BY TRAIN: ***High-speed trains departing from Rome*** connect with the cities of Bari, Brindisi, and Lecce in Puglia. All trains destined for Brindisi and Lecce first pass through Bari. | ***Trenitalia's high-speed Frecciarossa trains*** operate approximately 6 times per day from Rome to Bari (and Brindisi and Lecce).

These trains depart from Rome's Termini train station and the journey typically takes around 4 hours. Advance tickets for these trains can be as low as 13.90 euros. Traveling to Brindisi takes an additional hour (5 hours total), while reaching Lecce adds another 1.5 hours (5.5 hours total). | *ItaloTreno*, a private company, also offers daily departures from Rome to Bari with similar travel times and prices.

BY BUS: *Direct buses are available from Rome, Naples, and neighboring regions such as Basilicata and Molise*. In Basilicata and Molise, transport hubs into Puglia include Matera, Potenza, and Termoli. The bus journey from Rome to Bari takes approximately 6 hours, while it's around 3.5 hours from Naples. Flixbus offers bus tickets from Rome starting at just 4 euros.

BY CAR: The journey from Rome takes just under 5 hours, while it's around 3 hours from Naples. The roads are in good condition and driving is straightforward. From Rome, you'll take the A1 superhighway south to the outskirts of Naples, where you'll switch to the A30 and E842. Following the E842 will take you across the Campania region, through Basilicata, and into Puglia. The final stretch of the journey to Bari (or beyond) is a short drive on the E55 highway.

GETTING AROUND PUGLIA

Puglia is undeniably ideal for embarking on a road trip, making it practically essential to have a car during your visit. While public transportation does exist and can facilitate travel to most desired destinations, its availability is limited and journey durations are often lengthy. An exception to this is in the vicinity of Bari, where train services are relatively reliable, enabling convenient exploration of many towns north of the city.

However, as you venture southward, transportation options diminish, leaving you primarily dependent on buses. Although traveling from Lecce to Ostuni may be relatively straightforward, extending your exploration to destinations like Alberobello, Locorotondo, or Martina Franca often entails spending a significant portion of your day transferring between buses.

With only a week at your disposal, the inefficiencies of public transit become a notable concern, potentially detracting from your overall experience. Moreover, a considerable portion of the charm of visiting Puglia lies in exploring its countryside and coastline. To fully appreciate the serene country roads of the Itria Valley and the stunning coastal routes in Salento and the Gargano region, having your own vehicle is indispensable.

Relying solely on public transportation confines you to the cities and larger towns of Puglia, limiting your ability to explore its more remote and picturesque locales.

CHAPTER 3: EXPLORING PUGLIA

PART 1: THE GARGANO PENINSULA

The Gargano Peninsula is situated in the southeastern part of Italy within the province of Foggia in the Apulia region. Known for its stunning landscapes, medieval towns, and delicious cuisine. You can explore diverse attractions such as Gargano National Park, coastal areas like Cala Azzurra, and historic sites such as the Sanctuary of San Michele Arcangelo. The nearest airport is in Bari, with train and bus connections available to reach various towns on the peninsula. While public transportation options are limited and often unreliable, renting a car is recommended for efficient exploration. The best time to visit is from late April to May or in June and September, avoiding the busiest tourist months of July and August. Gargano is characterized by a vast mountain massif, notably featuring Monte Calvo, its highest peak at 1,065 meters. Covering around 1,200 square kilometers, Gargano National Park protects much of its upland terrain since its establishment in 1991. Along its coastline, It offers various tourist attractions, including popular resorts like Vieste, Peschici, and Mattinata, as well as notable landmarks such as the shrine of Monte Sant'Angelo sul Gargano, San Giovanni Rotondo, the Abbey of Santa Maria of Ripalta, the "Black Stones" volcanic rocks in Lesina, and the Sanctuary of San Nazario.

VIESTE

Situated on the eastern shoreline of the Gargano Peninsula in Puglia, Vieste is a captivating coastal town blending medieval allure with sun-drenched beaches and rugged coastal vistas. Picture-perfect scenes of whitewashed houses tumbling down cliffsides into turquoise waters, ancient remnants whispering stories of yore, and vibrant sunsets painting the heavens nightly characterize Vieste – a picturesque retreat in the heart of the Mediterranean.

LOCATION

Vieste can be found on the easternmost tip of the Gargano peninsula, positioned along the shores of the Adriatic Sea, Vieste's municipal territory stretches from the Sfinale bay in the north, adjacent to Peschici, to the bay of Vignanotica in the south, bordering Mattinata. Towards the western inland area, it is bordered by the Umbrian forest and neighbors Monte Sant'Angelo and Vico del Gargano. Notably, Vieste lies within the Gargano National Park and is approximately 93 kilometers away from Foggia, the capital of the province.

HOW TO GET TO VIESTE

BY AIR: Bari Karol Wojtyla Airport (BRI) serves as the nearest airport to Vieste, situated approximately 180 km away. From there, travelers can opt for a bus or train journey to Vieste, taking approximately 6 or 7 hours, respectively. | **BY TRAIN:** Although Vieste lacks direct train service, travelers can board a train to Foggia, located around 80 km away, and then proceed to Vieste via bus or taxi. The train journey from Rome to Foggia spans roughly 3 hours, followed by a 1-hour bus trip to Vieste. | **BY CAR:** Renting a car provides flexibility for exploring the Gargano Peninsula at one's leisure. The drive from Rome to Vieste typically lasts about 5 hours.

GETTING AROUND VIESTE

Public Transportation: Local buses connect Vieste to neighboring towns, beaches, and attractions. | **Summer Shuttle:** A dedicated shuttle operates during peak season, linking Vieste to Baia delle Zagare beach. | **Car Rental:** Renting a car allows freedom for exploring Gargano National Park and coastal areas, though parking in the old town can be challenging. | **Taxis**: Readily available for shorter journeys or transfers to and from the airport or train station. | **Bike Rental:** Ideal for active travelers, offering a chance to explore the coastline and countryside at their own pace, with dedicated bike paths and scenic routes. | **Boat Tours:** Discover hidden coves, caves, and marine reserves along the Gargano coast with boat tours, providing stunning views and opportunities for swimming and snorkeling.

WHERE TO STAY IN VIESTE

Accommodation in Vieste varies from hotels with pools to cozy apartments and beachside campgrounds. Hotels offer local cuisine and extensive amenities, while families and groups can opt for resorts with bungalows and villas by the sea. For a rustic experience, farmhouses and campgrounds provide peaceful retreats in nature, while private homes and bed and breakfasts in the town center offer tranquility and privacy. My recommended places for a memorable stay in Vieste include: **Residence B&B Maresol:** Hilltop location with stunning views of Castello beach and Pizzomunno rock. Surrounded by pine trees, close to the center, and a short distance to the beach. Amenities include a well-equipped kitchen, wifi, and spacious terrace for cooking. | **Relais La Pretura:** Elegant accommodations with a rooftop terrace for breakfast and scenic views. Hosts provide attentive service, and guests enjoy complimentary beach loungers in the summer. | **Casa Giulia:** Budget-friendly rooms with ocean views and breakfast served on the rooftop terrace. | **Hotel Seggio**: Cliff-top location in the historic district, featuring a pool, private beach access, and breathtaking views. | **Navicri B&B:** Welcoming establishment with a pool, rooftop hot tub, and beach proximity. A 15-minute walk from the city center with convenient parking. | For more accommodation options in Vieste, visit *https://www.visitvieste.com/dormire-vieste*

TOP 21 PLACES TO SEE IN VIESTE

The historic district known as "Vieste Vecchia" resides atop a rocky perch overlooking the sea, adjacent to the Castle Beach. | *Pizzomunno*, a towering limestone monolith standing at 25 meters tall, is situated at the southern tip of Vieste's castle beach. | *Marina Piccola*, a captivating bay nestled in Vieste's center, spans from Punta San Francesco to Punta. | *Along the Gargano coast*, particularly from Vieste to Mattinata, lies one of Puglia's most captivating landscapes, characterized by towering cliffs and sea caves. | *the Lighthouse of Vieste*: Dominating much of Vieste's skyline, the Lighthouse of Vieste sits upon the islet of Santa Eufemia. | The bay and arch of San Felice present a serene oasis, featuring a small beach with shallow, sandy shores, enveloped by lush greenery. | **Punta San Francesco**, a small peninsula jutting into the sea, is a must-see destination while exploring Vieste's historic center. | *The Scala dell'Amore:* The "Stairway of Love" was crafted during the inaugural Vieste in Love event, adorning one of the staircases connecting the upper city gate. | The Coastal Towers of the Gargano: Built in response to Saracen pirate threats, construction of ten coastal towers commenced in 1563 along the Gargano coastline. | *The Swabian Castle of Vieste* perches on a cliff's edge, commanding panoramic views of the sea and Scialara Beach. | The Cathedral of Vieste: situated in the upper reaches of the medieval village, stands adjacent to the Swabian Castle. | *The Porticello Tower*, nestled between Vieste and Peschici, overlooks a rocky coastline dotted with ancient quarries. | *Trabucchi*, ancient fishing contraptions, dot the coastline from Vieste to Peschici, serving as a testament to traditional fishing practices. | *The nineteenth-century village of Vieste* retains its authenticity amidst the tourist influx, offering a glimpse into the town's past. | Santa Maria di Merino Sanctuary, located north of Vieste, holds significant symbolic value and stands amidst the plains. | *The Michele Petrone Archaeological Civic Museum*, housed in the former Capuchin convent, offers insight into Vieste's rich archaeological heritage. | *Petrone Square*, a charming corner of Vieste's historic center, holds historical significance and cultural allure. | *La Salata Necropolis*, situated near the sea, is the principal burial site in the Gargano region. | *"La Chianca Amara,"* a rock adjacent to Vieste's Cathedral, serves as a somber reminder of past atrocities. | *The Defensola Mine,* renowned in European mining archaeology, played a pivotal role in flint extraction for centuries. | *The Necropolis of Saint Nicholas of Myra*, alongside the well-known

La Salata Necropolis, offers a fascinating glimpse into Vieste's ancient past.

DINING RECOMMENDATIONS

<u>Agriturismo Chalet degli Ulivi:</u> Set amidst olive trees, offering a variety of dishes including grilled and marinated vegetables, frittata, bruschetta, and Puglian specialties like fava e cicoria and orecchiette pasta. Currently temporarily closed. | *Country House Tavernola:* Surrounded by olive-covered hills, this farmhouse serves abundant antipasti plates and hearty home-cooked meals. Advance booking recommended. €25 per person, including wine and digestivi. Located a 15-minute drive from central Vieste. | **IN VIESTE CENTER:** *Pizzeria Notte e Di*: A friendly takeaway pizza joint offering decent pizzas and local specialty paposcia sandwiches. | *Sweet Temptations – Le Dolci Tentazioni*: A quaint shop in the old town selling large cornetti filled with cream, Nutella, or jams. | **OTHER RECOMMENDATIONS**: *Tutto in un Calice*: Wine bar offering generous antipasti platters. | *Antichi Sapori:* Café with freshly baked paposceria sandwiches. | *Piétra Vieste:* Cozy pizzeria with vaulted ceilings. | *Ritual:* Beach bar and restaurant north of Vieste offering a vegan multi-course menu upon request. | *Casual Dining: Osteria al Vico del Gargano:* An authentic trattoria serving hearty dishes like orecchiette con cime di rapa and succulent grilled fish.

TOP FOOD CHOICES

Orecchiette con cime di rapa: Traditional Puglian pasta paired with turnip greens, olive oil, and a hint of chili flakes. | **Panzerotti:** Crispy fried dough pockets filled with tomato, mozzarella, and ricotta, ideal for a quick bite. | **Pesce crudo:** Fresh raw fish marinated in zesty lemon juice, olive oil, and aromatic herbs, a delight for seafood enthusiasts. | **Spaghetti alle vongole:** Simple yet satisfying spaghetti dish with clams in a garlic-infused white wine sauce. | **FOCACCIA:** Soft and fluffy flatbread, perfect for dipping in olive oil or topped with fresh tomatoes and cheese. | **Burrata:** Indulgent creamy mozzarella cheese filled with stracciatella and cream, offering a decadent treat.

TOP MUST-DO ACTIVITIES IN VIESTE

Explore Gargano National Park: Embark on trekking adventures to uncover hidden waterfalls, ancient forests, and awe-inspiring coastal vistas. | *Kayak through Marine Grottoes:* Navigate turquoise waters and marvel at mesmerizing cave formations. | *Visit Tremiti Islands:* Experience the beauty of this archipelago with its pristine beaches and crystal-clear waters. | *Attend a cooking class:* Learn the secrets of Puglian cuisine from a local chef and prepare a delectable meal yourself. | *Explore Castello Svevo:* Wander through the ruins of this medieval castle, offering stunning views of the Adriatic Sea. | *Shop at local markets:* Discover vibrant stalls brimming with fresh produce, handmade crafts, and unique souvenirs. | *Take a coastal boat trip:* Admire dramatic cliffs, secluded coves, and picturesque fishing villages from a different perspective. | *Explore Vieste Old Town:* Visit the 11th-century Cathedral of Santa Maria Assunta and the historic site of Chianca Amara. Consider joining a guided walking tour to delve deeper into the town's rich history. | *Enjoy Scenic Walks:* Start by the Norman castle, descend to Castello Beach, and witness Pizzomunno rock. Stroll through old town for panoramic views at Belvedere Ripa and Piazza Seggio. Continue to Punta San Francesco for the Church of San Francesco and a charming fishing platform. | *Relax on Vieste Beaches:* Unwind at Castello Beach or San Lorenzo Beach for tranquil sunbathing. Opt for quieter months like June and September. Explore nearby Gargano beaches for varied experiences. | *Take a Boat Trip to Grottoes:* Embark on a boat excursion to Baia delle Zagare for sea stacks and colorful caves. Swim in clear waters and enjoy the coastal beauty. Tours depart from Vieste Port.

Engage in Water Sports: Experience kitesurfing, windsurfing, scuba diving, and more. Rent equipment or take lessons from Free Surf at Capo Vieste private beach club.

MONTE SANT'ANGELO

Perched on the slopes of Monte Gargano in Italy's Puglia region, Monte Sant'Angelo exudes a captivating blend of historical richness and religious significance. This quaint town offers a wealth of medieval architecture, ancient caverns, and awe-inspiring natural landscapes, making it an irresistible destination for travelers seeking authentic experiences.

WHY SHOULD YOU VISIT MONTE SANT'ANGELO?

Designated UNESCO World Heritage Site: Home to the Sanctuary of San Michele Arcangelo, a magnificent basilica constructed around a revered grotto where Archangel Michael is believed to have appeared. This UNESCO-listed sanctuary attracts pilgrims and art enthusiasts alike. | **Medieval Charm**: Roam the winding streets of the Junno district, characterized by its picturesque whitewashed dwellings adorned with vibrant flowers. The ancient arches and inviting squares transport visitors to a bygone era. | **Natural Oasis:** Explore the Gargano National Park, a sanctuary teeming with diverse flora and fauna, or bask in the sun on the pristine Adriatic coastline. Discover secluded bays and dramatic cliffs offering breathtaking vistas. | **Culinary Delights**: Delight in the flavors of Puglian cuisine, renowned for its fresh seafood, handmade pasta, and robust spices. Indulge in local specialties such as orecchiette con cime di rapa, burrata cheese, and taralli biscuits. | **Hospitable Atmosphere:** Experience the genuine warmth of Puglian hospitality as locals eagerly share their customs and narratives, accompanied by friendly smiles.

TOP ATTRACTIONS

Sanctuary of San Michele Arcangelo: Explore the sacred grotto where the Archangel appeared, admire the intricate Byzantine bronze doors, and marvel at the medieval frescoes embellishing the basilica. | **Monte Sant'Angelo Castle:** Ascend this imposing fortress for panoramic vistas of the town and surrounding landscapes, while uncovering its rich history spanning from Longobard to Angevin reigns. | **Tomba di Rotari:** Journey back in time at this 7th-century mausoleum, likely a former baptistery, showcasing Lombard craftsmanship and architectural prowess. | **Gargano National Park:** Immerse yourself in the park's diverse terrain, from verdant forests and limestone caves to secluded lakes and rugged shores. Embark on hikes, bike rides, or simply revel in nature's splendor. | **Junno District:** Lose yourself in the enchanting labyrinth of whitewashed residences, adorned with charming balconies and floral arrangements. Discover tucked-away squares, artisan boutiques, and local eateries.

GETTING AROUND

The town is compact and easily navigable on foot. For day trips to nearby areas, buses or rental cars provide convenient transportation options.

TOP ACCOMMODATIONS

LA DIMORA DI MICHELE: A boutique B&B housed in a restored historical edifice, offering cozy accommodations and a rooftop terrace boasting panoramic vistas. | **PALAZZO DEL TAURO:** An elegant hotel situated within a former 16th-century palace, featuring spacious rooms, a spa, and a gourmet dining establishment. | **HOTEL CONVENTO SAN MICHELE:** Offering a unique stay within the Sanctuary complex, providing comfortable lodgings and access to the historic site.

TOP DINING ESTABLISHMENTS IN SANT'ANGELO

Osteria del Corso: Delight in authentic Ischitan cuisine featuring dishes such as rabbit cacciatore and linguine with clams, all within a welcoming

Osteria known for its convivial ambiance. | *Ristorante Medioevo*: Transport yourself to another era at this medieval-themed eatery, where you can relish hearty pasta dishes, fresh seafood, and local wines amidst a charming stone setting. | **Al Battistero:** Indulge in exquisite seafood delicacies like lobster ravioli and grilled octopus while enjoying picturesque sea views at this refined restaurant situated adjacent to the historic Sant'Angelo Baptistery. | **Li Jalantuùmene:** Experience authentic island cuisine at this family-operated trattoria, serving up wood-fired pizzas, homemade pasta, and fresh local ingredients amidst a lively atmosphere. | **Al Barone:** Elevate your dining experience at this upscale restaurant boasting an extensive wine cellar and innovative dishes like sea bass carpaccio with citrus fruits and pistachio pesto, perfect for special occasions. | *Cibus:* Discover contemporary interpretations of Italian classics at Cibus, where gourmet appetizers, fresh fish entrees, and delectable desserts are served in a chic and modern setting. | *Cantine Cippone:* Set within a historic cellar, Cantine Cippone offers an intimate dining experience centered around locally sourced ingredients, featuring handmade pasta dishes and regional wines. | *La Rocca Restaurant Bar Pizzeria*: Enjoy a diverse menu and stunning sea views at La Rocca, where fresh pizzas, grilled meats, seafood, and pasta dishes cater to all tastes. | *Templari Ristorante:* Immerse yourself in history at Templari, housed in a former Knights Templar church, and savor innovative dishes like black ravioli with sea urchin mousse and monkfish wrapped in pancetta, presented with sophistication. | *Borgo Antico:* Experience the charm of the old town at Borgo Antico, where traditional Ischitan fare such as rabbit stew and mixed seafood fry is served in a rustic setting with friendly hospitality.

WHAT TO DO & SEE IN MONTE SANT'ANGELO

RELIGIOUS SITES: *Sanctuary of San Michele Arcangelo:* Positioned as the town's pinnacle attraction, this UNESCO World Heritage site encompasses a remarkable cave complex where, according to legend, Archangel Michael manifested in 490 AD. The basilica, constructed in intricate Byzantine style atop the grotto, along with the striking 86-step stairway leading downwards, offer awe-inspiring sights.

Rione Junno: This historic medieval quarter, characterized by its maze-like pathways and whitewashed residences, provides insight into the town's heritage. Noteworthy sites include the Chiesa Santa Maria Maggiore, the

Tomba di Rotari (tomb of a Lombard king), and the META museum, showcasing local customs and artisanal crafts.

HISTORICAL AND CULTURAL GEMS: *Monte Sant'Angelo Castle:* Overlooking the town from its elevated position, this formidable Norman-Swabian fortress offers sweeping vistas of the surrounding landscape. Explore its towers, battlements, and inner courtyards, envisaging the medieval knights who once safeguarded its walls. | *Museum of Popular Arts and Traditions*: Immerse yourself in the essence of Gargano culture at this museum, housed within a former convent. Marvel at traditional attire, artisanal implements, and displays elucidating the region's folklore and historical narratives. | **OUTDOOR PURSUITS:** *Foresta Umbra:* Traverse the verdant expanse of this ancient national park on foot or by bike, encountering primeval beech groves, diverse fauna, and secluded cascades. Ascend Monte Sant'Angelo for unparalleled panoramas of the Gargano coastline. | **Gargano Coastal Region:** Drive or cycle along the picturesque coastal route, pausing at idyllic villages like Vieste and Peschici to relish beachside interludes, delectable seafood, and mesmerizing vistas of the Adriatic. | **GASTRONOMIC DELIGHTS:** Indulge in the local culinary scene, renowned for its bounty of fresh seafood, pasta specialties such as orecchiette with cime di rapa (turnip greens), and robust cheeses. Treat yourself to "ostie ripiene," the famed sweet delicacies of Monte Sant'Angelo brimming with ricotta and fruit preserves. | **FESTIVALS AND CELEBRATIONS**: *Feast of San Michele Arcangelo (September 29th)*: Immerse yourself in the spirited festivities honoring the town's patron saint, replete with processions, religious rituals, and traditional music and dance performances. *Medieval Days (August):* Transport yourself to a bygone era during this annual medieval celebration, featuring costumed enactments, artisanal demonstrations, and street pageantry.

FORESTA UMBRA

The Foresta Umbra nature reserve, nestled in Gargano National Park, boasts lush greenery and rugged terrain across 10,000 hectares. Italy's largest deciduous forest, it's home to over 2,000 plant species, including majestic beech trees towering over 40 meters. The diverse landscape includes Cerro beech and oak woodlands, with coastal Aleppo pine and Mediterranean maquis. Wildlife thrives here, with Italian roe deer, wild cats, wild boars, and various bird species like eagle owls and woodpeckers.

HOW TO GET TO UMBRA FOREST

Starting from Vieste, you can access the forest via Garganica State Road 89, covering approximately 9 kilometers, before turning onto SP52 Bis towards Monte Sant'Angelo. Alternatively, from Scialmarino Bay, you can directly take the 52Bis route, which traverses the forest and offers a breathtaking spectacle from the outset.

REASONS TO EXPLORE THE UMBRA FOREST

Experience UNESCO Heritage: Dive into pristine beech forests, honored by UNESCO for their ecological significance. Encounter diverse wildlife, from deer to birds of prey, amidst over 20,000 plant species, including towering beech trees. | **Nature Lover's Haven:** Explore 100+ kilometers of trails winding through valleys, ancient caves, and the tranquil shores of Lago d'Umbra. | **Historical Exploration:** Uncover medieval villages like Vico del Gargano and delve into legends at the 12th-century Hermitage of Pulsano. | **Culinary Delights:** Indulge in Puglia's rustic cuisine, savoring orecchiette pasta, fresh seafood, and creamy burrata cheese.

MAIN ATTRACTIONS

Lago d'Umbra: Embark on a picturesque boat ride, try your hand at local fishing, or simply bask in the tranquility of this woodland oasis.

Sentiero dei Giganti: Trek amidst the towering beech trees, some reaching heights of over 40 meters, and admire the ancient forest floor bathed in sunlight. | **Grotta di Pulsano:** Explore this enchanting cave adorned with stalactites and stalagmites, once a refuge for monks and rumored to hold hidden treasures. | **Foresta Umbra Visitor Center:** Gain insights into the forest's ecology, history, & conservation efforts through interactive displays & knowledgeable guides.

TRANSPORT OPTIONS

CAR: Opt for car rental for the freedom to explore the forest at your leisure, with ample parking available near the main entrances. | **BIKE:** Rent a mountain bike to tackle the challenging yet rewarding trails, experiencing the forest from a unique perspective. | **GUIDED TOURS:** Join organized hiking or biking tours led by local experts, who will reveal the forest's hidden wonders and captivating tales.

ACCOMMODATION

To explore the Umbra Forest, you can base yourself in Vieste, Vico del Gargano, Peschici, Giovanni Rotondo or the Umbra Forest Visitor Center. Vieste and Vico del Gargano are great choices if you want a bustling atmosphere with plenty of options for dining, nightlife, and shopping. Peschici and San Giovanni Rotondo offer a more laid-back experience, while the Foresta Umbra Visitor Center is perfect for nature lovers who want to be immersed in the forest.

WHAT TO SEE & DO IN UMBRA FOREST

FOR ADVENTURE ENTHUSIASTS: *Horseback Riding:* Traverse forest trails atop noble steeds, forging a bond with these magnificent animals amidst the natural splendor. | **Caving:** Venture into the depths of Grotta di Pulsano on a guided expedition, unveiling hidden caverns and geological wonders shaped over time. | **Zip-lining:** Glide through the forest canopy on an exhilarating zip-line adventure, capturing panoramic views of the verdant landscape from above. | **FOR NATURE ADMIRERS:** *Bird Watching:* Tune in to the harmonious melodies of various avian species, observing their vibrant plumage as they flit amidst the foliage. | *Forest Therapy:* Immerse yourself in the serene ambiance of the forest, embracing mindfulness and absorbing the restorative essence of nature. | ***Botanical Excursions:*** Accompany a botanist-led hike, discovering the diverse flora and their vital roles within the forest ecosystem. | **FOR FAMILIES:** ***Educational Workshops:*** Participate in engaging activities at the visitor center, delving into wildlife education, conservation initiatives, and traditional craftsmanship.| ***Play Area Delight:*** Allow children to frolic in a nature-inspired playground, crafted from organic materials and seamlessly integrated into the forest environment. | ***Enchanted Trail:*** Follow the whimsical Fairy Trail, spotting charming wooden characters nestled among the trees to ignite youthful imaginations. | **FOR HISTORY ENTHUSIASTS:** ***Medieval Village Exploration:*** Wander through the historic towns of Vico del Gargano and Monte Sant'Angelo, adorned with ancient walls, churches, and labyrinthine alleyways. | ***Hermitage of Pulsano Discovery:*** Uncover the secrets of this secluded refuge, once inhabited by monks and rumored to conceal cryptic passages and lost treasures. | ***Visit the Gargano National Park Museum***: Dive into the cultural and natural heritage of the Gargano region through captivating exhibits and archaeological relics.

PESCHICI

Peschici is a charming coastal town perched 90meters above the sea level atop a limestone cliff overlooking the Adriatic Sea. Its historic center is characterized by narrow cobblestone streets, ancient buildings, and a Norman fortress. The town boasts pristine beaches and secluded inlets with Blue Flag certification for water quality, all within the biodiverse Gargano National Park. Peschici offers a lively ambiance with traditional festivals and delicious Puglian cuisine.

REASONS TO EXPLORE

A harmonious fusion of historical allure and natural wonders: Delve into the charm of the old town, delve into the ancient Norman castle, and unwind on idyllic beaches, all within close proximity. | **_Outdoor enthusiasts' haven:_** Trek or cycle through the Gargano National Park, uncover hidden coves via kayak, or dive into the azure depths. | **_Culinary delight:_** Indulge in fresh seafood, tantalizing pasta dishes, and local specialties like orecchiette with cime di rapa. | **_Immerse in authentic Italian culture:_** Witness traditional festivals such as the Festa del Mare, meander through bustling markets, and embrace the relaxed Puglian lifestyle.

MUST-SEE ATTRACTIONS

Peschici Historic Center: The old quarter of Peschici comprises a labyrinth of narrow streets, adorned with whitewashed houses and delightful squares. Take a leisurely stroll through its charming lanes, savoring the ambiance, and be sure to pause for a refreshing gelato or coffee along the way. | **_Baia_**

del Turco: Just a brief walk from the town center lies this picturesque beach renowned for its crystalline waters and fine sandy shores. With an array of beachside bars and restaurants, you can unwind while soaking in the scenic vistas. | **_Baia Calalunga:_** A bit farther from the town center, Calalunga Bay beckons with its secluded charm, offering a tranquil haven for those seeking relaxation. Explore the surrounding area's scenic hiking trails for added adventure. | **_Baia Zaiana:_** Situated close to the town center, this petite bay is a favored spot for swimming and sunbathing. Additionally, its small harbor provides opportunities for boat rentals and scenic excursions. | **_Baia Dei Trabucchi:_** These traditional fishing structures, unique to the Gargano coast, stand as a testament to centuries-old fishing practices. Several trabucchi dot the Peschici shoreline, some of which offer dining or beverage experiences for visitors. | **_Enoteca da Mario:_** Indulge in a tasting of local wines at this inviting wine bar, where knowledgeable and amiable staff are on hand to assist in selecting the perfect complement to your meal. | **_Baia di Sfinale:_** A secluded gem, Sfinale Bay is tailor-made for a romantic retreat, boasting clear waters and soft, white sands. As amenities are scarce, remember to bring along all essentials for your visit. | **_Peschici Castle_**: Dating back to the 11th century, Peschici Castle affords breathtaking panoramic views of the town and its coastal surroundings. Within its walls, a small museum recounts the rich history of Peschici. | **_Baia Jalillo:_** Well-frequented for swimming, sunbathing, and snorkeling, with two caves accessible by boat. | **_Chiesa di Sant'Elia:_** A diminutive Romanesque church dating back to the 12th century. | **_Torre di Monte Pucci:_** A medieval tower offering sweeping vistas of the town and its environs. | **_Al Vecchio Frantoio:_** A boutique specialty store offering local delicacies such as olive oil, wine, cheese, and ceramics.

HOW TO GET TO PESCHICI

To reach Peschici from Vieste, there are two primary routes. The first, an inland route, traverses ancient olive groves & the Mandrione plain before winding through a hilly area adorned with a captivating pine forest. | The second option is the coastal road, characterized by numerous hairpin bends that meander alongside beaches, cliffs, and bays such as the picturesque Sfinale, marking the boundary between Vieste and Peschici. | Alternatively, from the north, travelers can access Peschici via Vico del Gargano, leading to the Calenelle plain, or from Rhodes Garganico, following the coast of San

Menaio.

HOW TO GET AROUND PESCHICI

On Foot: Ideal for exploring the historic center's narrow streets, squares, and whitewashed houses, but wear comfortable shoes due to the hilly terrain. | **By Bus:** Local buses link the town center to beaches and villages; tickets are purchasable at newsstands or tobacconists. | ***By Car***: Renting a car is advisable for exploring the surrounding area, although parking may be challenging in the town center during peak times. | ***By Taxi:*** Convenient for short trips or carrying luggage, taxis are easy to find in the town center and at the train station. | ***By Bicycle:*** With numerous bike rental shops, cycling is an excellent way to explore the coastal and countryside scenery. | ***By Boat:*** Boat trips from the harbor offer scenic views of the Gargano coastline and access to nearby beaches and grottoes.I

THINGS TO EXPERIENCE IN PESCHICI

Explore The Umbra Forest: Lose yourself in the verdant heart of the Gargano National Park, where ancient beech trees create an enchanting ambiance. Trek diverse trails, spot local fauna, and uncover hidden waterfalls and caverns. | ***Kayak To Secluded Coves:*** Rent a kayak or paddleboard to discover the rugged coastline, finding hidden enclaves and beaches accessible solely by sea. Relax on pristine sands, swim in crystalline waters, and snorkel amidst vibrant marine life. | ***Discover The Trabucchi Coast:*** Encounter the distinctive fishing structures known as "trabucchi," perched dramatically on cliffsides. Learn about traditional fishing techniques, relish breathtaking ocean panoramas, and savor a seafood feast at a trabucco restaurant.

Venture To The Tremiti Islands: Embark on a day excursion to the Tremiti Islands, an idyllic archipelago renowned for its azure waters, marine sanctuary, and picturesque scenery. Explore by bike or boat, indulge in diving or snorkeling, and unwind on secluded shores. | ***Engage In Traditional Festivities:*** Immerse yourself in the vibrant ambiance of Peschici's festivals, such as the Festa del Mare in May or the Sagra del Pesce Azzurro in August. Enjoy live music, dance performances, local culinary delights, and dazzling fireworks displays. | ***Master Puglian Cuisine***: Enroll in a cooking class to uncover the secrets behind traditional Puglian dishes like orecchiette with cime di rapa or seafood stew. Revel in the fruits of your labor with a delectable homemade meal. | ***Stargaze:*** Escape light pollution to marvel at the celestial spectacle above the Adriatic Sea. Utilize a stargazing app to identify constellations and planets, and make a wish upon a shooting star. | ***Shop for Local Crafts:*** Peruse the vibrant stalls of Peschici's weekly market or quaint souvenir shops in the old quarter. Discover unique handmade ceramics, artisanal goods, olive oil, and other regional delicacies to commemorate your journey. | ***Unwind on the Beach:*** Bask in the sun on one of Peschici's exquisite beaches, such as Cala Lunga with its powdery sands and turquoise waters, or Cala Zaiana renowned for its smooth pebbles and tranquil ambiance. Enjoy swimming, sunbathing, and aquatic activities. | ***Embark on a Wine Tour:*** Immerse yourself in Gargano's winemaking heritage by visiting local vineyards. Learn about grape varietals, the winemaking process, and savor exquisite wines paired with regional gastronomic delights.i

TREMITI ISLANDS

The Tremiti Islands, also known as the Diomedee Islands, are a small archipelago situated in the Adriatic Sea, off the coast of the Gargano Peninsula in Puglia region of Italy. Comprising five main islands—**_St. Nicholas_**, **_St. Domino_**, **_Capraia_**, **_Pianosa_**, and **_Cretaccio_**—this picturesque destination is renowned for its natural beauty, rich history, and pristine beaches. With a history dating back to ancient times, the Tremiti Islands have served as a strategic outpost, a place of exile for political prisoners during the Roman Empire, and a refuge for monks seeking solitude during the Middle Ages. Over the centuries, various civilizations have left their mark on the islands, contributing to their cultural heritage. Characterized by rugged cliffs, hidden coves, and crystal-clear waters, the Tremiti Islands boast stunning landscapes and abundant marine life, making them a haven for nature lovers, divers, and outdoor enthusiasts. Visitors can explore charming villages, historic sites, and pristine beaches while soaking in the Mediterranean ambiance.

BEST TIME TO VISIT THE TREMITI ISLANDS

The best time to visit the Tremiti islands varies depending on the type of experience you seek. August is ideal for those who prefer a lively atmosphere, while May, June, and September offer pleasantly warm weather with fewer crowds, providing ample opportunity to enjoy secluded beaches and peaceful surroundings. However, the islands boast beauty throughout the year. Inclement weather or extreme cold are rare occurrences, and it's not uncommon for visitors to dine outdoors without coats even in December.

GETTING TO THE TREMITI ISLANDS

The islands are easily accessible either by ferry from Termoli (with occasional departures from ports like Vieste, particularly during peak season) or by helicopter from Foggia. It's important to note that in adverse weather conditions or rough seas, the ferry service from Termoli may be suspended. Even when the sea appears calm, Termoli's port is shallow, posing a risk of hull damage to ships. During high season, there are usually 2 or 3 daily ferry trips to and from the islands, while in low season, there's typically one trip per day. Tirrenia and Navigazione Libera del Golfo are the main boat operators. If unsure about weather conditions and trip status, contacting the Coast Guard on the day of departure (+39 0875706484) is advisable for guidance. Conversely, the helicopter service operates at least twice daily and generally operates regardless of weather conditions, except in cases of extremely poor visibility, which is rare, occurring perhaps only 2 or 3 times annually. For further information and tickets reservations, visit: ***https://traghetiisoletremiti.it***

PRACTICAL TIPS FOR TRAVELERS

Before traveling to the Tremiti Islands, monitor weather conditions, especially in the off-peak season when rough seas can affect ferry schedules. Book ferry tickets and lodging in advance, especially during peak tourist periods. Choose your island based on activities and attractions available, as each has its unique offerings. Pack essentials like sunscreen, comfortable shoes, swimwear, and medications as amenities may be limited on the islands.

ST. NICHOLAS ISLAND

San Nicola, the second largest island in the Tremiti archipelago off the coast of Puglia, Italy, holds a prominent status among its counterparts. With a past marked by hosting monks, serving as a penal colony, and functioning as a defensive stronghold, the island is steeped in historical narratives. The imposing Abbey of Santa Maria a Mare, a Benedictine monastery dating back to 1045, stands as a testament to the island's spiritual heritage. Surrounded by ancient walls and fortifications, San Nicola emanates a blend of natural beauty and historical allure. Despite its historical weight, San Nicola provides a serene refuge, perfect for unwinding and exploration.

ATTRACTIONS: *__Abbey of Santa Maria a Mare:__* This impressive Benedictine abbey showcases Romanesque and Byzantine architecture, intricate mosaics, and a serene cloister. | *__Chiesa di San Nicola:__* Dedicated to the island's patron saint, this quaint church charms visitors with its unassuming facade and peaceful ambiance. | *__Grotta degli Inglesi (Cave of the English):__* Descend into this natural sea cave, rumored to have once sheltered English pirates during storms. | *__Villaggio dei Conigli (Village of Rabbits):__* Wander through this picturesque fishing village, renowned for its colorful houses and laid-back atmosphere. | *__Natural Wonders:__* Immerse yourself in San Nicola's rugged cliffs, secluded coves, and crystalline waters.

ST. DOMINO ISLAND

St. Domino Island is renowned for its pristine beaches, turquoise waters, and lush vegetation, offering visitors a tranquil retreat in a natural paradise. The island boasts amenities such as restaurants, bars, and beach resorts, making it an ideal destination for sunbathing, swimming, and water sports. It holds the distinction of being the largest and most developed island among the group, boasting the sole sandy beach and a quaint port town brimming with charm. During the vibrant summer months, it pulsates with activity, offering visitors a blend of relaxation, historical intrigue, and breathtaking natural vistas.

KEY ATTRACTIONS: *__Cala delle Arene:__* Indulge in relaxation upon the golden sands of this premier beach, renowned as the island's focal point, where tranquil waters meet picturesque scenery. | *__Cala degli Inglesi:__* Delve into exploration at this intriguing cove adorned with natural rock formations and a clandestine cave accessible via swimming. | *__Grotta delle Viole:__* Uncover the beauty of this sea cavern adorned with violet-hued algae, reachable through guided boat tours. | *__Abbazia di Santa Maria a Mare:__* Delve into the annals of time at this 11th-century abbey, offering guided tours and panoramic vistas. | *__Marine Grotto:__* Peer into the depths of the underwater world through glass panels within this distinctive sea cave, accessible by elevator. | ***Porto Vecchio:*** Meander through the captivating old port town, adorned with vibrant restaurants, local boutiques, and colorful residences.

WHAT TO SEE & DO: ***Beachside Relaxation and Swimming***: Bask in the sun at Cala delle Arene or seek out secluded coves for unique aquatic adventures. | ***Snorkeling and Diving:*** Immerse yourself in the vibrant marine ecosystem thriving within the crystalline waters, replete with colorful fish and subaquatic caverns. | ***Boat Excursions***: Embark on exploratory journeys, uncovering the hidden nooks and crannies of the Tremiti Islands archipelago amid breathtaking vistas. | ***Hiking and Biking:*** Traverse the island's picturesque trails, offering sweeping panoramas and concealed grottos. | ***Cultural Exploration:*** Immerse yourself in the island's rich heritage through visits to the abbey, port town, and maritime museum. | ***Gastronomic Delights:*** Indulge in delectable seafood specialties and traditional Puglian cuisine at waterfront eateries exuding lively ambiance. | ***INSIDER'S TIP:*** For a truly memorable experience, consider timing your visit to coincide with the "Festa Patronale di San Silverio" in late June, a celebration honoring the island's patron saint featuring processions, fireworks, and culinary delights.

CAPRAIA ISLAND

Capraia remains uninhabited, hosting only a dilapidated lighthouse and a solitary hut. Until a few decades ago, a family resided in the lighthouse. Additionally known as Caprara or Capperaia, the former name suggests the island once teemed with wild goats (as "capra" means goat in Italian), while the latter hints at its abundance of caper plants. During May and throughout the summer, visitors have the opportunity to harvest kilos of capers. Capraia boasts remarkable natural rock formations, including the 'Grottone'—a sizable sea grotto—and the 'Architiello'—an archway extending over the sea. Capraia Island is a haven for scuba diving enthusiasts, with its crystal-clear waters teeming with marine life and underwater caves waiting to be explored. Excursions to nearby diving sites are readily available.

PIANOSA ISLAND

Pianosa Island is a protected marine reserve, home to diverse ecosystems and endemic species. Visitors can participate in eco-tours, birdwatching, and nature walks to discover the island's natural beauty.

CRETACCIO ISLAND

Cretaccio Island is steeped in legends and folklore, with tales of hidden treasures and ancient rituals adding to its mystique. Visitors can explore the island's rugged terrain and uncover its secrets.

WHAT TO DO ON THE TREMITI ISLANDS

Diving and Underwater Activities: The Tremiti Islands offer excellent diving opportunities, with vibrant coral reefs, underwater caves, and shipwrecks waiting to be explored by divers of all skill levels. | **Exploring Caves and Beaches:** Visitors can embark on boat tours to explore the hidden sea caves and secluded beaches that dot the coastline of the islands, offering a unique perspective of their natural beauty. | **Hiking and Nature Walks:** Hiking trails crisscross the islands, allowing visitors to explore their rugged landscapes, ancient ruins, and panoramic viewpoints while immersing themselves in the pristine Mediterranean wilderness. | **Cultural and Historical Sightseeing:** History enthusiasts can visit ancient monuments, churches, and archaeological sites scattered across the islands, providing insights into their rich cultural heritage & maritime history.

WHERE TO STAY ON THE TREMITI ISLANDS

While the archipelago comprises five islands, only two, namely San Domino and San Nicola, are inhabited. The remaining islands, Cretaccio, Caprara, and Pianosa, lack any amenities and are uninhabited. San Domino offers various accommodation options such as hotels, bed and breakfasts, Airbnbs, and rental apartments. On San Nicola, although fewer in number, accommodation services are still available for visitors. To book any hotel of your choice and budget, visit: *https://www.booking.com/region/it/isole-tremiti.html*.

GASTRONOMY OF THE TREMITI ISLANDS

The cuisine of the Tremiti Islands blends Mediterranean featuring fresh seafood as the highlight. Specialties include various fish dishes, grilled crustaceans, and seafood spaghetti. Local favorites like Scescille meatballs & Pesce Fe'jute soup offer unique tastes, while desserts include Treccine pastries and Pastiera Tremiti ricotta pie. Explore local markets, dine waterfront for stunning views, and try Vermiglio wine. Here are 10 recommended restaurants: ***Capatosta:*** Moderate to high-priced Italian cuisine, ideal for group gatherings. | ***A' Smerza Bar Ristorante***: Seafood dining with scenic views on San Domino. | ***Da Enrichetta:*** Italian and seafood eatery on San Nicola known for excellent desserts. | ***Architiello***: Comprehensive Italian & seafood menu on San Nicola with serene surroundings. | ***L'Altro Faro:*** Seafood and Mediterranean cuisine on San Domino, perfect for dinner. | ***La Fenice:*** Italian and pizza joint on San Domino with generous portion sizes. | ***Eraora***: Excellent bar offerings on San Domino with a pleasant atmosphere. | ***Da Elio Fish Bar&Restaurant***: Delicious Italian and seafood dining on San Domino. | ***Ristorante Gabbiano:*** Fresh seafood and Italian cuisine on San Domino, particularly good during the off-season. | ***Al Torrione:*** Italian and seafood restaurant on San Nicola, perfect for a dinner date.

OTHER TOWNS WORTH EXPLORING IN THE GARGANO PENINSULA

VICO DEL GARGANO

Nestled atop a hill within the Gargano National Park, the fortified enclave of Vico del Gargano is affectionately dubbed the "City of Love," paying homage to its patron saint, Saint Valentine. During February, visitors may have the chance to partake in the Festa di San Valentino, one of the many vibrant saints' day celebrations hosted in Vico. With roots tracing back to ancient times, Vico del Gargano offers a glimpse into its storied past. Its medieval streets, easily navigable and compact, invite leisurely strolls. Noteworthy landmarks include the 11th-century castle, repurposed into apartments with access to its courtyard, and a multitude of historic churches. Among them, the Chiesa di Santa Maria Pura, an 18th-century structure erected near the Fontana Vecchia, a site marking an ancient spring. Venturing beyond the historic district leads to the old Capuchin Convent on the town's outskirts, amidst vineyards and olive groves. En route, visitors encounter a venerable oak tree of indeterminate age, a First World War memorial arboretum, and a vantage point offering sweeping vistas of the hills cascading towards the coastline.

MATTINATA

Mattinata, perched atop a hill, boasts breathtaking vistas and is famed for its sandy beaches, traditional fishing vessels known as trabucchi, and a centuries-old castle. Constructed in the 13th century under the patronage of Frederick II of Hohenstaufen, the castle affords sweeping panoramas of the surrounding landscape.

WHAT TO SEE & DO IN MATTINATA: *Ascend Monte Sacro*, the highest peak in the Gargano region, standing at nearly 874 meters. | **_The Castle:_** Delve into the remarkable fortress for sweeping vistas of both the town and the surrounding countryside. | **_The Trabucchi_**: These indigenous fishing vessels are exclusive to the Gargano Peninsula. Embark on a boat excursion to observe them up close and gain insights into their operational mechanisms. | **_The Beaches:_** Mattinata boasts numerous exquisite beaches, ideal for indulging in swimming, sunbathing, and engaging in various water activities. | ***The Historic Center:*** Wander through the picturesque historic quarter, adorned with traditional stone dwellings and artisanal shops vending locally crafted goods and mementos.

STRADA PROVINCIALE 53 (SP53)

SP53 is a serpentine coastal route connecting Vieste and Mattinata, flanked by forested cliffs on one side and a sheer descent into the sea on the other. Currently, this road sees minimal traffic due to the construction of a new superhighway that burrows through the cliffs, reducing travel time by approximately 30 minutes. While the drive along SP53 offers an enjoyable experience, opting to bike along it allows for a leisurely pace, granting ample time to soak in the breathtaking vistas.

PART 2: TERRA DI BARI

The Terra di Bari, encompassing the metropolitan area surrounding Bari, the capital of Puglia, stands out as the region's most affluent and densely populated area. Its coastal towns and cities boast cosmopolitan vibes, showcasing rich architectural heritage, artistic treasures, and vibrant cultural scenes. Renowned for its exceptional cuisine, this region offers some of the finest dining experiences in all of Puglia. For travelers relying on public transportation, Terra di Bari proves to be the most accessible part of Puglia to navigate. Its hub revolves around Bari and extends northward to Barletta and southward to Monopoli. Home to over 1.5 million people, accounting for more than a third of Puglia's population, this bustling region beckons urban explorers with its diverse cityscape. If your interests lean more towards city exploration rather than beachside relaxation or countryside strolls, Terra di Bari is definitely a must-visit destination.

BARI

Bari often doesn't make it onto lists highlighting the most picturesque towns in Puglia, which is somewhat understandable, but also unfair. As the bustling capital city of Puglia, Bari boasts a population of nearly half a million residents and offers elegant boulevards, pedestrian-friendly shopping avenues, a picturesque boardwalk, and a maze-like old town that ranks among the region's finest. Additionally, the city is renowned for its **_vibrant culinary scene_**. Key attractions include the **_San Sabino Cathedral (Duomo)_**, **_the Basilica di San Nicola_**, the imposing **_Svevo Castle_**, and the **_Teatro Petruzzelli theater_**. Exploring the winding streets of the old town is a must for every visitor, as is a leisurely stroll along the bustling harbor. For excellent people-watching opportunities, meandering down **_Via Sparano and Via Argiro_**—two bustling pedestrian thoroughfares lined with shops and eateries—is an ideal late afternoon or early evening activity. Furthermore, Bari stands out as the primary nightlife hub in Puglia, offering ample options for those seeking a lively atmosphere after dinner. Historically, the Terra di Bari (Greater Bari) region has been one of the wealthiest areas in Puglia, and as a result, the city is surrounded by charming towns and cities that make for convenient day trip destinations. In essence, Bari is a destination not to be underestimated!

LOCATION OF BARI

Bari lies along the coast, nestled between the geographical formations known as the "spur" and the "heel" of the Italian peninsula. Located approximately 285 miles south of Rome, it takes about a 5-hour drive, while it is roughly 170 miles east of Naples, reachable in around 3 hours.

GETTING TO BARI

Bari serves as a vital transportation hub in Puglia and southern Italy, with an international airport connecting it to major European cities and domestic destinations. **BY AIR:** International travelers typically fly into Rome or Milan before continuing to Bari via domestic flights, trains, or rental cars. Bari's airport offers frequent flights to Rome, Milan, Venice, Bologna, and Pisa, with Rome and Milan providing the most connections. **BY TRAIN:** Travelers within Italy often prefer trains to reach Bari, with direct routes from Rome and connections from other major cities. Trains from Rome to Bari, operated by Trenitalia, take about 4 hours with advance tickets costing as low as 15 euros. Travel from Naples to Bari is possible by train, though slower with transfers in Caserta, or by bus, taking around 3.5 hours. **BY CAR:** Renting a car offers the freedom to explore Puglia at your leisure. The A14 highway links Bari with other prominent cities across Italy.

REASONS TO EXPLORE BARI

Bari, often overlooked by travelers to Puglia, offers a unique experience worth exploring. Here are four reasons why you should spend at least a day or two here:

1. RICH HISTORY: Bari thrived as a vital port city in the Middle Ages, with well-preserved architecture and traces of its significance during World War II. | **2. CULTURAL FUSION:** It's a blend of eastern and western cultures, highlighted by the church housing Saint Nicholas' remains and a diverse atmosphere attracting visitors from various backgrounds. | **3. CULINARY DELIGHTS:** The old town maintains its authenticity, offering a taste of vibrant history through traditional cuisine, including street food, seafood, and handmade pasta. | **4. STRATEGIC LOCATION:** Bari serves as a key transit point in Puglia, with extensive connections and efficient public transportation, making it an ideal base for exploring the region. Be aware of heavy traffic and assertive drivers if renting a car.

THE BEST TIME TO VISIT BARI

The best times to visit Bari are spring and early fall, offering pleasant weather and fewer crowds. December and early January are also enjoyable, with festive holiday atmospheres and fewer tourists. Avoid visiting in July and August due to extreme heat and large crowds from cruise ships. January to March tends to be rainy and cold, while November to December sees fewer tourists and a return to regular city life, making it a pleasant time to visit, especially during the Christmas season. Ultimately, April to June and September to October are the optimal times to experience Bari at its best, with favorable weather and vibrant local life.

DURATION TO SPEND IN BARI

When planning your stay in Bari, traditional sightseeing can be done in just a day, but the true essence of the city lies in immersing yourself in its atmosphere and enjoying its offerings. Unlike major tourist destinations like Rome or Florence, Bari's charm is best experienced by leisurely exploring its streets and savoring its cuisine over a couple of days. The vibrant local life comes alive in the late afternoon and evenings, with bustling bars, restaurants, and street vendors creating a lively ambiance. Basing yourself in Bari also allows for convenient day trips to nearby attractions in Puglia, such as Trani, Matera, Alberobello, and Polignano, enhancing your overall experience of the region. Therefore, staying in Bari for a few days not only lets you appreciate the city but also provides an ideal launchpad for exploring the surrounding areas.

WHERE TO STAY IN BARI

BEST AREAS TO STAY IN BARI: 1.BARI VECCHIA: Ideal for First-Time Visitors and Couples who want to immerse themselves in the historic charm of the city. | **MADONNELLA:** Great for Families seeking a quieter and residential atmosphere, away from the hustle and bustle. | **JAPIGIA:** Perfect for Budget Travelers looking for affordable accommodation options while still being within reach of the city center. | **MURAT:** The go-to choice for Nightlife enthusiasts, Shopaholics, and Foodies, offering a vibrant atmosphere with plenty of dining, entertainment, and shopping opportunities. | **QUARTIERE UMBERTINO:** Another excellent option for Foodies, offering a mix of traditional and modern dining experiences. | **BARI VECCHIA:** Also recommended for History buffs, offering a glimpse into the city's rich cultural heritage through its ancient streets and landmarks.

TOP ACCOMMODATION RECOMMENDATION: *BARI VECCHIA: Arvian B&B* offers spacious rooms with essential amenities such as air conditioning, a flat-screen TV, and a refrigerator. Situated on the ground floor, it's perfect for travelers with heavy luggage. | ***Dimora Arco Basso:*** Experience luxury in Bari Vecchia at Dimora Arco Basso, featuring private parking, concierge services, and upscale facilities including a coffee machine and minibar. | ***Dimora dei Veneziani:*** Offering budget-friendly accommodations, Dimora dei Veneziani is a cozy one-bedroom apartment near Basilica San Nicola, ideal for travelers seeking economical options.

MURAT: ***Travel B&B:*** Positioned across from Bari Centrale station, Travel B&B provides comfortable rooms with breakfast included, perfect for travelers using public transportation. | ***Fourooms Bari:*** Enjoy captivating city views at Fourooms Bari, boasting double-height windows and tasteful decor, ideal for midrange travelers. | ***Red Carpet Rooms:*** Budget-conscious travelers can opt for Red Carpet Rooms, offering affordable yet comfortable accommodations near Murat's vibrant nightlife scene.

QUARTIERE UMBERTINO: ***Celentano Suite:*** Experience mid-range comfort at Celentano Suite, equipped with a kitchen, laundry facilities, and amenities like air conditioning and complimentary WiFi. | ***70's Luxury Cavour:*** Embrace retro luxury at 70's Luxury Cavour, featuring spacious rooms adorned with 1970s-style decor and a balcony with city views. | ***Le BB:*** Conveniently located near trendy bars and cafes, Le BB offers a cozy one-bedroom apartment with a well-appointed kitchen and a balcony for enjoying city ambiance.

MADONNELA: ***Carulli 69:*** Offering great value for money, Carulli 69 provides a comfortable apartment with a large double bed and a sofa bed, perfect for small families. | ***Nuovissimo Appartamento Lungomare:*** Accommodating up to eight guests, Nuovissimo Appartamento Lungomare features a spacious layout with a large kitchen, dining area, and easy access to coastal attractions. | ***Marea 51 Apartment***: Modern and inviting, Marea 51 Apartment offers a one-bedroom layout with a partial sea view balcony and essential amenities for a comfortable stay.

JAPIGIA: ***Appartamento Claudia:*** Discover budget-friendly accommodations at Appartamento Claudia, featuring essential amenities & complimentary parking, conveniently located near Bari Centrale station. | ***Centro Città Concept:*** Experience comfort at an affordable price with cozy rooms and private bathrooms at Centro Città Concept, perfect for budget travelers. | ***La Clessidra B&B***: Enjoy breakfast-inclusive accommodations at La Clessidra B&B, with discounted rates for solo travelers seeking economical options.

THINGS TO SEE AND DO IN BARI

EXPLORE SAINT NICHOLAS CHURCH: Saint Nicholas Church stands as a remarkable example of Romanesque architecture and holds significant religious importance, attracting both devout pilgrims and curious visitors. Descend into the crypt to witness the saint's resting place, and marvel at the rare Greek Orthodox chapel nestled beneath the church. Don't miss the captivating XII Century sculpture resembling a seat held by miniature figures, among the church's esteemed treasures.

TOUR SAN SABINO CHURCH: Journey to the city's cathedral, San Sabino Church, a striking 13th-century architectural marvel. Witness the spectacle of sunlight streaming through the main rose glass window during the Equinox, illuminating a mosaic on the floor, creating a mesmerizing reflection of the window's image.

DISCOVER THE SWABIAN CASTLE: Uncover the rich history within the walls of the Swabian castle complex, housing various structures spanning different historical periods. Explore the collection of Romanesque decorations molds gathered from across Puglia, offering insights into the region's artistic heritage.

STROLL ALONG ORECCHIETTE STREET: Navigate the charming lanes of Orecchiette Street, where tradition intertwines with modernity. While a segment of the street caters to tourists with its performances, venture into the adjacent alleys surrounding the castle to uncover authentic local experiences and preserved authenticity.

SHOP ALONG VIA SPARANO WITH LOCALS: Indulge in a quintessential Italian shopping experience along Via Sparano, the bustling thoroughfare linking the old town to the train station. Enjoy a leisurely stroll sans traffic in this pedestrianized zone, browsing through the finest shops and boutiques that adorn the vibrant street.

ATTEND CULTURAL EVENTS: Immerse yourself in Bari's cultural tapestry by attending captivating shows and events. From opera and ballet performances to music concerts and art exhibitions, Piazza del Ferrarese and venues like Spazio Murat, Ex Mercato del Pesce, and Margherita Theatre offer a diverse array of cultural delights.

EXPERIENCE THE FISH MARKET: Delve into the sensory spectacle of the fish market near Margherita Theatre, where vendors communicate in the local dialect. Immerse yourself in the vibrant atmosphere and savor the authenticity of this local culinary tradition.

CATCH A SOCCER GAME AT SAN NICOLA STADIUM: Experience the fervent energy of a soccer match at San Nicola Stadium, home to SSC Bari. While the team competes in Serie B, Italy's second-tier professional league, the passionate atmosphere of the stadium promises an unforgettable sporting experience.

TAKE A LEISURELY STROLL ALONG THE LUNGOMARE: Embark on a leisurely stroll or bike ride along the picturesque lungomare, a scenic seaside promenade. Enjoy the serenity of the shoreline, soak in the Mediterranean ambiance, and revel in the simple joys of life amidst breathtaking coastal vistas.

ENJOY A BEACH PICNIC AT PANE E POMODORO: Relish a delightful beach picnic at Pane e Pomodoro, renowned for its idyllic shores. Grab a sandwich or a slice of focaccia from a local bakery, pack your favorite read, and unwind on the sandy shores, basking in the tranquil beauty of the Mediterranean coastline.

DINING IN BARI

A MUST-TRY DISH IN BARI IS THE COMBO OF PANZEROTTO AND PERONI BEER. This entails enjoying a cold Peroni beer (fun fact: Bari is home to a massive Peroni brewery!) alongside a fried calzone, stuffed with mozzarella and tomatoes. It's as delicious as it sounds! | **GRILLED OCTOPUS SANDWICH:** For a unique local delicacy, indulge in a grilled octopus sandwich. ***Mastro Ciccio*** on Vittorio Emanuele Street is a popular spot to savor this particular street food.| **ORECCHIETTE**, a pasta shaped like little ears, is a classic staple in Bari and throughout Puglia. It's typically served with olive oil, broccoli rabe, bay leaves, garlic, anchovy, and chili peppers. | **RISO, PATATE, E COZZE:** Another iconic dish is "riso, patate, e cozze" (rice, potatoes, and mussels), prepared by layering the ingredients in a casserole with olive oil, onion, cheese, black pepper, and tomatoes before baking. | For an authentic dining experience, visit **Osteria Travi Buco**, where you'll enjoy local recipes in an unpretentious setting, albeit with somewhat gruff service.

Barese people love seafood, often enjoying it fresh by the sea or at the market. While trying raw seafood from unofficial vendors can be exciting, hygiene should be considered. Restaurants offer safer options for raw seafood dishes. In Bari, locals can be assertive sellers, so confirm prices in advance and seek recommendations from the staff or owner for a pleasant dining experience.

Here are a few additional tips for dining in the city:
Be aware of the coperto charge, which includes expenses like bread and dishwashing. Confirm the amount beforehand to avoid surprises. | Some restaurants may suggest trying a variety of antipasti or recommend the catch of the day. Ensure you know the prices before ordering. | Trust the recommendations of the staff or owner for the best dishes. Opt for restaurants specializing in specific cuisines for an authentic experience. | Embrace the relaxed pace of dining in Bari, where meals are enjoyed over conversation. Choose casual spots if you're in a hurry, as formal meals can take longer.

BEST BARI RESTAURANTS

LE DUE AQUILE: This unassuming yet bustling eatery is a favorite among locals for its consistently high-quality dishes. While it may not boast rustic charm, Le Due Aquile exudes simplicity and authenticity, drawing patrons seeking excellent cuisine. | **BIANCOFIORE:** Offering a sophisticated dining experience, Biancofiore exudes romance and elegance, serving delectable gourmet fare. This upscale establishment is renowned for its exquisite culinary creations and refined ambiance. | **AL PESCATORE:** A longstanding institution in Bari, Al Pescatore has been delighting diners with fresh, flavorful seafood for over five decades. With an impressive display of fish on ice, patrons can select their preferred catch for a personalized dining experience. | **LA TANA DEL POLPO**: For an unparalleled seafood experience, whether cooked or raw, look no further than La Tana del Polpo. This casual, locals-frequented spot offers exceptional value, friendly service, and an authentic dining atmosphere. | **PANIFICIO FIORE:** Nestled behind the church of San Nicholas, Panificio Fiore is a historic bakery renowned for crafting some of the finest Bari-style focaccia in the city. Indulge in freshly baked delicacies while savoring the charming ambiance of this esteemed establishment.

TRANI

Trani, a city situated approximately 40 kilometers (25 miles) north of Bari is renowned for its charming seaport and historic cathedral, Trani experienced significant growth during the 11th century, with its strategic location playing a vital role during the Crusades. Trani boasts a rich Jewish heritage, having been home to a sizable Jewish population since the 12th century, establishing it as a prominent center of Jewish life in Southern Italy. The city produced many notable rabbis, and examples like the well-preserved Scolanova Synagogue underscore its historical significance, still in use to this day. While primarily celebrated for its historical significance, Trani has also gained recognition for its excellent produce, including figs, almonds, olive oil, and the delightful Moscato di Trani.

GETTING TO TRANI

Traveling from Bari to Trani via public transportation is remarkably convenient. To embark on your journey to Trani, simply make your way to Bari Centrale, the primary train station in Bari, and locate the next departing train. These trains operate at regular intervals, typically every half hour, heading northbound, with Trani being a common stop along the route. A second-class ticket for the Bari to Trani train ride costs €3.60 for a single trip. You can conveniently purchase your ticket directly from the station's ticket vending machine. The journey from Bari to Trani by train lasts approximately 39 minutes and follows the route toward Barletta. It's important to validate your ticket using the green Trenitalia Machines at the station before proceeding to the platform.

BEST TIME TO VISIT TRANI

During my visit to Trani in late February to early March, the weather was pleasantly mild, with temperatures averaging around 14°C (57°F) and plenty of sunshine, although occasional rain occurred. This period offered comfortable conditions for strolling around the area. However, it's worth noting that visiting Puglia during February coincides with the offseason, resulting in many establishments being closed for holidays or renovations, limiting available activities. In contrast, summers in Puglia and Trani are characterized by warmer temperatures and bustling activity, with everything open for exploration.

WHAT TO SEE AND DO IN TRANI

Explore Svevo Castle: The Svevo Castle built by Frederick II of Swabia in 1233, is a majestic medieval fortress overlooking the Adriatic Sea. It boasts a unique fusion of Romanesque and Gothic architectural styles. With its imposing stone walls and strategic position, the castle served as a defensive stronghold for centuries. | ***Visit Trani Cathedral:*** Located near the harbor and close to Svevo Castle, Trani Cathedral, also known as the Cathedral of San Nicolás, is a stunning 12th-century structure constructed from sandy, pink stones. With its towering 60-meter bell tower, the Romanesque cathedral offers a picturesque setting for exploration and photography. You can access the cathedral daily during specified hours 9 am–12:30 pm & 3:30–8 pm (Sunday 9 am–12:30 pm, 3:30–8 pm), making it a must-see destination in Trani. | ***Explore Trani Harbor:*** Trani Harbor offers a delightful surprise with its expansive waterfront bustling with fishing vessels, yachts, and cozy waterfront establishments. Unlike expectations based on previous experiences in Polignano a Mare and Monopoli, Trani Harbor captivates visitors with its vibrant atmosphere and array of dining options. It's recommended to allocate ample time to explore the harbor, enjoy a leisurely meal, and soak in the lively ambiance. | ***Wander the Quaint Streets of Trani:*** After exploring the harbor, take time to wander through Trani's charming streets. Despite limited opening hours, the city exudes cleanliness and charm, promising potential for bustling activity in the evening. Strolling through the quiet lanes offers glimpses into Trani's authentic character and architectural beauty. | ***Enjoy Villa Comunale di Trani:*** Situated opposite the harbor, Villa Comunale di Trani is a sprawling promenade and park adorned with scenic viewpoints, cafes, statues, and art installations. This tranquil oasis offers a welcome retreat from the city bustle and provides opportunities for leisurely walks and relaxation amidst picturesque surroundings. Don't miss out on experiencing the serenity and beauty of Villa Comunale di Trani during your visit to Trani, Italy.

TRANI RESTAURANTS AND GELATERIAS

Osteria La Banchina Osteria La Banchina is renowned for its exquisite seafood dishes and Mediterranean cuisine. With a prime location by the harbor, you can enjoy stunning views while savoring delicious meals prepared with fresh, locally sourced ingredients. | **Osteria La Perla Del Sud**, another harborside eatery, emerged as the go-to place for seafood enthusiasts in Trani. Offering a variety of dishes, the restaurant lets patrons pair their favorite pasta with the day's fresh catch or a medley of seafood. | **Bar Gelateria** became a guilty pleasure for me, despite being lactose-intolerant. Indulging in some of Italy's finest ice cream and gelato brought me joy during my visits to Trani and other parts of the country. My late snack at Bar Gelateria involved savoring a cone of gelato. | **Bubbles Bar / Three Palms Gelateria**, located at Republic Square, caught my attention with its aesthetic charm. Discovered during an evening stroll back to the train station, the hip decor both inside and outside the bar fascinated me. Though I only explored the place briefly, I regret not staying overnight in Trani to experience the vibrant nightlife this unique spot within Piazza della Repubblica had to offer.

WHERE TO STAY IN TRANI

Visiting Trani could be done as a day trip from Bari but spending a night or two in Trani to witness the city during both sunrise and sunset, and to explore its nightlife to some extent wont be a bad idea.

Trani provides various lodging options for travelers. Below are a couple of well-regarded choices catering to various budgets in Trani:

⇒ **LUXURY ACCOMMODATION: The Palazzo Filisio Hotel - Regia Ristorante**
The Palazzo Filisio Hotel - Regia Ristorante offers comfortable accommodation with modern amenities including minibar, air conditioning, and free Wi-Fi. You can enjoy complimentary breakfast and dine at the on-site restaurant known for its quality seafood dishes. Conveniently located near Trani's attractions such as Sinagoga Scolanova and Cattedrale di Trani,

the hotel overlooks the sea, providing stunning views of the cathedral.

⇒ **MID-RANGE ACCOMMODATION IN TRANI**: *B&B Palazzo Paciotti* offers a delightful accommodation experience in a recently renovated historic building. It features spacious rooms equipped with modern amenities including private bathrooms, televisions, air conditioning, Wi-Fi internet, mini-fridges, and hairdryers. Yo can enjoy complimentary breakfast served on a rooftop terrace with a picturesque view of the harbor. it also offer stylish decor, cleanliness, comfort, and friendly staff.

⇒ **BUDGET ACCOMMODATION:** *Il Sole* offers colorful rooms with free Wi-Fi and air conditioning, conveniently located just a 5-minute drive from Trani's center and train station, and 300 meters from the beach. Amenities include TV, work desk, private bathroom, and breakfast at a nearby bar. Various room types cater to different preferences, with some offering garden or courtyard views. Guests praise cleanliness, comfort, and value for money, along with helpful staff. Amenities include fast Wi-Fi, private parking, and airport shuttle. The property maintains a sustainable approach.

⇒ *Hotel San Paolo al Convento:* offers a breathtaking setting located adjacent to the charming port. It was once a historic monastery belonging to the Barnabite Fathers, the building has undergone a remarkable transformation into a hotel. With 33 rooms, the property exudes a truly distinctive charm and character.

NIGHTLIFE IN TRANI

During the summer, the nightlife in the port area is bustling and diverse, catering to various tastes with its array of breweries, pubs, cocktail bars featuring live music, and discos hosting international DJ sets. | *Portulaca*, boasting a waterfront setting, epitomizes Trani's nightlife scene. Serving as both a restaurant and a cocktail bar, it's a beloved spot frequented by locals. With its spacious outdoor area, Portulaca hosts DJ nights and live music events, making it a popular choice. | For those seeking an energetic post-dinner experience, the renowned *Il Vecchio e il Mare* is a must-visit. Situated in the dock area near Fortino, this venue offers a sizable outdoor terrace where patrons can dance into the early hours of the morning.

POLIGNANO A MARE

Polignano a Mare is arguably one of the most scenic coastal destinations in Italy, if not all of Europe. Positioned around 25 miles southeast of Bari, this quaint town sits atop expansive limestone cliffs that descend into the Adriatic Sea. Despite its modest population of approximately 24,000 residents, Polignano a Mare offers a wealth of activities to captivate visitors for several days. Whether exploring the enchanting historic district or basking in the breathtaking vistas of Lama Monachile Beach, there's something to enchant every traveler seeking experiences in Polignano a Mare. Polignano a Mare is pronounced *poh-lee-NYAH-noh ah MAH-reh.*

BEST TIME TO VISIT: The best times to visit Polignano a Mare are during late spring (April or May) or early fall (September or October). During these periods, you can avoid the summer crowds and excessive heat. If you are interested in attending the Festa di San Vito, it's important to plan your visit for June 14-16. Conversely, if you prefer to avoid large crowds and festivities, it's advisable to steer clear of Polignano a Mare during these dates.

GETTING TO POLIGNANO A MARE

There are two primary transportation options to conveniently reach Polignano a Mare, situated just 18 miles southeast of Bari: by car or by train. By Car: Starting from Bari, follow the SS16 route toward Brindisi/Lecce. Drive approximately 30 minutes southeast along the picturesque SS16, which winds along the cliff edges. Exit the SS16 at Polignano a Mare Sud, where you can then navigate to your accommodation. I recommend either obtaining an Italian SIM card or utilizing a GPS-equipped vehicle to facilitate navigation. Depending on traffic conditions, the approximately 25-mile journey typically takes around 36 minutes. You can visit: https://www.discovercars.com to rent a car. | BY TRAIN: To travel from Bari to Polignano a Mare, catch a train from Bari Centrale. The journey lasts between 30 to 45 minutes and costs €2.50 regardless of the train you choose. For more detailed information, refer to my comprehensive guide on how to travel from Bari to Polignano a Mare by train.

WHERE TO STAY IN POLIGNANO A MARE

While the options for accommodations in Polignano a Mare aren't abundant, there's still a selection to consider. However, it's worth noting that budget-friendly choices are somewhat limited. Below are my top picks for hotels in Polignano a Mare:

Hotel Grotta Palazzese (Luxury): This remarkable hotel, situated within a cave, offers a unique and luxurious experience. Though it comes with a higher price tag compared to other options, it's well worth a visit even if you can't stay overnight. Be sure to check out the restaurant for an unforgettable dining experience. | **_POSEA –_** Polignano Sea Suites (Mid-range): If you're searching for mid-range accommodations with a touch of luxury without breaking the bank, POSEA – Polignano Sea Suites is an excellent choice. Located by the beach, this hotel provides great value with its terraces, cozy rooms, and more. | **_Casa della Nonna (Budget):_** While Casa della Nonna might be considered a budget option, it leans towards the higher end of the spectrum, offering travelers all the essential amenities. With complimentary Wi-Fi, luggage storage, and clean, comfortable rooms, it's a solid choice for those on a tighter budget.

WHAT TO SEE & DO IN POLIGNANO A MARE

1. EXPLORE POLIGNANO A MARE'S ANCIENT QUARTER: Discover the rich history of Polignano a Mare as you wander through its enchanting ancient district. Stroll along labyrinthine alleys, admire whitewashed buildings, and soak in the vibrant atmosphere of squares like Piazza Dell'Orologio. As night falls, indulge in the town's lively nightlife with a taste of exquisite Italian wine.

2. **ENJOY COASTAL BEAUTY AT LAMA MONACHILE BEACH:** Relax on the stunning white pebble beach nestled within towering cliffs and clear waters. Take in panoramic views of perched houses and sea caves while savoring refreshments from a nearby beachside bar. Adventure awaits with opportunities for diving off adjacent ledges or exploring neighboring beaches near Monopoli.

3. **EXPERIENCE THRILLING CLIFF DIVING:** Witness the adrenaline-pumping sport of cliff diving against Polignano a Mare's dramatic coastal backdrop. Optimal cliffs and water depth attract daredevil divers, with the town hosting the Italian leg of the Red Bull Cliff Diving World Championships since 2014.

4. **UNCOVER ARTISTIC TREASURES:** Explore the artistic essence of Polignano a Mare's old quarter, adorned with poetic verses on walls and doorways. Look out for landmarks like the Poetry Stairs, where a poignant poem unfolds with each step. Seek guidance from locals for efficient navigation to these cultural gems.

5. **DINE IN A CAVE AT GROTTA PALAZZESE:** Experience an unforgettable dining experience at Grotta Palazzese, a renowned 5-star hotel and restaurant nestled within a remarkable sea cave. Dating back to the 1700s, this historic cave offers a refined atmosphere for enjoying delectable fresh seafood amidst mesmerizing Adriatic vistas. Adjacent to the restaurant, the luxurious hotel boasts captivating sea views, providing an extraordinary accommodation option in Polignano a Mare.

6. **DISCOVER BREATHTAKING VANTAGE POINTS:** Explore Polignano a Mare's old quarter to find stunning vantage points offering sweeping views of the sea and cliff-perched town. Terrazza Santo Stefano is a particularly renowned spot, providing panoramic views of the beach and quaint cliffside dwellings. Numerous enchanting spots throughout the town invite visitors to pause and admire the raw beauty of this gem often hailed as the "Jewel of Puglia."

7. **VISIT THE MUSEUM OF CONTEMPORARY ART:** Located on the southeastern fringe of the town, overlooking the coast, the Museum of Contemporary Art Pino Pascali showcases the minimalist contemporary art style of the celebrated artist born in Polignano a Mare. The museum,

housed within a former slaughterhouse-turned-art gallery since 1998, features Pascali's renowned sculptures alongside rotating exhibits by various contemporary artists, offering visitors a dynamic artistic experience.

8. EXPERIENCE SERENITY AT THE CHURCH OF SAINT MARY OF THE ASSUMPTION: Nestled in the heart of the old quarter, the Church of Saint Mary of the Assumption offers a serene atmosphere and understated elegance. Constructed in the 13th century atop an ancient pagan temple, the church boasts ornate art and sculptures dating back centuries, providing a glimpse into its rich historical legacy. Accessible only on Saturdays and Sundays, visitors can explore the church's exquisite interior free of charge, located at Piazza Vittorio Emanuele II, Number 21 in Polignano a Mare.E

9. PAY TRIBUTE TO DOMENICO MODUGNO: Celebrate the musical legacy of Domenico Modugno, born in Polignano a Mare in 1928. Best known for his iconic song "Volare (Nel blu, dipinto di blu)," Modugno's connection to the town is honored with a statue near the Scalinata "Volare" viewpoint. The statue, facing the town with outstretched arms, offers a brief yet rewarding visit.

10. MARVEL AT PONTE LAMA MONACHILE: Explore the ancient Roman legacy of Polignano a Mare through Ponte Lama Monachile, a Roman bridge crossing near Cala Porto/Lama Moncachile beach. Once part of the Via Triana, this bridge provides splendid views of the beach and cove, showcasing Roman craftsmanship over two millennia ago.

11. DELIGHT IN GELATO IN THE OLD QUARTER: Experience the renowned Italian gelato tradition in Polignano a Mare's old town. Sample exquisite flavors crafted by artisanal ice cream makers, including the prized Apulian fig gelato, available at Caruso Note d'Eccellenza.

12. EXPERIENCE SPECIAL COFFEE CULTURE: Discover Polignano a Mare's unique coffee culture with Special Coffee, exclusively served at "Il Super Mago del Gelo Mario Campanella." This local innovation blends coffee, cream, sugar, lemon zest, and amaretto for a delightful treat enjoyed by locals and tourists alike.

13. ENTER THE OLD TOWN THROUGH PORTA GRANDE: Step into Polignano a Mare's old town through Porta Grande, a historic gateway erected in 1530. While its defensive function has faded, the gateway remains a poignant relic, offering glimpses into the town's strategic past and enhancing the arrival experience.

REALISTIC ITINERARY FOR A DAY IN POLIGNANO A MARE

Upon arrival, park your vehicle at Parcheggio San Francesco, then proceed to Polignano by driving to the large pay and display lot, also known as Parcheggio San Francesco e Sant'Oronzo. It's just a brief 10-minute walk from there to the historic center.

TOP TIP: Utilize the EasyPark app for convenient parking management. It allows remote credit addition and refunds for early departures, ensuring hassle-free parking experiences. | *STAY INFORMED:* Note that from June to early September, certain main roads in Polignano a Mare, including the historic center, are part of a ZTL (Limited Traffic Zone). Pay attention to prominent signage upon entering the town.

EXPLORE LAMA MONACHILE: Begin your day by visiting the renowned Lama Monachile. To beat the crowds, arrive early and soak in the breathtaking views from the Ponte Borbonico bridge before descending the stairs to Ponte Romano. Enjoy a leisurely walk along the paved path leading to the picturesque stony beach, where you can relax and admire the scenic beauty. In case swimming isn't ideal due to weather, seize the opportunity to unwind with a book or snack while reveling in the captivating seaside vistas. Consider revisiting later in the day to avoid the bustling crowds. | *Insider's Tip:* The Porta Romana viewpoint of Lama Monachile offers equally stunning photo opportunities, particularly when framed by the arches of Ponte Borbonico. | *Exercise Caution:* Watch your step on the sandy and wet steps and pathways, as they can become slippery.

Indulge in Local Delicacies: After ascending from the beach, satisfy your cravings by heading to Il Super Mago del Gelo, a top-notch gelateria conveniently located near the Porta Vecchia entrance. Alternatively, if savory treats are more to your liking, visit the stand run by Katia and Francesco across the street. Sample their assortment of taralli and olives, including flavorful varieties like turmeric-infused taralli and the delectable bella di Cerignola olives.

STROLL THROUGH POLIGNANO'S OLD TOWN: Embark on a leisurely stroll through Polignano's historic center, commencing from Via Roma and traversing Via Anemone towards Piazza San Benedetto. Continue onwards to

Piazza Vittorio Emanuele II, where you can admire the Palazzo dell'Orologio and the Chiesa di Santa Maria Assunta in Cielo (Duomo). Don't miss the opportunity to detour to the terrazza con vista mare for panoramic views overlooking Lama Monachile.

SAVOR SEAFOOD DELIGHTS AT PESCARIA: Treat yourself to a seafood feast at Pescaria, a renowned sandwich shop offering delectable seafood options. Whether you opt to dine in or grab takeout, be prepared for a short wait, approximately 30 minutes, for your order. Alternatively, for a sit-down meal, consider L'Osteria di Chichibio, a Michelin-starred restaurant renowned for its seafood dishes.

ADMIRE VIEWS FROM LARGO ARDITO: Enjoy spectacular views of Polignano a Mare, including the Grotta Palazzese and the scenic coastline, from the panoramic viewpoint at Largo Ardito. Take a leisurely stroll along the lungomare to further appreciate the coastal beauty.

PAY TRIBUTE TO DOMENICO MODUGNO: Pay homage to the renowned Italian singer Domenico Modugno at his statue, set against the backdrop of the sea. Descend the scalinata behind the statue to reach the rocky pietra piatta area overlooking the water.

RELISH APERITIVO WITH A VIEW: Indulge in a refreshing aperitivo while enjoying vistas of the sea or the bustling piazzas. Opt for La Casa del Mojito for a change with their specialty mojitos, or return to Piazza Aldo Moro for classic Aperol spritzes at Spritz e Polpette.

DEPARTURE OR DINNER DECISION: Conclude your day by either returning to Parcheggio San Francesco to head back to your accommodation or opting to stay for dinner in Polignano. There are numerous dining options available, including L'Osteria di Chichibio for a leisurely seafood dinner or Il Quadrifoglio for excellent pizza.

ADDITIONAL ACTIVITIES: Depending on your time and interests, consider embarking on an Ape Tour for an informative local experience, exploring San Vito for a change of scenery, or taking a boat tour to explore the fascinating caves along the coastline. Additionally, keep an eye out for special events such as the Festa di San Vito or the Red Bull Cliff Diving World Series for added excitement during your visit.

MONOPOLI

Monopoli is a charming coastal town known for its picturesque old town, stunning beaches, and historic architecture, Monopoli offers visitors a mix of cultural richness and seaside relaxation. With its winding streets, colorful buildings, and vibrant atmosphere, it's a popular destination for tourists seeking authentic Italian experiences. The quaint village lies approximately 47 minutes southeast of Bari and is famed for its visually appealing white-painted dwellings, which create a striking contrast against the azure waves gently lapping the shoreline.

GETTING TO MONOPOLY

Getting to Monopoli is most convenient from Bari, the main city in Puglia, which boasts an airport and excellent connections across Italy. Situated approximately 29 miles southeast of Bari, there are several straightforward methods to reach Monopoli efficiently.

⇒ **BY CAR:** If you're utilizing a rental car, Monopoli is just a 47-minute drive from Bari. Departing from Bari, follow the SS16 towards Brindisi/Lecce. Take the Monopoli North exit and follow signage or use a navigation system to reach your destination. Enjoy the scenic coastal views along the way, and if you have spare time, consider stopping by charming towns like Polignano a Mare.

⇒ **BY TRAIN:** Direct trains operate regularly from Bari Centrale to Monopoli, with fares starting as low as €3.60. The journey duration ranges from 25 to 55 minutes, depending on the train type, though the standard ticket price remains consistent regardless of train selection.

THINGS TO SEE AND DO IN MONOPOLI

⇒ *__Discover the Charm of Monopoli's Historic District:__* Monopoli's Old Town enchants with its winding streets, hidden churches, and centuries-old buildings, making it a must-visit in Puglia. Delve into its rich history, enjoy a moment of relaxation at a local café, or opt for a personalized walking tour for a deeper exploration.

⇒ *__Experience the Magnificence of Monopoli's Landmark Cathedral:__* Basilica of the Madonna della Madia, Monopoli's landmark cathedral, boasts a storied past dating back to the 12th century. Admire its awe-inspiring interior adorned with frescoes depicting miraculous events. Don't miss the festival honoring the Madonna icon, celebrated twice a year. Access may vary during mass times.

⇒ *__Marvel at the Scenery from Castello di Carlo:__* Castello di Carlo, overlooking Monopoli, offers stunning views of the sea and harbor. Once a fortress and later a prison, it now hosts conferences and exhibitions. Explore the castle grounds for panoramic vistas or visit the exhibition center for artistic offerings.

⇒ *__Marvel at the Scenery from Castello di Carlo:__* Monopoli's beaches, like Cala Porta Vecchia and Lido Colonia, offer serene escapes with pristine sands and clear waters. Enjoy sunbathing or rent a sun lounger for a relaxing day. Adjacent bars and taverns provide refreshing beverages and delicious bites.

⇒ *__Explore the Ruins of Il Bastione del Molino:__* Il Bastione del Molino, a historic fortress in Monopoli, showcases cannons & defensive walls from bygone eras. Despite its compact size, it offers a captivating glimpse into the city's defensive history. Located near the coastline, it provides panoramic views of the ancient walls encircling the city.

⇒ *__Step Into History at Chiesa di San Salvatore:__* Chiesa di San Salvatore, one of Monopoli's oldest churches, exudes minimalist beauty and serves as a venue for cultural events. Despite its turbulent past, including theft and disuse, the church has been restored and remains a significant historical site.

⇒ *__Indulge in Fresh Seafood Delights at Komera, Cucina Nostra:__* Komera, Cucina Nostra offers fresh seafood delights in a modern setting. Enjoy generous portions of succulent fish, octopus, and mussels. The restaurant's ambiance and attentive staff make for a memorable dining experience in Monopoli.

⇒ *__Savor Exquisite Craft Beer at Birra Del Console:__* Birra del Console, a craft brewery in Monopoli, offers meticulously crafted beers. Collaborations with local restaurants create exclusive brews tailored to their menus. Explore their selection at Illuppolati craft beer bar and support local entrepreneurship.

⇒ **Explore the Egnazia Archaeological Park:** Egnazia Archaeological Park, south of Monopoli, showcases ruins spanning from the Messapian to the Roman periods. Marvel at its ancient history and ongoing excavations, providing insights into its past.

⇒ **Experience the Sunrise at the Historic Old Harbor:** Witness the beauty of sunrise at Monopoli's historic old harbor, with blue fishing boats against whitewashed buildings and a charming lighthouse guiding boats.

⇒ **Appreciate the Grandeur of Palmieri Palace:** Palmieri Palace, though now in disrepair, offers glimpses of its former grandeur through magnificent frescoes and architecture. The courtyard provides a serene retreat from the bustle of the old town.

⇒ **Enjoy a Coffee at Piazza Giuseppe Garibaldi:** Piazza Giuseppe Garibaldi, nestled in the old town, invites visitors to savor coffee or wine while people-watching. The vibrant square offers a glimpse into Italian daily life amidst cafes and bars.

⇒ **Embark on a Journey to the Museo e Sito Archeologico Cripta Romanica:** Museo e Sito Archeologico Cripta Romanica beneath the Monopoli Cathedral showcases 4,000 years of history, including remnants of a Roman temple and artifacts from the Bronze Age. Limited opening hours offer a unique opportunity to explore tangible history.

WHERE TO DINE IN MONOPOLI

Rosso Granato Monopoli: This eatery boasts an impressive nearly 5-star rating, renowned for its outstanding service and fresh, authentic Italian cuisine, making it an ideal choice for those seeking an introduction to Italian culinary delights. | **La Locanda dei Mercanti (Via Giuseppe Garibaldi, 44)** – A classic spot for seafood dining in Monopoli. Casual ambiance with quality dishes like seabream and grilled veggies. Reserve ahead to snag one of the cozy outdoor tables along Via Garibaldi. Despite its bustling atmosphere, this restaurant remains a popular choice due to its delectable offerings, ranging from fresh seafood to traditional Italian pasta dishes. They offer exceptional service and quality meals. | **Ristorante Piazza Palmieri:** Offering a convenient spot for a swift lunch, this restaurant presents a diverse menu featuring pasta, appetizers, seafood, and more. Diners can relish the inviting ambiance while savoring a taste of Italian cuisine. | **Al Maré:** Situated in proximity to the sea, Al Maré attracts many patrons eager to sample its exquisite seafood offerings while enjoying picturesque views of the azure waters. | ***Pinsotti (Via Santa Caterina, 9)*** – Enjoy delicious Roman-style hand-pressed pizza known as pinsa in a lively setting just off Via Garibaldi. Don't miss the pasta straws – a hit with kids! Perfect for a casual meal, with gluten-free options available. | ***Munz Munz BiOstrot (Via Cimino, 33)*** – Vibrant vegan and organic dishes await you in this cheerful eatery, also great for breakfast. | **Piazza Garibaldi** – Spend leisurely moments in this square. ***Vini e Panini*** offers excellent aperitivo and sandwiches, while ***Caffè Venezia*** serves up relaxed breakfasts. For gelato, don't miss Bella Blu Gelateria on the corner – our top pick in town.

FINDING YOUR PERFECT STAY IN MONOPOLI, ITALY

Choosing the right accommodation in Monopoli depends on your budget, travel style, and desired amenities. There is a wide array of hotel and apartment options available in Monopoli. Among MY personal recommendations are: **Palazzo Cesare** - Recently renovated 19th-century palace turned B&B apartments in Monopoli, Italy. Prime location just 200 meters from white beaches, spacious rooms with modern amenities, and attentive host Francesco ensure a memorable stay. | **Hotel Don Ferrante** - Romantic retreat in an ancient fortress overlooking the sea in Monopoli. Spacious, beautifully decorated rooms with top-notch amenities. Rooftop terrace and pool offer breathtaking ocean views. Excellent service and dining options make for an unforgettable stay in Puglia. | **Kees Apulian Stay** - Exceptional accommodation in the heart of Monopoli, Italy. Air-conditioned holiday home with a spacious terrace and well-equipped kitchen. Complimentary WiFi, flat-screen TV, and private bathroom with free toiletries. Easy access to beaches and attractions with friendly hosts for a memorable stay in Apulia. For more accommodation options in Monopoli, visit: ***https://www.myboutiquehotel.com/en/boutique-hotels-monopoli***

Visiting Monopoli with Kids: Monopoli is a must-see destination for families traveling in Puglia. While it may not have specific kid-centric attractions, children can enjoy exploring the charming streets of Monopoli, providing a delightful day out for both parents and kids alike.

CASTEL DEL MONTE

Enigmatic and perfectly octagonal, this structure stands out as one of the most intriguing landmarks in southern Italy, recognized as a UNESCO World Heritage Site. Despite its fame, the purpose behind Frederick II's construction remains a mystery. Situated far from any significant settlement or strategic point, the castle lacks typical defensive features such as a moat, drawbridge, arrow slits, or trapdoors for defensive measures like pouring boiling oil on attackers.

Various theories suggest that, in the context of the mid-13th-century fascination with geometric symbolism, the octagonal shape symbolized the fusion of the circle and square, representing the convergence of divine perfection (the infinite) and human perfection (the finite). Consequently, the castle was interpreted as a symbol of the profound connection between humanity and the divine.

Comprising eight octagonal towers, the castle boasts interconnecting rooms adorned with ornate marble columns and fireplaces, while its doorways and windows are elegantly framed in corallite stone. Notably, many towers feature washing rooms equipped with what are believed to be Europe's earliest flushing toilets – a testament to Frederick II's appreciation for cleanliness, influenced by the hygiene practices of the Arab world he admired. For a comprehensive understanding of the castle's history and significance, investing in the audio guides (€3) is highly recommended to enrich your visit.

HOW TO GET THERE

There are several transportation options to reach Castel del Monte from Bari, catering to various preferences and budgets: **BY CAR:** This offers the fastest and most flexible journey, typically taking around 55 minutes via the SS96 and SP231 roads, covering approximately 56 kilometers. While there is a parking lot near the castle, it tends to fill up quickly, so arriving early is advisable. | **BY TRAIN AND TAXI:** For a more leisurely travel experience, albeit longer (approximately 1 hour and 20 minutes), one can board the Ferrovie Nord Barese train from Bari Centrale station to Andria station. From there, a taxi ride to Castel del Monte is necessary. | **BY BUS AND TAXI:** Opting for the most economical but time-consuming route (around 1 hour and 30 minutes), passengers can take the Flixbus from Bari to Corato and then proceed with a taxi to Castel del Monte. | **BY TOUR:** Various tour operators offer excursions from Bari that encompass a visit to Castel del Monte, ideal for those seeking guided insights into the castle and its surroundings.

TIPS: When planning your trip to Castel del Monte, consider the following: The castle is open from Tuesday to Sunday, operating from 9:00 am to 7:00 pm. | Tickets can be purchased either online or at the ticket office. | Guided tours in English are available for an additional fee. | It is advisable to wear comfortable footwear as some walking is involved during the visit. **PHONE NUMBER:** 0883 56 99 97 | **WEBSITE:** https://www.casteldelmonte.beniculturali.it

WHAT TO SEE AND DO AT THE CASTEL DEL MONTE

1. Explore the castle's architecture: The primary highlight undoubtedly lies in exploring the castle itself. Wander through the octagonal courtyard, marvel at the intricate stonework, and ascend to the rooftop for sweeping vistas of the surrounding landscapes.

2. Dive into its historical significance: Erected by Holy Roman Emperor Frederick II in the 13th century, Castel del Monte's exact purpose remains shrouded in mystery, speculated to serve as a hunting lodge, military bastion, or a symbol of imperial authority. Delve deeper into its historical narrative by visiting the on-site museum.

3. Embark on a guided exploration: For a more immersive experience, opt for a guided tour available in both English and Italian, lasting approximately an hour, to gain deeper insights into the castle's heritage and secrets.

4. Revel in panoramic panoramas: Perched atop a hill, the castle offers breathtaking panoramas of the surrounding countryside, extending as far as the Adriatic Sea on clear days.

5. Unwind amidst tranquil gardens: Take respite in the castle's serene gardens, where you can bask in tranquility amidst nature's embrace.

6. Indulge in a picturesque picnic: Adjacent to the castle lies a designated picnic area, perfect for savoring a packed lunch while soaking in the ambiance.

7. Explore Andria's charms: Extend your excursion by visiting the nearby town of Andria, boasting a captivating cathedral and vibrant main square, enriching your cultural experience beyond the castle's confines.

OTHER TERRA DI BARI TOWNS WORTH EXPLORING

Among the numerous treasures that adorn Puglia's coastline are the sparkle towns of Barletta, Giovinazzo, Molfetta, and Bitonto. Each of these towns possesses a distinct character, offering a delightful fusion of history, culture, and coastal allure.

BARLETTA

Barletta, a city of nearly 95,000 people located approximately an hour north of Bari, immediately impresses visitors with its numerous grand monuments scattered throughout the area, indicating its historical significance. The standout attraction is the remarkably well-preserved castle dating back to the 1200s, which is highly recommended to explore. Additionally, Barletta boasts a charming cathedral, the impressive Palazzo della Marra museum, and the renowned Colossus of Barletta. This colossal bronze monument, depicting a Roman emperor, was accidentally discovered by a local fisherman after being dragged out of the sea.

GIOVINAZZO

Undergoing a significant revitalization effort, Giovinazzo is witnessing residents returning to its historic quarter, much to the delight of visitors who discover this hidden gem. The picturesque old town features cobblestone streets, pedestrianized for leisurely strolls, flanked by charming whitewashed buildings. Along the lungomare, or boardwalk, visitors can enjoy a delightful waterfront promenade. What's more, the town remains relatively undiscovered outside of the peak tourist season, offering a serene atmosphere for much of the year.

BITONTO

Bitonto may not always be the most aesthetically pleasing destination in Puglia, but its authenticity and historical significance make it a compelling stop for travelers exploring the northern towns and cities around Bari. The highlight of Bitonto is the Duomo di Bitonto, a Norman cathedral constructed in the 1100s, renowned as one of the finest examples of Romanesque architecture in the region.

MOLFETTA

Molfetta, situated in the northern region of the Metropolitan City of Bari, Apulia, Southern Italy, lies at the northwest corner of its province. It shares borders with Bisceglie (BT), Giovinazzo, Terlizzi, and Ruvo di Puglia along the Adriatic Coast. Molfetta is approximately 27 kilometers from Andria, 31 kilometers from Barletta, and 34 kilometers from Bari. Molfetta boasts several significant landmarks. ***Il Pulo***, a Neolithic site, features a circular cave with ancient constructions. ***The Old Cathedral***, built in the 12th–13th centuries, showcases Apulian-Romanesque architecture. Watchtowers like ***Torre Calderina*** and ***Torrione Passari*** stand as historical sentinels. ***The New Cathedral***, constructed by Jesuits in 1610, houses relics of San Corrado. Other notable sites include ***the church of San Bernardino da Siena***, ***Palazzo Giovene,*** and the ***church of Santa Maria Consolatrice degli Afflitti***. Additionally, ***the Temple of Calvary*** and the ***basilica-sanctuary of the Madonna dei Martiri*** hold religious and historical significance. The ***Molfetta Lighthouse*** remains operational on the eastern pier.

PART 3: THE ITRIA VALLEY

The Itria Valley, nestled in the picturesque region of Apulia in Southern Italy, boasts a landscape rich in history, culture, and natural beauty. Stretching across the provinces of Bari, Brindisi, and Taranto, this enchanting region offers visitors a glimpse into the region's ancient past and vibrant present. One of the most iconic features of the Itria Valley is its distinctive trulli, traditional round stone dwellings with cone-shaped roofs. These unique structures, recognized as UNESCO World Heritage sites, dot the landscape, offering a glimpse into the region's architectural heritage. Wander through the labyrinthine streets of towns like Alberobello and Locorotondo in the Province of Bari, where clusters of trulli create a fairy tale-like atmosphere. Beyond its architectural wonders, the Itria Valley is renowned for its agricultural bounty. Olive groves stretch as far as the eye can see, their gnarled trees bearing witness to centuries of cultivation. Vineyards, too, flourish in the fertile soil, producing crisp white wines that delight the palate and reflect the region's dedication to viticulture. Key towns overlooking the Itria Valley include Alberobello & Locorotondo in the Province of Bari, Cisternino & Ostuni in the Province of Brindisi and Martina Franca, in the Province of Taranto.

ALBEROBELLO

Nestled in the picturesque Valle d'Itria (Itria Valley), Alberobello stands as one of Puglia's most iconic towns, renowned worldwide for its enchanting Trulli houses. Alberobello, situated in the southern Italian region of Puglia, is renowned for its extraordinary Trulli houses. These dry-stone residences, characterized by their iconic conical roofs, have earned recognition as a UNESCO World Heritage Site, attracting visitors from around the globe. The Trulli district of Alberobello is divided into two principal areas: Rione Monti and Aia Piccola. Rione Monti, the larger and more frequented area, boasts narrow streets adorned with Trulli shops, eateries, and cafes. In contrast, Aia Piccola offers a smaller, quieter ambiance, preserving a more authentic feel. Exploring either area promises enchantment with the unique architecture of the Trulli. The combination of whitewashed walls, conical rooftops, and vibrant symbols adorning some of the houses creates a truly magical environment. Beyond its Trulli, Alberobello presents a plethora of other attractions, including the 17th-century Church of Santa Maria dei Cosmi, featuring a stunning Baroque facade. The Museo del Territorio Casa Pezzolla provides insight into Alberobello's history and its Trulli dwellings. Additionally, visitors can enjoy panoramic vistas of the town and surrounding countryside from the Belvedere lookout point. For travelers seeking an unforgettable experience, Alberobello offers a compelling destination. Its charming Trulli houses, delectable cuisine, and welcoming locals ensure a memorable visit that lingers in the memory long after departure.

According to UNESCO, which designated Alberobello as a World Heritage site in 1996, the distinctive trulli (singular: trullo) represent: "exceptional instances of drywall (mortarless) construction, an ancient building method still practiced in this area. These trulli are constructed from roughly shaped limestone rocks gathered from nearby fields. Notably, they exhibit pyramid-shaped, domed, or conical roofs constructed using stacked limestone slabs."

IS ALBEROBELLO WORTH A VISIT?

Our experience in Alberobello left us slightly underwhelmed. As expected, it's heavily touristed, which somewhat alters its charm. We explored for a couple of hours, browsed shops, snapped photos, and grabbed a late breakfast. However, we found ourselves eager to move on to nearby towns like Locorotondo, especially as large tour groups began to flood in after 10 a.m. That said, Alberobello is undeniably unique with an important story, and we don't regret visiting. We recommend arriving before 9 a.m or after 5 pm to avoid the crowds or coming in the late afternoon once they've thinned out. While I must admit my reservations about recommending a visit due to its overt touristy atmosphere, I understand its inevitable inclusion on your itinerary. Alberobello's historic center, predominantly composed of meticulously restored and preserved Trulli structures, offers a captivating sight and has earned recognition as a UNESCO World Heritage site. However, it's essential to acknowledge the overwhelming tourist influx, particularly during the peak season from May to October, which can diminish the authenticity of the experience. I typically advise allocating around 30 minutes to an hour for a brief exploration of Alberobello. This allows time to admire the unique architecture, enjoy a leisurely stroll, and perhaps indulge in a coffee break before venturing to more captivating nearby towns like Locorotondo, Martina Franca, and Ostuni. During these peak hours, the influx of tour buses and day-trippers from cruise ships can detract from the charm of the town.

HOW TO GET TO ALBEROBELLO

BY CAR: Opting for a car rental is the most convenient way to explore Alberobello, especially if you're touring Puglia extensively. Renting a car grants you flexibility and access to remote areas that may not be reachable by public transport. There are two paid parking lots near Rione Monti, costing €6 per day, which can be easily located by following the signs upon entering Alberobello or using Google Maps. However, be mindful that these lots tend to fill up quickly, particularly after 11 am. In case these lots are full, there are alternative parking options just a short walk away. When renting a car, it's advisable to compare deals across various platforms like **_AutoEurope_** or **_RentalCars_** to secure the best rates and vehicle options.

USING PUBLIC TRANSPORT: BY TRAIN: Alberobello is accessible by train, especially from nearby towns like **_Martina Franca_** and **_Locorotondo,_** which offer regular services taking around 10 to 20 minutes. If coming from **_Bari_**, you can catch a train to **_Putignano_** and transfer to a direct train to **_Alberobello_**, which takes a little over two hours. Alternatively, there's a direct bus service from **_Bari to Alberobello_**, departing from a station within the new town. **BY BUS:** There's a direct bus route connecting Bari to Alberobello, departing regularly from a station in the new town. | **_JOINING ORGANIZED TOURS:_** If you prefer guided tours, there are various options available from different locations in the region.

WHAT TO SEE & DO IN ALBEROBELLO

Certainly, the primary allure drawing visitors to Alberobello is undoubtedly the opportunity to stroll through its streets adorned with trulli, a sight unparalleled anywhere else in the world.

THE RIONE MONTI QUARTER: Upon reaching the heart of the town, one immediately recognizes the focal point - **_the Rione Monti quarter_** nestled within the 'trulli zone'. Positioned slightly uphill, it boasts over 1,000 trulli structures, dominating the architectural landscape. Despite its touristy ambiance, characterized by gift shops lining the streets, the area exudes an undeniable charm. For those vertically challenged, like ourselves, navigating among the trulli imparts a sense of grandeur akin to that of a giant. The best approach is to embrace spontaneity, aimlessly wandering through the streets, uncovering serene alleys or picturesque corners away from the main thoroughfares. In Rione Monti, proprietors leisurely bask in the sunlight, enticing passersby to explore their establishments. While there's a subtle expectation of patronage, there's no aggressive sales tactics employed, providing an opportunity to peek inside these unique buildings. Tourism evidently sustains the local economy, thus supporting local businesses by purchasing souvenirs or items of interest is encouraged. | **TIP:** Be sure not to overlook "il trullo più piccolo" (the smallest trullo for non-Italian speakers), now converted into a souvenir shop, easily locatable on Google Maps this GPS Coordinates: 40.782572, 17.236800 | **RIONE AIA PICCOLA DISTRICT:** For a more authentic immersion into trulli living, venture into the Rione Aia Piccola district, where around 500 trulli stand with less commercialization. Here, one can observe locals inhabiting these gnome-sized dwellings and witness elderly Italian men leisurely strolling the streets, a scene reminiscent of the town's pre-tourist era. Additionally, this area offers the most panoramic views overlooking the clustered trulli patches of Alberobello. For those intrigued by the historical background of Alberobello and its trulli, a guided tour is recommended. A highly praised two-hour walking tour encompassing the aforementioned neighborhoods provides valuable insights at a reasonable cost.

OTHER NOTABLE ATTRACTIONS WITHIN ALBEROBELLO INCLUDE:

⇒ **Trullo Sovrano:** The sole trullo in the village boasting two floors, now serving as a heritage museum. | ⇒ *Sant'Antonio Church:* The town's church, uniquely constructed in trullo style. | ⇒ *Casa d'Amore:* A historical landmark symbolizing the end of feudalism in Alberobello. | ⇒ *Arte Fredda:* Renowned for serving the finest gelato in town. | ⇒ *Pasqualino:* Sample the town's signature sandwich, a culinary creation since 1966. | ⇒ *Food Tours and Cooking Classes:* Opportunities to savor local delicacies and learn traditional recipes. | ⇒ *Santuario di Santi Medici Cosma e Damiano:* An impressive sanctuary dedicated to the Saints Medici Cosma and Damiano. | ⇒ *Trullo Siamese:* The only trullo with two connected domes, now a souvenir shop. | Additionally, don't miss the Thursday morning street market along Via Barsento from 7:30 am to 12:30 pm.

WHERE TO STAY IN ALBEROBELLO

For a serene escape from the crowds, consider spending the night in a charming traditional trullo. Here are our top picks:

GUESTHOUSES & B&Bs: **BUDGET:** *Trulllieu Guesthouse* offers clean and tastefully decorated accommodations starting at £56 per night. Ideal for couples or families seeking a quiet retreat close to the tourist area. | **MID-RANGE:** *Trulli Casa* provides self-catering facilities and a garden for 2-4 guests, starting at £68 per night. Located just outside the trulli zone, it offers a convenient stay. | *Grandi Trulli Bed & Breakfast* offers a unique trulli experience with an en-suite bedroom, outdoor terrace, and breakfast included. Prices start at £80 per night for two people, accommodating up to four. | **LUXURY:** *Astra*, a 16th-century trullo, offers a romantic getaway in a peaceful setting, starting at £117 per night. Perfect for couples or honeymooners seeking a unique experience. | *Il Trullo dell' Agricoltore* boasts rustic luxury and authentic Italian charm, with rates starting at £126 per night. Experience the beauty of Alberobello in this unique trullo accommodation. | AIRBNBS: There are several trulli accommodations listed on Airbnb, both in Alberobello and its vicinity. We've selected three options within the village to cater to various budgets: ***Hermanas Relais***: Positioned as the epitome of luxury within Alberobello's center (albeit with a corresponding price tag of £172 per night for two guests), this accommodation boasts a meticulously restored interior that exudes a boutique hotel ambiance. | *Il Trullo della Massaia:* Despite its 400-year-old heritage, this trullo surprisingly offers ample space and seamlessly blends historical charm with contemporary amenities. Renovated with great care, it caters well to the needs of modern travelers. | *I trulli di nonna Totò*: Situated a bit away from the village, this accommodation offers exceptional value for money. Recently renovated, it features all modern conveniences along with a charming terrace. Rates start at £55 per night.

SCAN THIS QR CODE TO EXPLORE THE FULL MAP OF ALBEROBELLO

LOCOROTONDO

Locorotondo, a charming town in the Metropolitan City of Bari, celebrated for its population of around 14,000 residents and its picturesque location between Martina Franca and Alberobello in the Valle d'Itria. Designated as one of the most beautiful villages in Italy, Locorotondo has received the Orange Flag from the Touring Club of Italy, acknowledging its harmonious architecture and easily accessible historic old town. The town's appeal lies in its intricate narrow streets adorned with historic buildings, and it is renowned for its unique houses, "Le Cummerse," featuring regular geometric shapes and distinctive sloping roofs made of two layers of limestone slabs. These traditional dwellings have been renovated and transformed into scattered hotels, offering visitors a unique and immersive experience in this idyllic Italian setting.

REASONS TO EXPLORE LOCOROTONDO

For those who appreciate leisurely strolls, Locorotondo offers a unique charm with its absence of easily identifiable tourist attractions. It is a town that encourages you to wander aimlessly for a few hours, transitioning from the new town to the old, meandering through narrow streets, basking in the sun with a couple of aperol spritz, and perhaps exploring the numerous captivating workshops or dining al fresco at one of the incredibly charming side-street restaurants. Above all, Locorotondo is a place to relish the simple joy of being there. Amidst the various villages, towns, and cities we explored in Puglia, this hill-perched gem stood out as one of the most breathtaking.

In a region renowned for its spectacular beauty, the allure of Locorotondo is reason enough to pay it a visit, even if only for a few fleeting hours.

HOW TO GET TO LOCOROTONDO FROM BARI

BY CAR: There are three primary routes for reaching Locorotondo by car from Bari, each varying slightly in travel times and distances. The quickest option is via the SS16, covering 69 km in approximately 52 minutes. For a more scenic drive, the SP240 and SP146 offer a route taking about 1 hour and 12 minutes, spanning 69.2 km. Alternatively, the shortest route is through the SS172, covering 63.6 km in approximately 1 hour and 5 minutes. Car rental services are available at Bari and Brindisi airports through Auto Europe or RentalCars.

Parking in Locorotondo, like many small Italian towns, can be a bit challenging. While street parking is abundant, securing a free space can be difficult. Unless you arrive early or travel during the off-season, we recommend utilizing one of the larger parking lots located slightly outside the old town.

BY TRAIN: There are currently no direct trains from Bari. You'll have to take a bus to Putignano and then transferring to a train, turning what seems like a manageable distance into a somewhat lengthy day trip. However, there are regular, swift trains connecting Locorotondo to other tourist-centric towns and villages in the Valle d'Itria, such as Alberobello and Martina Franca. Alberobello station is conveniently located a short walk from the centro storico. It's important to be aware that on Sundays, the train service is replaced by a bus.

BY BUS: Another option is reaching Locorotondo by bus from Bari, with a direct journey taking approximately 1 hour and 20 minutes and costing around €5 per person. It's worth noting that the buses depart from a station on the outskirts of the old town rather than the city center of Bari. **TIPS:** For booking train tickets in Puglia, I recommend using Trenitalia or the Omio app, which provides comprehensive information on bus and train schedules throughout Europe.

WHERE TO STAY IN LOCOROTONDO

Staying in Locorotondo may pose a slight challenge for those on a tighter budget. While it doesn't necessarily require spending hundreds, the more upscale lodging options can be relatively pricier. However, given its proximity to other must-visit places like Martina Franca and Alberobello, Locorotondo serves as an excellent base for a day or two. | <u>**APARTMENTS IN LOCOROTONDO:**</u> Without a doubt, the most cost-effective lodging in Locorotondo is available through Airbnb, where you can secure an entire house, apartment, or trulli starting at around £50 per night—a notably economical choice compared to hotels in the area. Here are 5 recommended Airbnb options in Locorotondo: **_Ughetto:_** A traditional one-bedroom property in the heart of the old town, featuring a stylish and contemporary makeover. | **_Bel Panorama:_** Another traditional apartment with two bedrooms and a small balcony overlooking the lungomare, providing incredible views. **_Trulli Nannì:_** Ideal for those dreaming of a trulli experience, this option is located in the countryside but still a short distance from the center of Locorotondo. Set amidst olive groves, it boasts beautiful interiors and even offers access to a jacuzzi. | **_Central Apartment:_** A modern three-bedroom apartment just a few minutes' walk from the old town, suitable for families and equipped with parking. | **_Dimora Palmisan:_** A one-bedroom apartment with a vintage and traditional design, featuring a lovely outdoor space. While it currently isn't available, we'll keep an eye on the listing for any updates. | Other noteworthy Airbnbs include **_Umberto's Roof_**, **_Casa Lina_**, and **_Trullo di Flora and Nino_**. If you prefer a more traditional booking platform, booking.com also offers a variety of apartments.

<u>HOTELS / B&Bs IN LOCOROTONDO:</u> In Locorotondo, traditional hotels are not prevalent, so the following selection includes B&Bs and small trulli, some with self-catering facilities, all providing breakfast—ideal for short stays: **_Da Concavo e Convesso:_** A beautiful B&B in the center of the old town, lovingly restored and run by a local family. Francesco, who speaks perfect English, and his 'mama' are always available to offer freshly made Italian treats. | **_B&B Lamie Di Olimpia_**: Located a short walk from the town center, this modernized traditional trullo is suitable for those without a car but seeking a countryside trulli experience. Guests praise the helpful owner.

WHAT TO SEE AND DO IN LOCOROTONDO

After parking our rental car in the shade of a palm tree, we leisurely strolled from the newer yet equally charming part of the town into the historic centro storico. Amidst the maze of whitewashed lanes, crumbling facades, and grand baroque archways, we spent hours exploring. While the primary allure of Locorotondo lies in the joy of aimless wandering, Below are some suggestions on other things to see and do in Locorotondo: **_Lungomare Views:_** Being situated atop a hill, Locorotondo offers fantastic panoramic views of the surrounding countryside. Head to the limit of the hill-top town, known confusingly as the 'lungomare,' for the best vistas. This route provides spectacular panoramas of the valley below, featuring vineyards, olive groves, and trulli. _Don't miss the 19th-century gardens (Villa Comunale) on your way, especially if visiting in the summer._ | **_Photography:_** The narrow streets east of Piazza Vittorio Emanuele host an engaging open-air photography exhibit, showcasing old and new images depicting life in the town. Check the tourist office in the Piazza for more information. | **_Church Exploration:_** Chiesa Madre di San Giorgio, Santuario di San Rocco, and the Romanesque Chiesa della Madonna della Greca are the most impressive in town. Note that opening times can vary, so visiting in the early morning is advisable. | **_Wine Tasting:_** Locorotondo's renowned sparkling white wine, Bianco Locorotondo DOC, is available in many regional restaurants. While the main wine producer Cantina Sociale del Locorotondo has closed, Pavì wine restaurant, La Bottega de I Pastini, and Tò - Aperitivi e affini offer highly rated alternatives. | **_Festival Participation:_** Experience the local culture during patron saint days with a grand market fair for San Giorgio on April 22nd and 23rd or music and fireworks for San Rocco on August 16th. | **_Walking Tours:_** While group walking tours for Locorotondo may be scarce, consider a private guide for a two-hour walking tour.

SCAN THIS QR CODE TO EXPLORE THE FULL MAP OF LOCOROTONDO

CISTERNINO

Cisternino, located in the Brindisi province of Apulia along the southeastern coast of Italy, lies approximately 50 kilometers northwest of Brindisi city. Renowned as one of Italy's most picturesque villages, it thrives primarily on tourism, olive and grape cultivation, and dairy farming. Nestled within the historic confines of the Itria Valley, Cisternino boasts a landscape adorned with iconic trulli, ancient dry stone dwellings, recognized and safeguarded by UNESCO for their cultural importance. The region also showcases intricate dry stone walls and fertile soil, contributing to its distinction as part of the esteemed Salento wine region. Notably, in 2014, Cisternino earned the prestigious title of "cittaslow city of the year." Cisternino epitomizes the essence of a hidden gem in Puglia, deserving a prominent spot on any traveler's bucket list. Its unassuming and genuine charm, coupled with a distinct local flavor, make it one of the region's best-kept secrets. Embracing a laid-back ambiance, Cisternino welcomes more locals than tourists, offering an authentic glimpse into southern Italian life. Perched atop a hill, overlooking the picturesque Valle d'Itria adorned with trulli, this white-washed town promises a delightful afternoon exploration. Wandering through its enchanting historic center, characterized by narrow labyrinthine streets, indulging in delectable Puglian cuisine at local tavernas, and savoring sublime vistas, visitors are encouraged to unwind, immerse themselves in the local rhythm, and truly live like a native.

HOW TO GET TO CISTERNINO

BY CAR: If traveling from Bari, follow the SS16 towards Brindisi, then take the

SS77 towards Martina Franca, and finally turn right onto the SP61 leading to Cisternino. From Brindisi, take the SS77 towards Martina Franca and then the SP61 to Cisternino. If coming from Taranto, take the SS106 towards Martina Franca and then follow the SP61 to Cisternino. | **BY TRAIN:** The nearest train station to Cisternino is located in Fasano. You can catch a train from Bari or Brindisi to Fasano and then transfer to a bus or taxi to reach Cisternino. | **BY BUS:** There are bus services available from Bari and Brindisi to Cisternino. The journey takes approximately 2 hours from Bari and 1 hour 30 minutes from Brindisi. | **BY PLANE:** Brindisi Airport (BDS) is the closest airport to Cisternino. Upon arrival, you can opt for a bus or taxi to reach Cisternino, with the bus journey lasting about 1 hour and the taxi ride about 40 minutes.

WHAT TO DO IN CISTERNINO

While Cisternino is not teeming with tourist attractions, its allure lies in its simplicity and authenticity, making it an ideal place to visit when you are visiting Puglia. Whether you have just a few hours or a day to spare, Cisternino invites you to immerse yourself in its historic center, where narrow cobblestone streets adorned with laundry and flower pots lead to hidden gems. | ↠ *Exploring Cisternino's Historic Center:* The historic center, or Centro Storico, is a labyrinth of alleys waiting to be explored. Lose yourself in its enchanting streets, starting perhaps from the renowned Porta Piccola, and let the town reveal its secrets at every turn. While wandering, you'll stumble upon quaint piazzas and charming corners that epitomize the essence of Cisternino. | ↠ *Unveiling Hidden Gems:* Within this maze lies the Church of San Nicola di Patara, a modest yet significant landmark showcasing local artistry. Step inside to admire its Romanesque interior and the exquisite Madonna and Child sculpture by Stefano Putignano. Adjacent to the church stands the Torre Normanno, a medieval tower steeped in history, offering insights into Cisternino's past. | ↠ *Embracing Nature's Beauty:* For panoramic views and tranquility, venture to Villa Comunale Guiseppe Garibaldi, a verdant oasis atop a hill. Take a leisurely stroll through its lush gardens, soak in the serene atmosphere, and savor breathtaking vistas of the Itria Valley—a perfect spot to unwind and capture memorable moments. | ↠ *Savoring Local Flavors:* Indulge in a leisurely walk along Ponte della Madonnina, a charming promenade boasting picturesque surroundings and a selection of cozy eateries. Treat yourself to a refreshing Spritz at a hilltop bar, relishing the flavors while admiring the mesmerizing landscape. | ↠ *Exploring Puglian*

Wine Culture: No visit to Cisternino is complete without sampling its renowned wines. Head to Il Cucco, a reputable enoteca offering an array of local and regional wines. Engage with knowledgeable staff who are eager to guide you through their selection or opt for a wine tasting experience paired with delectable antipasti.

WHERE TO STAY IN CISTERNINO: The finest accommodations in Cisternino are often found in the picturesque countryside that surrounds the town, offering an ideal base for exploring not only Cisternino but also the neighboring towns of the Itria Valley, including Ostuni, Locorotondo, Alberobello, and Martina Franca. | ⇢ ***Borgo Canonica*** – Offering an opportunity to reside in one of the most stunning trullo homes, this exceptional property captivates with its characteristic conical roofs, low ceilings, and exposed stone. Perfect for design enthusiasts, staying here promises an unforgettable experience that might just inspire you to purchase your own trullo and never leave. | ⇢ ***Casa del Maestro*** – This budget-friendly option is ideal for those seeking a local, unpretentious yet comfortable stay. Positioned conveniently in the heart of Cisternino, this quaint abode ensures easy access to the town's attractions and amenities, making it a great choice for those who prefer staying within town limits. | ⇢ ***Il Campanile*** – Exuding charm, this cozy split-level apartment is perfect for short stays in Cisternino. Boasting a blend of traditional local architecture and modern décor, it features a well-equipped kitchen, a comfortable living area, and a bathroom downstairs, with a cozy bed nestled upstairs. | ⇢ ***Masseria Peppeturro*** – Offering the chance to immerse yourself in the authentic Puglian experience, this Masseria combines the charm of a trullo with the grandeur of a traditional Puglian farmhouse mansion. Featuring beautifully appointed rooms and a refreshing swimming pool, it provides a serene retreat just a short drive from town, making access to this countryside haven easy with a car.

WHERE TO DINE IN CISTERNINO: ⇢ ***Vattelappesca Restaurant & Wine*** – Situated on Ponte della Madonnina, this cozy eatery stands out as one of Cisternino's finest. Specializing in local Puglian cuisine with a focus on pasta and seafood, it offers an ideal setting to savor a glass of chilled white wine alongside fresh seafood or pasta dishes as you admire the sunset over Valle d'Itria. While not budget-friendly, the experience is certainly worth the indulgence. | ⇢ ***Micro*** – Catering to vegetarians and plant-based diners, this restaurant located on the northern edge of the historic center offers a thoughtful selection of dishes, ranging from sandwiches and Asian-inspired fare to soups and local favorites. | ↠ ***Cremeria History Vignola*** – Perched on a hilltop terrace along Via San Quirico, this establishment boasts one of the town's premier spots for enjoying sunset drinks with a panoramic view. Treat yourself to a refreshing spritz, secure a prime table, and relish your beverage while soaking in the picturesque vistas of the entire Itria Valley. | ↠ ***Sandrino*** – Positioned right on the bustling Piazza Vittorio Emanuele II, this local gem is the go-to destination for cooling off with gelato during the afternoon heat. Be sure to also admire the nearby clock tower dating back to 1850, adding historical charm to the plaza.

TOP TIPS FOR EXPLORING CISTERNINO: ↠ Respect the traditional siesta time observed in Cisternino, where virtually everything shuts down between 2:30 pm and around 6 pm, including restaurants, delis, and shops. Plan your visit accordingly by arriving in the morning or after 4 or 5 pm to make the most of your time, perhaps staying into the evening. | ↠ Parking is generally ample and hassle-free in Cisternino, unlike some busier towns in the Itria Valley such as Ostuni or Locorotondo. You may even find free parking spots along the streets. | ↠ While the outskirts of Cisternino lack significant charm, the real beauty lies in the historic center (centro storico). Focus your exploration there for the most rewarding experience. | ↠ Accessing Cisternino and other towns in the Itria Valley is best done by car, as public transportation options, such as buses, are limited and may require careful planning of your itinerary. Note that Cisternino station is not directly connected to the town itself but is a 15-minute drive away.

SCAN THIS QR CODE TO EXPLORE THE FULL MAP OF CISTERNINO

OSTUNI

Perched on a hill for defensive purposes, Ostuni forms an authentic labyrinth —a complex network of narrow pathways, staircases, and arches, where houses are intricately layered upon one another, unveiling centuries of history in a manner that eludes accurate representation on any map. With dead ends, charming gardens, fleeting views of the Adriatic Sea, vibrant green doors, and expansive blue skies, each corner turned in Ostuni may reveal both everything and nothing. Ostuni is an ideal destination for those with an explorer's spirit, beckoning to be savored slowly over a couple of days. It caters to history enthusiasts and individuals who relish meandering through beauty and embracing spontaneous Italian moments. This city is an essential inclusion in every Puglian itinerary. Ostuni, known as Ostune in Barese and Stune in Salentino, is a city and municipality situated approximately 8 km inland from the coast within the province of Brindisi, in the Apulia region of Italy. With a winter population of around 32,000 residents, the town experiences a significant surge in numbers during the summer, attracting up to 200,000 inhabitants and establishing itself as one of the prominent tourist destinations in Apulia. Ostuni is home to a steady community of British and German immigrants, along with an industrial zone. Renowned for its production of high-quality olive oil and wine, the region holds a strong agricultural presence.

BEST TIME TO VISIT OSTUNI

For an ideal visit to Ostuni, consider planning your trip in the months surrounding the peak summer period of July and August. September, extending into mid-October, offers a pleasant atmosphere with open restaurants, vibrant city life, and warm temperatures. Late May and June are also good options to avoid crowds, though the sea may not have reached its optimal temperature. If visiting during peak summer, embrace an Italian lifestyle by enjoying afternoon breaks, seeking shade, and dining later in the evening to escape the heat and crowds. Overall, September remains a prime time for a delightful Ostuni experience.

GETTING TO OSTUNI

BY CAR: Upon arriving in Puglia, both Brindisi Airport and Bari Airport serve as viable entry points to Ostuni, with Bari being slightly farther but still a convenient option. If you have a rental car, the journey takes approximately 40 minutes from Brindisi Airport and 1 hour and 10 minutes from Bari Airport.

BY TRAIN: There are frequent direct trains from Brindisi Airport to Ostuni, taking approximately 20 minutes at a cost of around €3.20 per person. Although there are no direct trains from Bari Airport, a transfer at Bari Centrale connects to a direct train to Ostuni in about 1 hour and 20 minutes, with tickets priced at approximately €11 per person.

WHERE TO STAY IN OSTUNI

If you are without a car and desiring proximity to the action, staying within Ostuni's old town, whether within the city walls or outside, is recommended. Recommended below are well-reviewed accommodations within walking distance of essential amenities.

OSTUNI HOTELS & GUESTHOUSES: *La Sommità Relais & Chateaux:* A luxurious choice with a prime location, featuring a Michelin Star restaurant on-site. | *Hotel La Terra:* A hotel option in central Ostuni with exceptional facilities. Learn more and check availability. | *Palazzo Altavilla:* A blend of hotel benefits and self-sufficiency within the fanciest apart-hotel in the White City. | *Tulipano Bianco:* A charming apartment with impeccable decor and a delightful roof terrace. | *I 7 Archi Guest House:* Budget-friendly guest house with several apartments/studios, some featuring lovely terraces.

OSTUNI AIRBNBS & APARTMENTS: Airbnb options in Ostuni have expanded significantly over the years, providing numerous choices for all budgets. Below is a curated selection with descriptions indicating: *Ottogradoni*: An excellent value studio apartment located just 300 meters from the main square, boasting a private roof terrace with city views. | ***Casa Mima***: A large one-bedroom apartment situated 150 meters from the main square, offering light, airy spaces and two balconies. | ***A House in the Sky:*** A historic house with three floors and modern features, highlighted by a private terrace with panoramic views. | ***Casa Palmira*** (££): A recently renovated one-bedroom apartment with stylish interiors and a panoramic rooftop terrace. | ***Terrazza Ariafina:*** A two-bedroom apartment steps away from Porta Blu, featuring contemporary styling, excellent views, and a large roof terrace. | ***Casa Di Zia:*** A four-bed house within Ostuni's old walls, modernized while preserving original features, suitable for families. | ***Vista Mare:*** A three-bedroom property with separate apartments, ideal for a group of friends seeking shared spaces and ocean views. | ***White Dream:*** A luxurious option with a private cave pool and a stunning terrace for a romantic getaway.

OSTUNI MASSERIAS: Masserias, historically farmsteads, now often converted into tourist accommodations, dot the countryside surrounding Ostuni. Notable options with excellent reviews include:

Masseria Ayroldi | Masserie Maresca | Masseria Valente | Masseria Cervarolo | Masseria Donna Nina | Masseria Le Carrube | Masseria Spesseto | Masseria Corte degli Asini | Masseria Spetterrata

EXPLORING OSTUNI: THINGS TO EXPERIENCE

Ostuni, unlike many nearby towns, is more than a day-trip destination; it beckons for a stay of at least two or three nights, promising continuous discovery of hidden gems on return visits. Below are my top recommendations for experiencing Ostuni.

1. Stroll through the Old Town: Like any Puglian town, Ostuni's beauty unfolds as you wander through its historic center, especially in the morning during low season or the balmy summer evenings when locals embrace the streets for meals and conversations. Opt for a guided tuk-tuk tour or explore on foot to unveil the town's charm.

2. People-Watch in Piazza della Libertà: The main square, dominated by an 18th-century column & the statue of Saint Oronzo, hosts traditional restaurants and cafes. Visit in the early evening to witness the lively passeggiata, aperitivo, or dinner scene. Keep in mind that central square restaurants may be pricier, but the experience is worth it.

3. City Walls Exploration: Descend towards Ostuni's protective city walls for a unique perspective on the White City. Capture stunning photos at various spots, including the famous door and the city's most renowned stairs. In the evening, Borgo Antico Bistrot offers a popular viewpoint over the countryside.

4. Cathedral Visit: Atop the hill sits Ostuni's crown jewel, the impressive 15th-century Gothic cathedral. Ensure you step inside to witness its spectacular interior. Explore nearby landmarks like Palazzo del Seminario and Palazzo Vescovile, the latter housing the remains of a 12th-century Norman Castle.

5. Seek Special Views: Ostuni's beauty peaks at sunset. Head to Corso Vittorio Emanuele II for a panoramic view, or enjoy the scenery from Ristorante La Vecchia Terrazza or Bloom bistrot Cafè. Consider booking accommodations with a private rooftop for a more intimate experience. | **6. Indulge in Local Produce:** Escape touristy areas and explore the Saturday local market for fresh produce and crafts. Learn about Puglia's significant olive oil production, with many shops in the old town offering various varieties. Join tours for an in-depth understanding and tasting experience. | **7. Time Your Visit for Festivals:** Plan your trip around festivals like the Cavalcata di Sant'Oronzo in late August, featuring a costumed horseback procession. On August 15th, the Sagra dei Vecchi Tempi offers a chance to savor traditional dishes. Consider exploring galleries and museums if you have extra time. | **8. Day Trips from Ostuni:** Ostuni's strategic location makes it an ideal base for day trips to nearby attractions like Locorotondo, Martina Franca, Alberobello, and the Adriatic coastline. Rent a car for a convenient exploration of Puglia's highlights. | **9. Beach Retreat:** Don't forget Ostuni's proximity to stunning beaches along 'Marina de Ostuni.' Explore Lido Morelli, Quarto di Monte, and Torre Pozzella for a relaxing seaside experience. | **10. Sip Cocktails in Style:** Visit Via Cattedrale for a delightful restaurant and drinks street. Gabo and Il Posto Affianco offer excellent cocktails and ambiance. Make reservations for Bar Perso for a daytime view over the countryside during weekends or the summer season.

PLACES TO EAT AND DRINK IN OSTUNI

During the peak tourist season, deciding where to dine in Ostuni can be challenging due to the abundance of restaurants catering to various budgets, some of which are highly popular. Most options are concentrated in Piazza della Liberta or along Via Cattedrale and its adjoining narrow alleys. While this recommendations are our favorite bars and restaurants, additional ones that we would eagerly revisit are added. ***1. Il Vizio del Conte***: This establishment is more of a hole-in-the-wall than a traditional restaurant, offering excellent pizza and focaccia. The best experience is on the small bench outside, paired with a cold bottle of beer. | ***2. Borgo Antico Bistro:*** Tucked away in tiny alleyways, this photogenic spot provides some of the best sit-down views in the city. Known for delicious sharing plates and great cocktails, it has become a popular spot in Ostuni, especially among a younger crowd. | ***3. La Pastasciutta:*** A no-frills place for a quick lunch, this restaurant on Via Vito Tamborrino offers daily changing menus with pasta bowls for around 5 Euro and glasses of red wine for 3 Euro. | ***4. Casbah Risto Cafè:*** A cool hangout spot with cocktails and two charming tables overlooking the old town's action. | ***5. Impasto Napoletano Pizzeria:*** Though a bit of a walk from the center, this place is renowned for its excellent Neapolitan pizza, making it a top choice for pizza lovers in Ostuni. | ***6. Ciccio:*** Known for its outstanding gelato, this place has moved premises but still delivers the same incredible taste. Worth the wander into the newer part of Ostuni. | ***7. Cremeria La Scala:*** A gelateria in Piazza della Libertà, offering a good choice if you're looking for a sweet treat, though not quite on par with Ciccio.

SCAN THIS QR CODE TO EXPLORE THE FULL MAP OF OSTUNI

MARTINA FRANCA

Martina Franca is a delightful white town nestled in the heart of Southern Italy's Puglia region. Although smaller and less frequented compared to popular destinations like Alberobello or Lecce, Martina Franca offers an authentic taste of Puglia. Its winding white streets, rich Baroque architecture, and delectable cuisine make it a must-visit on your Puglia itinerary. Martina Franca is a municipality in the province of Taranto, Apulia, Italy. It ranks as the second most populous town in the province, with a population of 49,086 as of 2016. Since 1975, the town has been home to the annual summer opera festival, the Festival della Valle d'Itria. Situated in the picturesque Itria Valley, near the provinces of Bari and Brindisi, Martina Franca shares borders with several municipalities including Alberobello, Ceglie Messapica, Cisternino, Crispiano, Massafra, Mottola, Locorotondo, Ostuni, Villa Castelli, Grottaglie, and Noci.

BEST TIME TO EXPLORE MARTINA FRANCA

Martina Franca welcomes visitors throughout the year, yet certain periods offer distinct advantages. Spring and autumn emerge as prime seasons to discover Martina Franca, characterized by mild weather and fewer crowds. Particularly noteworthy is November 11th when the city commemorates **_San Martino Delle Sementi_**, a harvest festival honoring local produce and community bonds. | Summer stands out as the busiest period, attracting a surge of tourists. However, around July 4th, Martina Franca hosts **_San Martino dell'Aia e Santa Comasia_**, a captivating four-day festival featuring street performances, culinary delights, and a breathtaking light exhibition illuminating the town. This event proves especially delightful for families visiting Martina Franca with children.

HOW TO GET TO MARTINA FRANCA

BY CAR: The nearest major cities to Martina Franca are Bari, which is also home to the closest international airport, Brindisi, which has both an airport and a bustling port, and Taranto. The most convenient way to reach Martina Franca is by car, as the roads in this region of Puglia are well-maintained and clearly signposted. Pay-and-display parking facilities are readily available just outside the city walls. Martina Franca is approximately 1.5 hours away from Bari by car, and it's only a short 15-minute drive between Locorotondo and the renowned Alberobello. Once parked, you can explore Martina Franca's historic center on foot. | **BY TRAIN:** Martina Franca can be accessed by train from Bari or Taranto via Ferrovie Sud and Sud Est, with services stopping at Martina Franca railway station. It's worth noting that the railway station is approximately 1 kilometer from the town center, so if you're traveling with bulky luggage, you might want to consider taking a taxi to get closer to your accommodation. | For transportation options, you can check the following: Main Railway Service: **_trenitalia.it_** | Local railway and bus service: **_fseonline.it_** | Bus services provided by **_Autolinee Marozzi_** and **_FlixBus_** | Ferry services, which can be accessed via Porto di Bari (Bari Port), Porto di Brindisi (Brindisi Port), and Autorità Portuale di Taranto (Taranto Port).

ACCOMMODATION OPTIONS IN MARTINA FRANCA

1. Masseria San Michele: For an authentic stay in Martina Franca, consider Masseria San Michele. Nestled in the picturesque Puglian countryside amid olive groves and vineyards, this charming farm stay occupies a beautifully restored 19th-century farmhouse. Retaining its original features and traditional architecture, Masseria San Michele offers a tranquil retreat.

2. Agriturismo Masseria Aprile in Locorotondo: Located just a 15-minute drive from Martina Franca in Locorotondo, Agriturismo Masseria Aprile provides a memorable experience. This family-owned farm stay, boasting a rich history, offers both traditional masseria accommodations and iconic trulli, cone-shaped stone buildings. Hosts Stefania and Anna extend warm hospitality, ensuring a truly unforgettable stay. Guests can indulge in activities such as cooking classes, wine and olive oil tasting, and yoga sessions.

3. Masseria San Michele: This stunning traditional country retreat, offering a four-star experience, features a pool and various amenities such as cooking classes, wine and olive oil tasting, and yoga sessions. Family suites are also available for those traveling with children.

4. Trulli D'Autore: A delightful countryside retreat with a pool and charming trulli-style accommodations. Transfer and taxi services are available for an additional fee.

5. Masseria Trulli e Vigne: An upscale resort and winery boasting luxurious amenities including a pool, restaurant, and wellness offerings, providing guests with an indulgent escape.

WHAT TO SEE & DO IN MARTINA FRANCA

↠ **Martina Franca City Walls and Gates:** Martina Franca, established in 1310 by Prince Filippo D'Angio, retains much of its medieval heritage. Positioned atop a hill for defensive purposes, it was encircled by protective city walls featuring 24 watchtowers overseeing the surrounding landscape and four city gates. While the walls and gates have undergone changes over time, remnants of their original structure remain. The gates, named after saints—Porta Santo Stefano, Porta San Nicola, Porta San Pietro, and Porta Santa Maria—are notable landmarks. Among them, Porta Santo Stefano, dating back to the 15th century but rebuilt in the 18th century with a distinctive Baroque style, serves as a prominent entry point into the old town center. | ↠ **Palazzo Ducale:** Palazzo Ducale, situated in the heart of Martina Franca's old town overlooking Piazza Roma, is a remarkable edifice. Initially conceived by the Caracciolo family to resemble a royal residence with plans for 365 rooms, the palace now houses Martina Franca's city hall and museum. Though the palace never realized its ambitious scale, its Baroque architecture exemplifies the town's distinctive aesthetic, known as Barocco Martinese. | ↠ **Other Impressive Buildings and Palazzi:** Several other notable buildings enrich the architectural landscape of Martina Franca, including **Palazzo dell'Università and the city tower**, **Palazzo Martucci**, **Palazzo Ancona**, and **Palazzo Blasi**. These structures are easily identifiable while exploring the town. | ↠**Basilica di San Martino:** For an immersive experience of Martina Franca's local Baroque style, a visit to the Basilica of San Martino, dedicated to the city's patron saint, is highly recommended. The basilica's elaborate interior showcases significant artworks by local painters, while its exterior facade boasts intricate carvings that captivate visitors, especially when illuminated by sunlight. | ↠ **Piazza Maria Immacolata:** Piazza Maria Immacolata stands out as one of Martina

Franca's most beautiful and renowned squares. Bordered by semicircular buildings adorned in elaborate Baroque style, the square offers a picturesque setting for dining at its shaded porticoed cafes and restaurants. Additionally, the square hosts performances and local parades on certain occasions, adding to its vibrant atmosphere. | ⇾ ***Martina Franca's Whitewashed Streets and La Lama:*** Martina Franca, known as one of Puglia's "città bianche" or white towns, features a charming whitewashed neighborhood called La Lama, located below the main square. Although lacking major landmarks, La Lama exudes a quaint allure with its narrow alleys revealing hidden courtyards, adorned balconies, and intriguing staircases. Despite its maze-like layout, exploring La Lama is a rewarding experience, offering insights into the town's architectural evolution from its humble origins to its present-day charm.

EXPLORING MARTINA FRANCA WITH CHILDREN:

⇾ The old town of Martina Franca is pedestrian-friendly, making it safe and enjoyable for children. The main streets and squares provide ample space for them to play and run around freely. Additionally, the upper part of town near the gates and Piazza Immacolata is accessible with a stroller, offering convenience for families with toddlers. | ⇾ The charming whitewashed area of the town creates a fairy tale-like atmosphere that kids adore. While older children can explore ahead safely, navigating this part of town with a stroller can be challenging due to uneven terrain and slopes. | ⇾ Although Martina Franca doesn't offer specific children's activities, its picturesque streets, quaint shops, and gelato spots provide plenty of entertainment for little ones. Some recommended spots to visit in Martina Franca with kids include: ***1. Villa Comunale (park)*** | ***2. Acropoli di Puglia olive oil mill***, where children can observe the olive oil-making process and sample the renowned local olive oil. | Using Martina Franca as a base, families can also explore nearby attractions such as:

1. Riserva Bosco Delle Pianelle: Formerly a hideout for bandits, this nature reserve now features walking trails, cycling paths, and picnic areas, perfect for outdoor family adventures. | ***2. Fasano Amusement and Safari Park:*** This popular attraction offers a thrilling safari experience and various amusement rides, making it a favorite among children visiting Puglia.

WHERE TO EAT IN MARTINA FRANCA

Martina Franca boasts numerous bistros and eateries where you can savor the region's culinary delights, such as orecchiette con le Cime di papa (pasta), capocollo (pork), Ceci e fave (chickpeas and broad beans), and more. Here are some recommended dining spots:

→ **Osteria del Coco Pazzo:** This cozy restaurant specializes in delectable traditional dishes, including the renowned bombette, a local delicacy crafted from pork. | → **Ristorante Garibaldi:** Situated in the heart of Martina Franca's historic center, this restaurant offers a seasonal menu highlighting local ingredients and an extensive selection of regional wines. | → **Ristorante Dal brigante By Enrico:** A rustic trattoria celebrated for its homemade pasta and generous portions. Don't miss the orecchiette with turnip greens, a beloved Puglian classic. | → **Other establishments where you can enjoy delicious fare include** Caffe' Tripoli for coffee and pastries, Garibaldi Bistrot, Dal Brigante, Caseificio Gentile (offering sandwiches and cheeses), and Macelleria Braceria Granaldi, which serves as both a butcher shop and restaurant.

SCAN THIS QR CODE TO EXPLORE THE FULL MAP OF MARTINA FRANCA

OTHER ITIRA VALLEY TOWNS WORTH EXPLORING

CEGLIE MESSAPICA

Nestled near Ostuni, Ceglie Messapica, a historic gem often overlooked by beachgoers, dates back to the 15th century BC. Its extensive, well-preserved center, originally known as Kailia Messapi by the Greeks, combines influences from its Greek settlers and indigenous tribes. Surrounded by Puglian hills and Salento plains, it's conveniently located between Brindisi and Taranto, near Ostuni and Martina Franca. Unlike its trulli-adorned neighbors, Ceglie Messapica boasts Moorish-inspired architecture highlighted by the imposing Ducal Castle. Its labyrinthine streets lead to ancient churches, palatial buildings, and hidden grottoes. The Giovedi Settembre festival in autumn marks a rustic celebration of food and wine, depleting old barrels for the upcoming harvest. Renowned for its gastronomy, the town offers excellent dining experiences showcasing local cuisine, adding to its allure as a cultural and culinary destination.

PUTIGNANO

Situated on Puglia Murgia, Putignano is a historic city famed for its Carnevale, possibly the world's oldest, with roots dating back to ancient Greek worship of Dionysus. Dating to 1394, this celebration begins on December 26th. Putignano's history includes Roman and Benedictine influences, flourishing under Frederick II and later the Carafa dynasty. The town's layout, fortified walls, and numerous churches reflect its rich past. Piazza Plebiscito, with its Sedile and vibrant atmosphere, is a focal point. Culinary delights abound, featuring local specialties like tarallini and orecchiette pasta, complemented by Puglia's renowned wines. Its economy thrives on textiles and agriculture. Putignano offers easy access to nearby attractions like Alberobello and Monopoli. Its lively Carnevale festivities, showcasing elaborate floats, add to its charm as a top destination.

PART 4: SALENTO

Salento, also known as Terra d'Otranto, is a culturally rich and historically significant region located at the southern end of Apulia in Southern Italy, resembling the "heel" of the Italian "boot". It encompasses the entire administrative area of the province of Lecce, a significant portion of the province of Brindisi, and part of the province of Taranto. Transportation is facilitated through international airports in Brindisi and Bari, with a 2-lane freeway linking Salento to Bari and the main railway line ending at Lecce. Leisure ports include Taranto, Brindisi, Campomarino di Maruggio, Gallipoli, Santa Maria di Leuca, and Otranto. The region is characterized by its coastal towers, built as watchtowers against maritime attacks, and its cuisine, featuring dishes such as orecchiette, parmigiana di melanzane, pitta di patate, turcinieddhri, and purciaddruzzi. Tourism highlights include the Ciolo cave in Lecce province, while festivals like Salento's sagre showcase local cuisine and culture. Salento is also a popular holiday destination for the Italian gay community, particularly around Gallipoli and the lidos at Baia Verde, with the annual Salento Pride celebration.

LECCE

Located in the southern part of Puglia, within the picturesque Salento peninsula, lies the captivating city of Lecce. Its charm is immediately evident as you stroll through the stunning city center. With a population of only 100,000 inhabitants, Lecce offers a serene escape from the hustle and bustle of larger cities. The city's baroque and rococo architecture, pedestrian-friendly streets, elegant boulevards, and numerous squares create an inviting ambiance. Locals leisurely wander the streets, enjoying the plethora of cafes, pastry shops, gelaterias, and al fresco bistros. In the early evening, it seems as though everyone is out savoring a pre-dinner Aperol Spritz, and you're encouraged to join in. For a delightful wine tasting experience, be sure to visit Enrico's chic enoteca, Crianza. Don't miss the historic city gates - Porta Rudiae, Porta San Biagio, and Porta Napoli - along with the beautifully restored Basilica di Santa Croce and the magnificent Duomo. Lecce also serves as an excellent home base for exploring nearby coastal gems like Otranto and Gallipoli.

WHERE IS LECCE?

Positioned in the southernmost part of Italy, Lecce lies approximately 150 km (93 miles) south of Bari, the capital of the region, and around 605 km (375 miles) south of Rome. More precisely, Lecce serves as the principal city in the "Salento" sub-region of Puglia. This area, known for its arid terrain dotted with millions of olive trees, stretches from slightly north of Lecce to Santa Maria di Leuca at the tip of the peninsula, where the Adriatic and Ionian seas converge.

WHY VISIT LECCE?

Lecce is celebrated for its stunning Baroque and Rococo architecture, crafted from unique tan-white sandstone, and its bustling pedestrian zones filled with shops and cafes. Positioned at the heart of Salento, it's an ideal starting point for exploring the region. Recent government investments have revitalized the once-deserted city center, offering an elegant setting for leisurely exploration. While lacking major landmarks, Lecce invites visitors to embrace its ambiance, encouraging relaxation and enjoyment of local culture. Travelers can connect with local expert Paolo for personalized trip planning and insider tips.

HOW TO REACH LECCE

Lecce is easily accessible by car, plane, or public transportation. While the city lacks its own airport, its modest train station limits direct connections with major cities in Italy and within Puglia. | **BY AIR:** Travelers flying into Puglia can choose between two international airports: Bari or Brindisi. Direct flights to Bari or Brindisi are available daily from various Italian cities such as Milan, Rome, Venice, Bologna, and Pisa, as well as European destinations like London, Zurich, and Paris. From either airport, options to reach Leece include train, bus, or taxi services. Brindisi Airport is approximately a 40-minute drive away, while Bari Airport is about a 2-hour drive. Both cities boast train stations offering direct routes to Lecce. | **BY TRAIN:** Trenitalia's high-speed Frecciarossa trains depart from Rome's Roma Termini station, completing the journey to Lecce in approximately 5.5 hours. These trains typically offer 4-6 daily departures, with ticket prices starting from 25 euros and varying based on booking time. Although train journeys are direct, they include stops in Bari and Brindisi before reaching Lecce. | **BY BUS:** Buses departing from Rome to Bari offer frequent services, with fares starting from ***10 euros*** for a journey lasting 6-7 hours. Passengers must disembark in Bari and transfer to local trains or buses for the remainder of the trip to Lecce. | **BY CAR:** Lecce is approximately a 2-hour drive from Bari, a 40-minute drive from Brindisi, a 3.5-hour drive from Naples, and a 6-6.5-hour drive from Rome.

WHEN TO VISIT LECCE

When planning a visit to Lecce, timing is crucial. From January to March, chilly temperatures and closures of various facilities deter visitors. April, post-Easter, offers longer days and pleasant weather, ideal for exploring the city adorned with blooming flowers. May and June bring hotter temperatures and tourist crowds, though beach trips are still enjoyable. July and August are best avoided due to intense heat and overcrowding, especially during the Ferragosto holiday period. September and October resemble May and June, with warmer seas despite a drier countryside. November sees rainfall and a quieter atmosphere, earning it the nickname "month of the dead." December, often overlooked, presents favorable weather and festive charm, making it an underrated time to visit.

WHERE TO STAY IN LECCE?

Staying in the *old town of Lecce* is highly recommended due to its extensive restoration efforts, offering a variety of accommodations. Different parts of the district provide distinct atmospheres, with some areas bustling with activity and others offering a tranquil ambiance. The central district features numerous landmarks, shops, and eateries, while areas near churches offer a serene environment with subdued lighting at night. The Porta Napoli area strikes a balance between vibrancy and tranquility. For those seeking centrality with a local atmosphere, lodging near *Mazzini Square* or just outside **Porta Napoli** is recommended, as it's popular among university students. *Our Recommended Accommodations in Lecce are:* Patria Palace Lecce | Palazzo Rollo | ReLuxe Private Wellness | Masseria Vittoria

PATRIA PALACE LECCE: is a Top-Rated 5-Star Hotel in Lecce where you can njoy a scenic view from the restaurant terrace overlooking the basilica. Patria Palace Hotel in Lecce epitomizes luxury with its modern amenities and lavish ambiance, guaranteeing a delightful stay. Featuring well-appointed rooms, impeccable service, and an exceptional on-site dining experience, it stands out as a premier choice. Its central location offers convenient access to local attractions, making it ideal for leisure and exploration.

PALAZZO ROLLO: is a tranquil hideaway in Lecce's Heart where you can step into the serene interior courtyard adorned with lush greenery. There's a certain allure to the secluded courtyards found within Italian cities, offering a tranquil escape bathed in sunlight. Palazzo Rollo, nestled in the heart of

Lecce, is a 4-star hotel housed in a historic building adorned with antique furnishings, exuding charm and elegance.

RELUXE PRIVATE WELLNESS: is an idyllic retreat with Poolside Bliss where you can indulge in the underground pool of the spa. ReLuxe Private Wellness offers a unique experience, particularly in their private suite featuring an exclusive pool nestled within the Renaissance Palazzo's limestone arches. Perfect for a honeymoon or a romantic getaway, the ambiance and setting justify the price tag.

MASSERIA VITTORIA: offers tranquility Amidst Lecce's Countryside where you can relish in the serene garden setting of the hotel. Escape to the countryside at Masseria Vittoria, just a bike ride away from Lecce's pristine beaches and a nature reserve teeming with wildlife. Offering immaculate accommodations, a splendid pool, and gracious hosts, it's an ideal choice for those seeking peace and quiet outside the bustling city center. | For more affordable, midrange and luxury hotels to satisfy your ego, visit: *https://www.thehotelguru.com/best-hotels-in/italy/lecce*

THINGS TO SEE AND DO IN LECCE

1. APPRECIATE BAROQUE ARCHITECTURE: For enthusiasts of art history, immersing oneself in Lecce's baroque architecture is a must. To fully appreciate the splendor, consider hiring a local guide for a private city tour. Alternatively, conducting some preliminary reading will enhance understanding of this distinctive architectural style and its historical context. Iconic landmarks such as the Basilica di Santa Croce, the Cathedral, Chiesa di Santa Chiara, and Chiesa di San Matteo, along with the city's four historic gates, are worth exploring. Even for those less inclined toward art, the ornate beauty of Lecce's churches, governmental buildings, and private residences is impossible to ignore, offering a glimpse into the frozen time of the 1600s. The architecture's deliberate asymmetry and intricate details beckon visitors to pause and admire, with designs crafted to surprise and delight from various perspectives. | **2. SHOP FOR PAPIER MÂCHÉ AND CRAFTS:** Lecce is renowned for its artisans, particularly in the old town where craftsmen specializing in ceramics, ironwork, design, and tailoring abound. However, the city's true highlight is its association with Papier Mâché, a quintessentially baroque craft evident in shrines, church statues, and even St. Clair's church ceiling. Visitors can witness artisans at work in their workshops, crafting elaborate statues of saints and smaller figurines, often used in nativity scenes during Christmas. | **3. VISIT THE JEWISH MUSEUM AND FAGGIANO MUSEUM:** While these museums are noteworthy, indulging in an aperitivo or gelato might be equally appealing alternatives. | **4. SAMPLE PUGLIESE WINES:** Puglia boasts significant wine production, with numerous wineries in the vicinity of Lecce offering tours and tastings. Alternatively, explore local wine bars to savor the region's renowned reds, such as "Negroamaro" and "Primitivo," or opt for distinctive rosé wines. | **5. EMBRACE THE SIESTA TRADITION:** Following a leisurely lunch, partake in the traditional Southern Italian siesta between 2 PM and 4 PM to recharge for the evening. | **6. EXPERIENCE LECCE'S COCKTAIL SCENE**: Explore Lecce's vibrant cocktail bars, with a concentration found behind the cathedral or near Porta Napoli. | **7. DELIGHT IN LOCAL CUISINE:** Indulge in regional specialties like horse meat stew, raw shellfish, snails, chicory greens, and roasted lamb organs. Satisfy your sweet tooth with gelato or local pastries like "pasticciotto." | **8. VENTURE ON DAY TRIPS:** Explore the Salento peninsula with day trips to Otranto, Gallipoli, Gallatina, Nardò, or embark on a scenic coastal drive along SP358, offering breathtaking views of the Adriatic and Albania's mountains. | **9. EXPLORE THE BEACHES**: Discover the diverse coastal landscapes near Lecce, ranging from sandy shores in Porto Cesareo and San Foca to rocky formations around Torre Sant'Andrea.

WHERE TO DINE IN AND AROUND LECCE

Selecting restaurants can be challenging without insight into individual preferences, so I've curated a diverse selection to cater to varying tastes. **1. VECCHIA OSTERIA (LU TOTU):** For a taste of history, consider Vecchia Osteria, affectionately known as Lu Totu after its owner. Renowned for its rustic ambiance and vibrant atmosphere, this locale offers a quintessential experience of Salentina cuisine, featuring iconic recipes. | **2. OSTERIA DA COSIMINO E FIGLI (LU COSIMINU):** If Vecchia Osteria is unavailable or if you seek a more localized experience, venture to Osteria Da Cosimino e Figli, fondly referred to as Lu Cosiminu. Located a short walk from the main square, this establishment is favored by locals for its authenticity. | **3. LA CUCINA DI MAMMA ELVIRA:** For a blend of tradition and modernity in a tranquil setting, La Cucina di Mamma Elvira is an excellent choice. Situated at the outskirts of the old town, this restaurant boasts an impressive wine selection and innovative dishes crafted from local ingredients. | **4. ALEX:** For an elegant dining experience suitable for special occasions, Alex offers refined cuisine expertly curated by chef Alessandra. Indulge in exquisite dishes like tagliolini pasta with lemon, stracciatella cheese, and shrimp, artfully presented to tantalize the senses. | **5. CRIANZA:** Seeking a more casual atmosphere? Consider Crianza, a bistro-style eatery renowned for its gourmet offerings. From delectable bruschetta to expertly curated drink selections, this establishment promises a delightful culinary experience. | **6. QUANTO BASTA:** Among Lecce's cocktail bars, Quanto Basta stands out for its artful mixology and vibrant ambiance. Let the skilled bartenders craft a bespoke cocktail tailored to your preferences, transforming your evening into a memorable affair. | **7. ALVINO**: In Lecce, where bars and cafes seamlessly blend, Alvino stands as a prime example of culinary versatility. Located in the bustling Piazza Sant'Oronzo, Alvino offers an array of delights, from pastries and gelato to aperitivos. Indulge in a cappuccino paired with their renowned pasticciotto for a quintessential Lecce experience.

SHOPPING IN LECCE

There are array of independent clothing, jewelry, and craft stalls, perfect for leisurely browsing. Via Palmieri and Via Vittorio Emanuele II are recommended streets to explore for unique finds. For mainstream clothing and lingerie outlets, venture beyond the central area along Via Salvatore Trinchese, where several chain stores cater to shoppers, with many staying open throughout the afternoon. **CARTAPESTA:** One of Lecce's renowned specialties is papier mâché, known as "cartapesta" in Italian, traditionally used for crafting lightweight religious statues for festivals. You can discover small studios scattered around town, such as *Cartapesta Riso on Via Vittorio* Emanuele II, offering distinctive souvenirs. **FOOD SHOPPING:** In terms of food, a morning market awaits just outside Porta Rudiae, providing an opportunity to purchase fresh local produce. However, the biweekly market on Mondays and Fridays, situated further from the city center near the stadium, primarily features inexpensive clothing, though it does offer some worthwhile stalls for fruits, vegetables, olives, nuts, and dried beans. Unless equipped with a car and self-catering, it may not justify a special trip. For everyday grocery needs, **Dok** stands as the largest supermarket conveniently located in the city center.

WHERE TO GO RUNNING IN LECCE

To maximize comfort and avoid crowds, it's advisable to embark on your run as early as possible to escape the heat and bustling city center. While Villa Comunale, a small park near the center, seems suitable for laps, it unfortunately doesn't open until 9 am, rendering it unsuitable for early morning runners like myself. For shorter runs, I opted instead for Parco di Belloluogo, situated adjacent to the cemetery (accessible by exiting the old city from Porta Napoli). Opening at 8 am, this park provides facilities such as toilets and water taps. A complete circuit spans approximately 1.5 km and offers views of a tower and scenic olive trees. For longer distances, I ventured beyond the city limits into the countryside via Via Vecchia Frigole, located north of the center. Initially paved, the route transitions into a cycle path before evolving into a tranquil country road. Although crossing a highway is necessary at one juncture, traffic was minimal during early Sunday mornings.

BEACHES IN LECCE

The closest beach to Lecce is **_San Cataldo_** on the Adriatic Coast, just a 20-minute drive away, offering both a free section and lidos (beach clubs) where you can rent umbrellas and sun loungers. However, for a superior beach experience, it's recommended to head west to the **Ionian Coast**. The nearest options to Lecce are the picturesque beaches located north of Porto Cesareo, such as **_Torre Lapillo_** and **_Punta Prosciutto_**, renowned for their soft white sands and stunning turquoise waters. Torre Lapillo is approximately a 35-minute drive from Lecce. If the free beach was overcrowded, we opted for the luxurious amenities of the beach club, **_Bahia del Sol Porto Cesareo_**. If you seek a more secluded and natural setting amidst pine forests, **_Porto Selvaggio_** offers a pebble beach just 30 minutes south of Lecce. Additionally, to the north of Otranto, there are charming beaches including **_Torre dell'Orso_**, reachable within 30 minutes from Lecce. Torre dell'Orso stands out as one of the finest beaches near Lecce and pairs well with a visit to Otranto, offering a captivating blend of white cliffs, soft sandy shores, and crystal-clear blue waters.

DAY TRIPS FROM LECCE

Lecce, strategically situated between the Adriatic and Ionian Seas, offers easy access to all the highlights of the Salento region, with travel times ranging from 30 to 60 minutes to reach various destinations on the peninsula. Below are some of my preferred destinations to visit from Lecce, along with approximate driving durations: **Otranto (40 minutes)** – A picturesque coastal town boasting breathtaking views of the turquoise sea. | **Coast North of Otranto (approximately 35 minutes)** – This area features splendid beaches, including Torre dell'Orso, and the unique Cave of Poetry swimming hole. | **Gallipoli (35 minutes)** – Another enchanting seaside town offering a blend of sandy beaches and a historic olive press. | **Castro (40 minutes)** – A delightful coastal gem, often overshadowed by Otranto and Gallipoli, offering its own charm. | **Galantina (25 minutes)** – A quaint town showcasing a picturesque baroque center, often overlooked by visitors. | **Coriglione d'Otranto (25 minutes)** – An off-the-beaten-path destination boasting an intriguing medieval castle. | To facilitate convenient day trips from Lecce, having a car proves to be the most efficient and expedient option, as public transportation options are limited. Alternatively, if you prefer to explore without the hassle of driving, you may opt for a guided tour.

SCAN THIS QR CODE TO EXPLORE THE FULL MAP OF LECCE

OTRANTO

Otranto is nestled along the Salento coast in Puglia boasting a rich historical and cultural tapestry alongside its stunning natural scenery. Its cathedral, home to the famed Apocalypse mosaic, stands as a testament to its artistic legacy. This seaside gem attracts tourists with its sun-kissed beaches, clear waters, and delightful Mediterranean climate. Situated within the province of Lecce, Otranto hosts approximately 5,700 residents and serves as a gateway to the region's captivating landscapes. Its renowned beaches, such as Spiaggia degli Alimini and Spiaggia di Baia dei Turchi, allure visitors, while landmarks like the Cathedral of Santa Maria Annunziata and the Castle of Otranto offer glimpses into its storied past. Otranto, situated as the easternmost municipality in Italy within Salento, features an ancient village tracing its roots back to the Middle Ages. Recognized by UNESCO in 2010 as a "Messenger Site of Peace," this historic enclave holds a special significance. The unspoiled beauty of the Salento coastline has earned Otranto the prestigious title of "Most Beautiful Village in Italy," bestowed by the Club of Most Beautiful Villages in Italy during a broadcast on RAI 3. Its historical significance is evident in its architectural marvels, reflecting influences from the Messapian, Roman, Byzantine, and Aragonese periods.

HOW TO REACH OTRANTO IN PUGLIA

BY CAR: Our preferred method for reaching Otranto is via a road trip through Puglia, particularly if journeying south from Bari or Brindisi. While Otranto is just under a 30-minute drive from the baroque city of Lecce, it's also easily accessible from other nearby towns and villages. | **BY TRAIN**

AND BUS: Otranto is reachable by public transport, although most journeys will involve at least one change (e.g., taking the train from Lecce requires a transfer in Maglie). The small station is located in the modern part of Otranto, approximately a 15-minute walk from the old town center. Train schedules and tickets can be checked and booked via the Trenitalia website, or alternatively, both train and bus options are available on the Omio site.
| **PRIVATE TRANSFER:** If you're based in Lecce and prefer not to rent a car, you might consider arranging a private transfer for a full-day excursion to Otranto, allowing you the flexibility to explore independently. More information on private transfer options can be found here.

TOP THINGS TO EXPERIENCE IN OTRANTO

THE ARAGONES CASTLE: While the exterior of the Aragones Castle may not be the most aesthetically pleasing, its historical significance far outweighs its architectural charm. Following the Ottoman invasion and subsequent recapture of the city, the castle underwent extensive reconstruction to fortify its defenses, reflecting the resilience of its inhabitants. Today, it serves as the primary hub for arts and culture in the town. The ground floor offers a comprehensive history of the castle, including its strategic improvements, along with a small exhibition featuring Horace Walpole's seminal Gothic novel, "The Castle of Otranto." Upstairs, visitors can explore rotating art exhibitions, showcasing works from esteemed artists like Sebastião Salgado and Mark Chagall. While the panoramic views from the rooftop are noteworthy, the castle's entrance fee of €12 per person may deter some visitors, making it advisable to check the current exhibitions before purchasing tickets.

ENJOY SUNBATHING IN THE CITY: Otranto boasts several picturesque spots for sunbathing, ranging from sandy beaches to rocky outcrops. Spiaggia dei Gradoni, with its powdery white sand, is a popular choice for beachgoers, while Lido Camillo offers a more intimate setting for lounging. Families often gravitate towards Spiaggetta Del Molo, known for its shallow, clear waters and soft sand. The Lungomare, a scenic waterfront promenade, provides a tranquil setting for a leisurely stroll or a refreshing dip in the turquoise waters.

CHIESA DI SAN PIETRO: Tucked away amidst Otranto's narrow streets lies the Chiesa di San Pietro, a hidden gem showcasing remarkable Byzantine frescoes. Dating back to the 10th century, this modest church boasts some of the region's finest examples of Byzantine artwork. Despite centuries of wear, recent restoration efforts have preserved the church's vibrant frescoes, making it a must-visit for art enthusiasts. Admission is free, with donations appreciated, allowing visitors to admire these ancient treasures at their leisure.

TAKE A SCENIC STROLL ALONG THE LUNGOMARE: The Lungomare degli Eroi offers a picturesque pathway along Otranto's coastline, perfect for a leisurely passeggiata before indulging in an evening aperitivo. Whether you're drawn to the azure waters or the charming seaside vistas, this scenic route offers a delightful escape from the bustling city streets. Venture beyond the main thoroughfare to discover hidden gems like the Cappella della Madonna dell'Altomare, which offers panoramic views of the city from across the bay.

EXPLORE THE HISTORIC CENTRE: Immerse yourself in Otranto's rich history by exploring its historic center, a labyrinth of narrow alleys and ancient landmarks. From the imposing *__Cathedral__* to the fortified walls and *__Porta Alfonsina__*, there's no shortage of architectural marvels to discover. For a quieter experience, venture off the beaten path to discover hidden *__piazzettas__* and whitewashed streets, offering a glimpse into the town's storied past. Don't miss the *__Monument to the Martyrs of Otranto__*, a poignant reminder of the city's resilience in the face of adversity.

DISCOVER NEARBY BEACHES: Expand your Otranto adventure by exploring the nearby beaches and swimming spots, each offering its own unique charm. From the rocky cove of *__Porto Badisco__* to the sandy shores of *__Torre dell'Orso__*, there's a beach to suit every preference. For a secluded escape, venture to *__Baia dei Turchi__* or *__I Faraglioni di Sant'Andrea__*, where pristine sands and crystal-clear waters await.

ACCOMMODATION OPTIONS IN OTRANTO

AIRBNB RENTALS: **Cottage Donna Pina**: Nestled in a serene street within the historic center, Cottage Donna Pina is a charming and sought-after accommodation, ideal for couples seeking a cozy retreat. Despite its compact size, this cottage boasts a well-appointed interior and a delightful patio garden. Other properties by the same host within the centro storico come highly recommended, offering various amenities and receiving excellent reviews. | **Il Balconcino di Otranto:** This two-bedroom apartment exudes modern elegance and features tasteful decor, including unique artwork and vintage furniture pieces. Situated in the heart of the centro storico, it offers enchanting views of the Byzantine church of San Pietro from its quaint balcony. | **JANELA BLUE:** Comprising three one-bedroom apartments within a historic building, Janela Blue combines modern comforts with period details like vaulted roofs. These apartments, priced affordably even during peak season, offer a popular choice for travelers seeking a budget-friendly yet stylish accommodation option. | If you prioritize a splendid terrace experience, options such as a two-bedroom historic house, ***the one-bedroom Palazzo Borgomonte***, or the Magnificent Penthouse with sea view offer irresistible settings for dining and relaxation. While properties like ***Dimora Lopez*** and ***Riva Mediterranea Domus*** boast stunning features and newness, lacking reviews may warrant cautious consideration. | Several other favorites among Airbnb options include Le Nicchie, Romantic Studio, La Piccinna, and U Purpu, each offering distinct charms and convenient locations.

HOTELS & GUESTHOUSES: *Palazzo De Mori:* Steeped in history, this meticulously restored palace offers elegant accommodations with period furnishings and picturesque views of Otranto's harbor from its private terrace. Palazzo De Mori promises a refined stay, capturing the essence of Otranto's rich heritage. | ***Corte Di Nettuno:*** Adorned with pink walls and a nautical theme, Corte Di Nettuno presents a popular mid-range option within the heart of Otranto. While its decor may not appeal to everyone, its central location and favorable reviews make it a sought-after choice. | Alternatively, for a resort-style experience within walking distance of Otranto, ***Relais Valle Dell'Idro*** offers a compelling option. | ***Hotel San Giuseppe Dimora Storica:*** Set within a sensitively restored 16th-century farmhouse, this hotel offers stylish and contemporary rooms within the historic center. With its proximity to the sea and affordable rates for its 4-star status, Hotel San Giuseppe Dimora Storica provides a comfortable base for exploring Otranto's attractions. | ***Budget-conscious travelers*** may consider options like ***B&B Ophelia*** and ***Hotel Albània,*** which offer simple yet clean accommodations with excellent reviews. ***Hotel Miramare*** provides another budget option, particularly favorable outside the peak season. | For a tranquil countryside retreat within easy reach of Otranto, ***Baglioni Masseria Muzza*** offers luxurious accommodations amid scenic surroundings. ***Masseria dei Monaci*** presents a similarly appealing alternative for those seeking a refined stay outside the city center.

WHERE TO DINE AND UNWIND IN OTRANTO

The dining scene in Otranto, particularly along the seafront, is predominantly influenced by seafood, although vegetarians can typically find a selection of meat-free pasta dishes on most menus.

Here are our top picks for restaurants and bars in Otranto:

L'Ortale Ristoro Salentissimo: Tucked away in a charming deli, L'Ortale Ristoro Salentissimo boasts a hidden gem—a private rooftop terrace perfect for enjoying delightful aperitivos. With a fantastic wine list and tasty, fresh platters, it's an experience not to be missed. They also offer local wine tastings, adding to the allure of this spot.

Maestrale: While not necessarily recommended for food during the day, Maestrale's waterfront location makes it an ideal spot for watching the sunset with a refreshing spritz in hand.

Retro Gusto: Although we didn't dine here, Retro Gusto earns a spot in the Michelin guide, making it a noteworthy option for those seeking a more gourmet experience. | Alternatively, **_Icon Restaurant_**, located near the castle, is widely acclaimed as one of Otranto's best dining establishments. Offering a popular tasting menu and excellent value for the quality of food, it's a top choice for discerning diners. | **_Classe 80:_** Situated just a short stroll from the historic center, Classe 80 is a popular seafood restaurant known for its upscale dining experience without the inflated prices often found in tourist areas. | **_L'Altro Baffo:_** Nestled along one of the quieter streets of the historic center, L'Altro Baffo offers a contemporary dining experience with a focus on seafood prepared with creative flair. While vegetarian options are limited, they usually offer a meat-free orecchiette dish. | **_Gelateria Fisotti:_** Since its establishment in 2012, Gelateria Fisotti has become a local favorite, offering artisanal gelato with unique flavors like pasticciotto leccese. Their pistachio gelato comes highly recommended. | **_Friggitoria Otranto_**: Indulge in freshly caught and fried seafood served in a cone while enjoying the seaside ambiance at Friggitoria Otranto—an experience not to be missed. | **_Sosta e Gusta Pucceria:_** For a quick and satisfying lunch, grab a puccia from Sosta e Gusta Pucceria. Their simple yet delicious mozzarella, fresh tomato, and arugula option are sure to please. | **_Spinnaker:_** While the cocktails may be hit or miss, Spinnaker remains a popular spot for aperitivos, thanks to its stunning sunset views and inviting atmosphere. Opt for wine or beer to make the most of the experience.

TIP: If you have a couple of days in Otranto, consider joining a highly-rated cooking class in a local's home. You'll learn to prepare traditional recipes and taste everything you make, accompanied by wine, of course.

SCAN THIS QR CODE TO EXPLORE THE FULL MAP OF OTRANTO

GALLIPOLI

The etymology of Gallipoli traces back to the Greek "Καλλίπολις" (Kallípolis), translating to "beautiful city." Situated in the province of Lecce, Apulia, this southern Italian town had a population of 31,862 in 2014 and is among the locales where the Greek dialect Griko is spoken. Positioned along the Ionian Sea on the western coast of the Salento Peninsula, Gallipoli is characterized by two distinct areas: the modern city and the historic old town. The modern section boasts the latest infrastructure, including a notable skyscraper, while the ancient town lies on a limestone island, connected to the mainland via a 16th-century bridge. Gallipoli's municipal boundaries encompass Alezio, Galatone, Matino, Sannicola, and Taviano, with additional hamlets such as Baia Verde, Lido Conchiglie, Lido San Giovanni, Rivabella, and Torre del Pizzo. Gallipoli captivated me with its enchanting allure and vibrant ambiance. Within the old town, I found myself immersed in a realm reminiscent of a fairytale, where the essence of an idyllic Italian getaway materialized. This enchanting enclave boasts a rich historical tapestry, adorned with medieval landmarks, picturesque churches, sandy beaches lapped by crystalline waters, and delectable seafood offerings at local eateries.

HOW TO GET TO GALLIPOLI

BY CAR: To reach Gallipoli by car, you can utilize the state highways linking it to Lecce and Santa Maria di Leuca. These highways are toll-free, with a maximum speed limit of 110 km/h (68 mph). If you're driving, note that the old town operates as a ZTL (Zona a Traffico Limitato), meaning only vehicles with special permits, typically for residents, are allowed. Thus, you'll need to locate parking in the modern section of the city. The closest parking area to the old town is situated on the island, but be cautious not to inadvertently enter the ZTL. Off-season parking is free, while during the summer months, it costs 1.5 euros per hour or 10 euros per day. Remember to have enough coins, as the standard parking meters do not accept debit or credit cards. | **BY TRAIN:** Gallipoli's train station is managed by Ferrovie Del Sud Est, a part of Trenitalia. Although only slow regional trains operate, you can travel to Lecce, Brindisi, and Otranto. For schedules and online bookings, consult the official website of Ferrovie Del Sud-Est. | **BY BUS:** If you prefer bus travel, visit www.omio.com to explore all available connections.

WHAT TO DO AND SEE

WALK GALLIPOLI: Familiarize yourself with Gallipoli by taking a leisurely stroll along its perimeter on your first day. This allows you to discover some of the finest seafront cafes and restaurants, as well as observe fishermen tending to their nets on colorful boats in the harbor. | **LA FONTANA GRECA**, situated on the mainland just outside the historic city center. Believed by some historians to be Italy's oldest fountain, dating back to the 3rd century BC, its facade depicts characters from Greek mythology such as Dirce, Salmacis, and Byblis, although others argue it belongs to the Renaissance era. | **CASTELLO ANGIOINO DI GALLIPOLI**, a Byzantine castle from the 13th century that has undergone numerous renovations throughout its history. Today, it stands as one of Gallipoli's main attractions, housing a museum with an admission fee of 7 euros. | **THE GALLIPOLI CATHEDRAL**, dedicated to Saint Agatha the Virgin, offers a unique blend of Renaissance and Byzantine architectural styles within its baroque structure. Visitors can admire its interior adorned with frescoes depicting the life of Saint Agatha. | **IL FRANTOIO DEL VICERÈ:** For a glimpse into the region's olive oil production history, visit Il Frantoio del Vicerè, a subterranean museum showcasing a 16th-century olive oil press. Entrance is priced at just 1.5 euros. | **THE SANTA MARIA DELLA PURITÀ CHURCH**, though unassuming from the outside, boasts a lavish interior adorned with magnificent frescoes, paintings, ceramic floors, and an ornate chandelier. | **WITNESS SUNSET:** Don't miss the opportunity to witness the stunning sunset over the Mediterranean from Gallipoli's western coastline. Numerous seaside bars offer the perfect setting to unwind with fresh seafood and local wine after a day of exploration. | **SPIAGGIA DELLA PURITA:** Relax at Spiaggia della Purita, the charming city beach. Conveniently situated near the old town, it's just a short five-minute stroll from your doorstep. While we experienced strong winds during our visit, we recognize its allure as a delightful spot for a beach outing. | **IDEAL BASE FOR DAY TRIPS:** Gallipoli's strategic location also makes it an ideal starting point for day trips to several outstanding beaches or beach clubs, such as Spiaggia di Punta della Suina, Samsara Beach, or Spiaggia di Pescoluse (known as the "Maldive del Salento").

ACCOMMODATION OPTIONS IN GALLIPOLI

APARTMENT RENTALS: *Dimora Storica Briganti* presents chic apartments nestled in the heart of Brindisi's historic city center, boasting a seasonal rooftop pool as its highlight feature. | **Casa Nelly** offers a vintage-style apartment centrally located, providing travelers an opportunity to immerse themselves in the authentic ambiance of the city, just a 5-minute stroll from the beach. Additionally, it boasts a generous terrace equipped with BBQ facilities, parasols, and sun loungers. | *The Loft* is a snug yet inviting apartment situated in Gallipoli's modern district, conveniently close to the central train station and complemented by complimentary private parking. | *Poetic Salento Style House* is a charming ground-floor apartment in the historic city center, well-appointed and conveniently close to the beach.

HOTEL ACCOMMODATIONS: *Palazzo del Corso 5** stands as a luxurious boutique hotel in Gallipoli's contemporary zone, strategically positioned between the train station and the historic city center. Guests can savor their meals or unwind in a hot tub on the panoramic terrace. | *I Bastioni San Domenico 4** offers a sophisticated lodging experience within the historic city center, with select rooms affording breathtaking sea vistas. | *Xilhotel 4** presents a contemporary hotel experience near the train station, boasting a rooftop bar with scenic views of the Ionian Sea and the marina. | *Hotel Città Bella 3** provides a budget-friendly lodging option in Gallipoli's modern area, conveniently situated near the train station and featuring a terrace offering city views.

FARM STAYS NEAR GALLIPOLI: *Tenuta Ferraro* is the nearest farm stay to Gallipoli, just a 10-minute drive from the city, offering a genuine countryside experience where dogs, horses, and other animals freely roam. | ***Giardini di Marzo*** offers an authentic farm stay experience, a 20-minute drive from Gallipoli, surrounded by stunning beaches such as Spiaggia di Torre San Giovanni and Baia dei Diavoli. | ***Tenuta Monticelli*** presents a chic farm stay close to Gallipoli, nestled atop a hill with picturesque sea views and verdant fields. Guests can unwind by the pool or in their own outdoor hot tub, available in deluxe rooms.

WHERE TO DINE IN GALLIPOLI

Vecchio Ingrosso is an ideal spot for experiencing an authentic Apulian breakfast, renowned for its finest pasticciotto in the area. This traditional pastry, filled with either ricotta cheese or custard cream, is a must-try. Additionally, indulge in variations filled with pistachio cream or chocolate. | ***Baguetteria De Pace*** offers a quaint and cozy setting, perfect for a quick stopover while exploring Gallipoli's historic city center. Here, you'll savor what might just be the most delectable sandwich of your life. | ***Scafud-Terra*** presents another excellent option for a swift lunch break, serving up scrumptious sandwiches and platters featuring prosciutto and cheese, perfectly complemented by a glass of wine. | ***Le Garibaldine*** stands out as an authentic Italian eatery offering Mediterranean and seafood delights at reasonable prices. Delight in traditional Apulian dishes like pasta orecchiette with tomatoes, a fantastic vegetarian choice. | ***AMU Fish Restaurant & Store***, situated by the sea, provides an idyllic setting for a romantic evening meal. Immerse yourself in the freshest seafood offerings and attentive service for an unforgettable dining experience.

BEACH OPTIONS NEAR GALLIPOLI

SPIAGGIA DELLA PURITÀ, a compact free beach nestled within the historic city center, offers crystal-clear waters, though occasional seaweed may be present.

THE COASTLINE SOUTH OF GALLIPOLI boasts the most sought-after beaches, stretching along the Lungomare for miles, offering both sandy and rocky shores. Starting from Stabilimento Balneare Piccolo Lido and extending further southward. Among these, ***Spiaggia di Baia Verde*** stands out as one of the most popular, albeit crowded during peak summer months like July and August. Accessible via train from Gallipoli Baia Verde station. | Adjacent to Baia Verde lies ***Parco Naturale Regionale Isola di S. Andrea***, a nature park boasting numerous pristine beaches. | ***Punta Della Suina***, a petite rocky island adorned with parasols and sunbeds, is one such gem. Nearby private parking is available at a fixed rate of 6 euros, regardless of the duration of stay. | **TO THE NORTH OF GALLIPOLI**, the first beach is a brief 10-minute drive from the city center. Here, an expansive sandy coastline awaits, offering both free areas and beach clubs, accompanied by a plethora of bars and restaurants, beginning from Lido Torre.

SCAN THIS QR CODE TO EXPLORE THE FULL MAP OF GALLIPOLI

SANTA MARIA DI LEUCA

Santa Maria di Leuca, also known simply as Leuca, is a village in the Salento peninsula of southern Italy, within the comune of Castrignano del Capo. Historically, it was part of the comune of Gagliano del Capo. The area between Otranto and Santa Maria di Leuca is now a Regional Natural Coastal Park. Leuca's name comes from the Greek word "Leukòs," meaning white, referring to its high cliffs illuminated by the morning sun, making it the first land sighted by sailors from the east. It was known to the Romans as "de Finibus Terrae," meaning the end of the earth, their furthest outpost. The promontory of Leuca once housed a temple dedicated to the goddess Minerva, now transformed into the Basilica Minore. Legends associate Leuca with the landings of Aeneas and St. Peter. Archaeological evidence suggests Bronze Age settlement in the area. Popular belief holds that Leuca is the water divider between the Ionian and Adriatic Seas, but this distinction actually belongs to Punta Palascia, a few kilometers from Otranto, which is Italy's most easterly point.

WHY LEAUCA IS WORTH VISITING?

Santa Maria di Leuca offers a plethora of attractions, making it an enchanting holiday destination. The picturesque Port of Leuca serves as a docking point for both large fishing vessels and leisure yachts, while the nearby Caves of Leuca beckon exploration via boat rentals. Dominating the landscape is the striking lighthouse overlooking Punta Meliso, accessible by climbing the

250-step monumental staircase leading to the Sanctuary, where visitors can witness the mesmerizing cascading waters of the Monumental Waterfall. The azure hues of the sea, diverse seabeds, sandy bays, and pristine beaches further add to the allure. History enthusiasts can marvel at the ancient "Bagnarole" bathtubs on the beach, the sixteenth-century "Omo Morto" tower, and the exquisite nineteenth-century villas nestled amidst lush parks and gardens. Accommodation options abound, from luxurious sea-view villas to cozy holiday homes and hotels, including the traditional local trullo. Visitors can partake in the lively festivities honoring the Madonna, complete with captivating firework displays. To soak in the beauty of Santa Maria di Leuca, leisurely strolls along the splendid seafront offer breathtaking vistas and moments of serenity.

SANTA MARIA DI LEUCA LIGHTHOUSE

Accessing the port from the sanctuary involves ascending the 286-step Santa Maria di Leuca staircase, offering a memorable experience. Along the way, the town features a striking waterfall, marking the final segment of the Apulian aqueduct. Perched on the promontory is the impressive Santa Maria di Leuca lighthouse, erected in 1864 and towering at 47 meters tall. With its beam extending over 50 kilometers, the lighthouse has been instrumental in saving numerous vessels. Adjacent to the basilica, commonly referred to as the sanctuary, lies the Santa Maria di Leuca clinic, a nursing facility managed by religious personnel, boasting a breathtaking vista, ideal for providing solace in the twilight years of the elderly. This promontory serves as the historical nucleus of Santa Maria di Leuca, where local artisans have showcased their crafts for generations. However, Leuca is not solely steeped in history; it also thrives on gastronomy, craftsmanship, and, above all, its maritime allure.

THE ATTRACTIONS OF SANTA MARIA DI LEUCA

Exploring Santa Maria di Leuca entails a journey through its pristine beaches, secluded coves, and renowned caves.

SANTA MARIA DI LEUCA BEACHES: Describing the water as crystal clear would be an understatement. Those fortunate enough to witness the dawn spectacle are treated to an emerald-green sea, evoking a mythical ambiance akin to the phoenix rising. Perched upon rugged cliffs, Santa Maria di Leuca boasts a limited number of beaches. Among these is the stretch locally known as **"rena ranne,"** or the large beach, a mere hundred-meter expanse that stands in contrast to the kilometers of sandy shores along the Ionian coast, extending all the way to Gallipoli.

SANTA MARIA DI LEUCA CAVES: The area is adorned with an abundance of caves, natural marvels sculpted by Mother Nature around the perimeter and beyond of picturesque Leuca. Venturing into these caves is akin to stepping back millions of years, where the essence of time itself has shaped the landscape. | **BOAT TOUR:** Embarking on a boat tour in Santa Maria di Leuca allows you to explore the caves wonders. A few noteworthy mentions include the "***Le Tre Porte***" (the three caves of Santa Maria di Leuca), the "***Grotta del Diavolo***" (Devil's Cave), where the entrance transitions from land to sea, the "***Grotta del Soffio***" (Blowing Cave), where crashing waves create a unique spectacle, and the "***Gabbiano***" (Seagull Cave), among many others.

LOCAL HANDICRAFTS: The handicraft scene in Leuca revolves around olive wood creations, complemented by Salento's traditional rush and reed weaving for basketry, alongside terracotta pottery dating back to ancient times. Furthermore, the artistry of stonemasons working with Lecce stone, a remarkably soft tuff responsible for the region's stunning Baroque architecture, adds to the area's rich cultural tapestry.

WHERE TO STAY IN LEUCA

MONTIRO HOTEL: offers an intimate retreat amidst 12 acres of Mediterranean landscape. With 38 rooms featuring Trani Stone floors and scenic views, guests enjoy warm hospitality and delicious cuisine. | **MESSAPIA HOTEL & RESORT:** is a four-star hotel offers panoramic views and modern accommodations, including 110 units. While praised for its amenities, recent reviews on TripAdvisor present a mixed picture. | **HOTEL TERMINAL:** A waterfront hotel offering amenities like a private beach, pool, and spa. While some guests praise its convenient location and cleanliness, others express disappointment with aspects like food quality and outdated decor. | **MAREINCANTATO BED & BREAKFAST:** Highly rated for its cleanliness, friendly service, and convenient location near Santa Maria di Leuca's coastline. You will appreciate spacious rooms and amenities like air conditioning. The hosts, Ippazio and Caterina, are praised for their warm hospitality. | **B&B SANTA MARIA DI LEUCA:** this B&B is praised for its excellent location, cleanliness, and friendly service. With air-conditioned rooms and a sea-view terrace for breakfast, guests enjoy a cozy atmosphere and proximity to local attractions.

DINING OPTIONS IN SANTA MARIA DI LEUCA

Traditional cuisine reigns supreme in Leuca, featuring rustic dishes from the rural tradition infused with a blend of aromas, flavors, and colors reminiscent of divine feasts - the epitome of the Mediterranean diet. And for those craving fresh, local seafood, the options are aplenty. **For pizza aficionados**, here are a few options in Santa Maria di Leuca: La Conchiglia | Da Leo | Calura | Gnam | Athena | But the culinary journey doesn't end there. Santa Maria di Leuca is home to an array of restaurants offering delectable fare, including: **Osteria Terra Masci** – specializing in fish dishes | Osteria del Pardo – serving up typical cuisine | **Costa di Ponente Restaurant** – offering Mediterranean delights | **Mangiamare** – known for its seafood specialties | **Boccon di Vino** – showcasing typical local dishes | Fedele Restaurant – specializing in seafood | And let's not forget about dessert! Artisanal ice cream parlors, such as **Martinucci**, dot the landscape, offering sweet treats in picturesque settings worthy of a Flemish painting. As night falls, the seafront promenade comes alive, inviting leisurely strolls. For those seeking late-night revelry, **Bar Del Porto** stands as a beacon, one of Leuca's oldest establishments where the nightlife kicks off at midnight and carries on until the wee hours. | Perched overlooking the sea of Santa Maria di Leuca are magnificent late 19th-century villas, boasting impressive Arab and Baroque architectural features, adding to the allure of this enchanting coastal town.

2-DAY ITINERARY TO EXPLORE SANTA MARIA DI LEUCA

DAY 1: Commence your day by embracing the serenity of sunrise and immersing yourself in the awe-inspiring vista atop the Punta Meliso plateau, home to the towering Santa Maria di Leuca lighthouse, standing proudly at 102 meters above sea level. Operating since 1866, this beacon rises 48 meters, and on clear days, its intermittent beam extends a remarkable 40 kilometers. | Adjacent lies the **Sanctuary of Santa Maria de Finibus Terrae**, a must-visit destination revered by both religious and secular visitors alike. Erected upon the remnants of an ancient pagan sanctuary, it still harbors historical artifacts like the "Ara a Minerva," alongside captivating 17th and 18th-century paintings and a meticulously preserved organ dating back to 1855. Leuca Marina is renowned for its meticulously maintained and well-organized harbor, frequented by opulent yachts on numerous occasions. | Descend towards the town center via the two flights of stairs commemorating the culmination of the Apulian aqueduct, culminating in the grandiose Monumental Waterfall of Santa Maria di Leuca. This ambitious fascist-era project holds profound symbolic significance, blessing the waters as they cascade near the Basilica before merging with the boundless sea. | Conclude your exploration at one of the region's largest harbors, boasting over 760 mooring spots. Indulge in a brief respite with some local delicacies like ***pucce salentine***, serenaded by the gentle sea breeze, and continue your leisurely stroll along the picturesque seafront. Admire the charming manor houses, predominantly showcasing Art Nouveau architecture, once the summer retreats of affluent families that bestowed an exotic allure upon the seaside resort. Across the road, near the shoreline, marvel at the "bagnarole," carved into the rocks for discreet bathing in bygone eras.

DAY 2: Embark on the day with a breakfast overlooking the azure expanse, savoring a refreshing "caffé in ghiaccio" with almond milk and pasticciotto. | For an unparalleled perspective amidst the cerulean sea, opt for a boat excursion traversing the caves and rugged coastline. | Alternatively, delve into the "Parco Naturale Regione Costiera Otranto Santa Maria di Leuca e Bosco Tricase," spanning 3227 hectares and boasting a tapestry of diverse landscapes, vibrant hues, and flourishing flora. From Tricase, journey towards the coast to admire the majestic "Vallonea dei cento Cavalieri" (Vallonea of the hundred knights), Western Europe's sole centuries-old oak tree. | Cap off the weekend by indulging in the flavors of traditional cuisine, humble in ingredients yet opulent in taste, to conclude your Santa Maria di Leuca escapade on a delightful note.

SCAN THIS QR CODE TO EXPLORE THE FULL MAP OF LEUCA

OTHER SALENTO TOWNS WORTH EXPLORING

NARDO

Nardò remains relatively undiscovered by tourists, but this is likely to change soon. The city has invested significantly in restoring its historic center, boasting a magnificent main square adorned with charming rococo designs. The church of San Domenico exemplifies the local Baroque style, while the city hall occupies a splendid palazzo open for exploration.

GALATINA

Galatina is renowned as the epicenter of Puglia's regional dance, la pizzica. Its primary attraction is the church of Santa Caterina, showcasing breathtaking frescoes dating back to the 1300s. Don't miss the chance to indulge in delectable pastries at the renowned pastry shop "Ascalone," operating since 1745, especially their famous pasticciotto, a local delicacy.

CASTRO MARINA, SANTA CESARIA TERME, AND TRICASE

Castro Marina, Santa Cesaria Terme, and Tricase are best experienced through the scenic route of Strada Provinciale 358 (SP 358), spanning all three towns. This picturesque drive, stretching nearly 60 kilometers along the rocky coastline from Otranto to Santa Maria di Leuca, offers mesmerizing views over the Adriatic Sea. Consider exploring this route by bicycle for a more active adventure.

CHAPTER 4: THE BEST BEACHES OF PUGLIA

Puglia boasts Italy's finest beaches, from rugged Adriatic coastline to serene white sands and turquoise waters of the Ionian Coast. Balancing lazy beach days with evenings in charming coastal villages is quintessential to a Puglian beach holiday. Timing significantly shapes your beach experience. May offers uncrowded beaches, while August brings bustling scenes with high temperatures and plenty of activities. Optimal times for tranquility are May, early June, late September, and October, although amenities may be limited. July and August are vibrant but crowded, especially around Gallipoli. Mid-August is busiest, with overwhelming crowds. For balance, consider early June or mid-September, when weather is warm, atmosphere lingers, and crowds are manageable. Arriving early or enjoying sunset at the beach offers respite from crowds. Explore inland towns during midday or rent a villa with a pool for relaxation. Websites like Vrbo offer various holiday rentals to suit preferences and budgets.

LIDOS: ITALIAN BEACH CLUBS

For those unfamiliar with the Italian coastal scene, the sight of rows of beach chairs and umbrellas during summer can be surprising. These are the domain of privately managed beach clubs, known as lidos or stabilimenti balneari, which are integral to Italy's beach culture. They offer rentals for umbrellas and loungers, as well as amenities like toilets, showers, and bars. While some lidos opt for a straightforward setup, others offer upscale options with comfortable loungers, spacious arrangements, and personalized services. Prices for an umbrella and two loungers at a Puglia lido typically range from €20 to €30 for a full day, but luxury lidos can charge €200 or more for two people during peak periods. Prices often increase the closer your spot is to the sea, sometimes extending over 10 rows of chairs.

IS BOOKING A LIDO NECESSARY IN PUGLIA? In August, reservations are usually essential to secure a spot at a lido, while in July, early arrivals might secure a place, though it varies among different beach clubs. Some cater more to spontaneous visitors, while others are pre-booked by Italians for weeks, months, or the entire season. To explore the available beach clubs in Puglia, *Spiaggie.it* offers a platform for online bookings.

ARE LIDOS OBLIGATORY ON PUGLIA BEACHES? No, Italian beaches are public and must provide free sections (spiaggia libera). These areas may be found at one end of the beach or scattered among lidos. They are recognizable by the absence of uniform umbrellas seen in lidos. However, free beaches can get crowded in summer. Occasionally, independent vendors may rent chairs and umbrellas on these free sections, as we observed at Pescoluse Beach. While this option is more affordable than lidos and allows for early arrival to secure a good spot, facilities are typically not available.

TOP BEACHES NEAR BARI AND OSTUNI

1. PANE E POMODORO BEACH, BARI: Conveniently located just a short walk or drive from Bari's old town, this free beach offers powdery white sand and clear waters, perfect for a refreshing dip. Expect crowds on summer weekends.
2. LAMA MONACHILE, POLIGNANO A MARE: Nestled beneath a bridge in Polignano's old town, this picturesque pebbly cove surrounded by rugged cliffs is ideal for a quick swim during your visit to this charming coastal town.
3. CALA PORTA VECCHIA, MONOPOLI: Located south of Polignano, this free beach beneath 16th-century walls invites visitors to enjoy its golden sand and turquoise waters while exploring Monopoli's attractions.
4. LIDO MORELLI, OSTUNI: Within the Coastal Dunes Regional Natural Park, this beach offers a mix of lido facilities and free areas. While May offers uncrowded sands and free parking, peak season brings bustling activity. Torre Guaceto, known for its beauty, is another option nearby.

TOP BEACHES IN SALENTO

Torre Lapillo, Porto Cesareo: A stunning 4-kilometer stretch of white sandy beach with aquamarine waters. It can get crowded, but upscale beach clubs like Bahia del Sol Porto Cesareo offer comfort and amenities. | **Porto Selvaggio, Nardò**: A small, natural pebbly cove within a nature reserve, perfect for a tranquil beach experience away from crowds. | **Spiaggia della Purità, Gallipoli:** A convenient city beach with golden sands and clear waters, ideal for a quick dip while exploring Gallipoli's charming streets. Stay at Pascaraymondo Suite Palace for a memorable stay. | **Punta Pizzo, Gallipoli:** A serene beach within a nature reserve, offering peaceful stretches of free beach amid dunes and pine forests. Stay in nearby Marina di Mancaversa for affordability and convenience. | **Torre San Giovanni, Ugento**: A splendid sandy beach with free sections among beach clubs. | **Pescoluse Beach:** Known as the "Maldives of Salento," this beach boasts crystalline waters and golden sands. Plenty of free beach space is available. Stay in Marina di Pescoluse for convenient accommodations. | **Il Ciolo, Gagliano del Capo:** A scenic swimming spot amidst limestone cliffs and emerald waters. You can stay in nearby Castro for easy access to this picturesque cove. | **Castro Marina:** Rocky platforms ideal for sunbathing and swimming amid picturesque surroundings. You can stay at Hotel La Roccia for seafront views and access to Castro Marina's coastline. | **Otranto Beach:** Turquoise waters and sandy shores offer a refreshing swim amidst historic charm. You can Stay at Hotel Palazzo Papaleo for easy access to the beach and town attractions. | **Torre dell'Orso:** A km-long crescent of white sandy beach surrounded by cliffs and rock formations. | **Grotta della Poesia (Cave of Poetry):** A unique swimming experience in a natural pool carved into limestone rock. Enjoy tranquility during early or off-season visits.

BEST BEACHES IN GARGANO

16. SPIAGGIA DEL CASTELLO, VIESTE: A family-friendly beach south of Vieste, boasting calm, shallow waters and a picturesque setting overlooked by white cliffs. Stretching over 3 kilometers, it offers both beach clubs and spacious free sections. Stay at Residence Maresol for tranquil accommodations near Castello Beach.

17. BAIA DELLE ZAGARE, MATTINATA: Known for its dramatic white cliffs and secluded cove, this beach is accessible primarily by boat or through select hotels with elevators. Although the free section can be challenging to reach, guests at Hotel Baia delle Zagare enjoy convenient beach access via elevators.

OUR TOP BEACH RECOMMENDATIONS

For Beach Days: Torre San Giovanni, Pescoluse, Torre Lapillo
For a Scenic Swim: Lama Monachile, Castro Marina, Il Ciolo
For Exploration and Snorkeling: Porto Selvaggio
Most Picturesque Seaside Towns with Sandy Beaches: Monopoli, Otranto, Gallipoli, Vieste

As you can see, Puglia offers numerous stunning beaches, catering to those seeking relaxation on expansive shores or a refreshing swim in picturesque coastal towns. My foremost suggestion is to set realistic expectations. During July and August, the beaches in Italy become exceedingly crowded, and it's nearly impossible to avoid unless you arrive very early in the morning. Rather than fighting the crowds, it's advisable to embrace the vibrant beach atmosphere and make the most of your experience. However, if crowded beaches are not your preference, consider visiting during the shoulder seasons of May and October. During these months, the beach clubs dismantle, and you'll once again find tranquil stretches of sand awaiting your enjoyment.

TIPS FOR EXPLORING PUGLIA'S BEACHES

⇢ **OPT FOR CAR RENTAL:** Puglia's public transportation network isn't extensive, making it far more convenient to access the beaches with your own vehicle. You can easily scout for rental deals through *RentalCars.com*. For travelers arriving by air, car rental services are available at Bari or Brindisi airports. | ⇢ **PARKING:** Keep in mind that beach parking fees are applicable from June to September, typically ranging from €5 to €10 per day. While some beach towns offer metered street parking, many parking lots are managed by the beach clubs (lidos). It's possible to park at a lido even if you don't intend to rent an umbrella from them. | ⇢ **CASH:** Ensure you have cash on hand, preferably in coins for parking meters, as most parking facilities do not accept cards. | ⇢ **EARLY ARRIVAL IS KEY:** Italians approach beach outings seriously during the summer months. Those heading to free beaches tend to arrive early, well-prepared, and often stay for the entire day. In July and August, securing a prime spot in the free sections requires arriving before 9 am, preferably by 8 am. if you prefer a later start, consider pre-booking loungers at a lido. | ⇢ **BE PREPARED:** If you opt not to use lidos, it's advisable to purchase an umbrella as shade is scarce on the beaches. For rocky beaches along the Adriatic coast, beach chairs and water shoes may be appreciated. Beach towns in Puglia typically feature shops selling beach essentials, or larger supermarkets offer a selection. I personally acquired a snorkel set for €16 from Conrad supermarket. Keep an eye out for roaming vendors selling beach attire and inflatables at some beaches. Bringing ample water and a picnic lunch is wise, although certain beaches are within proximity to town facilities.

CHAPTER 5: SAVORING PUGLIA CULINARY DELIGHTS

Throughout its history, Puglia has been renowned for its abundant wheat production, earning it the moniker 'breadbasket of Italy'. It contributes significantly to Italy's olive oil output, accounting for 40-50% of the nation's total, and is home to Altamura, the sole producer of DOP bread in Italy. However, Puglia's culinary reputation extends beyond these staples to encompass a variety of traditional dishes, such as orecchiette with broccoli rabe. This cruciferous vegetable lends a mildly bitter flavor, which pairs exquisitely with the local focaccia, offering a truly authentic taste of Puglia. Benefiting from a distinct terroir and a warm, arid climate moderated by its coastal proximity, Puglia produces robust red wines that rank among Italy's finest. Moreover, this same climate fosters the production of crisp, dry white wines, equally celebrated for their exceptional quality. In the region, you'll encounter numerous impressive dishes that boasts a delightful simplicity. It relies on locally sourced ingredients, complemented by aromatic herbs and spices, resulting in incredible flavors. Let's explore some of the most prevalent dishes.

20 MUST-EAT PUGLIAN CUISINE

Below are 14 essential foods to savor in Puglia. Indeed, your visit to Italy's southernmost region wouldn't be complete without indulging in these culinary delights straight from the source.

FOCACCIA: Apulian focaccia stands out with its round dough, slightly thicker than the Genovese variety, boasting a crispy exterior and a soft, yielding interior. The traditional version features cherry tomatoes, but variations abound. When in Salento, be sure to try pucce, or in the Gargano, indulge in paposce – both are baked pizza loaves stuffed with a medley of delectable fillings.

CACIOCAVALLO: A delightful complement to bruschetta, caciocavallo is renowned for its distinctive shape & mild saltiness, unless aged extensively, which intensifies its flavor. Grilled caciocavallo is particularly exquisite. When visiting the Gargano peninsula, don't overlook Caciocavallo Podolico, crafted from the milk of Podolic cows, a lesser-known, endangered breed prized for its richly concentrated milk.

MOZZARELLA, BURRATA, AND STRACCIATELLA: Apulia's dairy craftsmanship extends beyond caciocavallo. Burrata has gained international acclaim, but its true essence is best experienced in Puglia. Stracciatella forms the creamy filling of burrata before being encased in mozzarella. Mozzarella, typically shaped into knots, boasts a uniquely crunchy texture when bitten into. These dairy delights abound throughout Puglia, with Andria and its environs particularly renowned for their quality.

PANZEROTTI: These fried, stuffed pockets of dough are a culinary delight, traditionally filled with tomato and mozzarella, though variants with prosciutto and mozzarella are also popular. When freshly fried, they are piping hot, with molten mozzarella eagerly escaping upon the first bite – a caution to avoid staining clothes or burning fingers. While oven-baked versions are available, they often lack the charm and flavor of their fried counterparts.

PETTOLE: Best enjoyed piping hot straight from the fryer, pettole are fried bread dough balls typically served with a sprinkle of salt or accompanied by tomato sauce and grated cheese. During the Christmas season, a sweet variation, dusted with sugar and sometimes drizzled with vincotto (sweet cooked grape must), is especially beloved.

PASTICCIOTTI: Although emblematic of Puglia, pasticciotti are predominantly found in and around Lecce. These shortcrust pastry tartlets are filled with cream and often feature a sour cherry, drawing comparisons to Lisbon's pasteis. Many Lecce bakers innovate with diverse fillings, including savory variations, showcasing the versatility of this beloved Puglian treat.

BREAD: Considered one of Puglia's most iconic culinary offerings, bread holds a special place in the region's gastronomic heritage. Notably, Pane di Altamura, a Protected Designation of Origin (PDO) bread hailing from the inland town west of Bari, enjoys widespread renown. Similarly, the bread from Monte Sant'Angelo, situated in the northern part of Puglia near the Adriatic coast, holds the esteemed designation of Traditional Agricultural Product (PAT). In truth, all of Puglia's durum wheat bread varieties are worthy of sampling. Fear not purchasing an entire loaf, fearing it may go to waste – chances are, you'll relish every last crumb.

CARTELLATE: Originating from the Gargano peninsula, cartellate epitomizes Puglia's rich culinary tapestry, showcasing influences from the region's historical connections with Arab culture. Originally a festive treat associated with Christmas, these intricately fried, rose-shaped pastries, flavored with honey or vincotto (sometimes both), are now enjoyed year-round. Variations may feature colorful sprinkles or toppings of shaved hazelnuts or almonds. Thanks to their extended shelf life, cartellate make for delightful souvenirs or gifts.

FRISELLA: Frisella, a type of bread, holds practical and significant culinary importance. Baked in a stone oven with a drizzle of olive oil, it yields a satisfyingly crunchy texture, ideal for long-term storage without compromising on flavor. It's readily available for purchase, even online, eliminating the need for homemade preparation.

TARALLI: Taralli, often likened to crackers, are circular treats akin to Italy's interpretation of pretzels. They come in a diverse range of flavors, from plain (perfect alongside vegetable and salami assortments for a traditional Italian appetizer) to fennel, poppy seed, or sweetened with sugar for a delectable alternative.

PUCCIA: Although visually unassuming, Puccia delights the palate with its divine taste. Essentially a sandwich, it features pizza dough as the 'bread,' generously filled with various ingredients such as meats, cheeses, and vegetables, appealing particularly to those on the move, served piping hot for maximum enjoyment.

ORECCHIETTE: No culinary exploration of Italy is complete without sampling the local pasta, and Puglia's Orecchiette stands out. Translating to "small ears" due to its distinctive shape resembling tiny ears, this pasta is often handmade and readily found being prepared on the streets of the region. Typically served with a classic combination of fresh tomatoes, garlic, ricotta cheese, and broccoli rabe, it offers a quintessential taste of Puglian cuisine.

BACCALÀ ALLA SALENTINA: A traditional dish originating from Puglia's Salentina area, Baccalà alla Salentina elevates dried and salted cod to new heights. Encased in breadcrumbs, tomato, and pecorino cheese before being baked to perfection, this rendition surpasses any previous encounters with dried and salted cod, offering a culinary masterpiece.

APULIAN BISCUITS: For an authentic Italian cookie experience, Apulian biscuits are a must-try. Crafted using almonds grown in the sun-drenched Puglia region of southern Italy, these cookies are coated in sugar and adorned with almonds, presenting a distinctive and delightful accompaniment to afternoon coffee.

RICCI DI MARE: Another oceanic delight worth sharing is the ricci di mare, a delicacy in Puglia that captivates both tourists and locals alike. These can be found at summer markets or even harvested directly from the water by those with diving skills. The edible portion is the vibrant orange/red part, traditionally enjoyed in pasta, with bread, or on its own with a spoon or directly with the tongue for the ultimate flavor experience.

VONGOLE: The finest fresh fish and shellfish are always discovered in the coastal villages. A well-prepared dish is so delightful that you'll find yourself cleaning the shells completely and ordering another basket of bread to savor every bit of the sauce.

FRISE: Frise exemplifies simplicity and purity in cuisine. Comprising only flour, salt, water, fresh tomatoes, and olive oil, this traditional Italian rustic bread from Puglia is simply delicious. It is typically consumed with an abundance of tomatoes, and sometimes enriched with burrata, taking it to the next level. A pro tip: bring some frise home, as it's perfect for long-term storage and easy preparation. In the past, it was a staple for field workers and fishermen; to soften, soak it in water.

ORECCHIETTE CON CIME DI RAPA: At *Boccaccio in Santa Maria di Leuca*, the handmade orecchiette secures a well-deserved second place. Almost always crafted by hand in Puglia, the freshness of the pasta makes a remarkable difference. When it's featured on the menu, don't hesitate to order it! | **FICHI:** Figs, or fichi, hold a significant place in the diets of southern Italians, being rich in antioxidants and vitamins. Consumed throughout the day in summer, they are considered a secret ingredient contributing to the region's longevity. While not frequently found on restaurant menus, that's no issue – you can pick them for free! Puglia's roadsides are adorned with fig trees where you can pluck one or two fresh figs by hand. Just be courteous, avoid taking all of them, and exercise caution when parking by the roadside. | **CAFFE LECCESE:** Caffe Leccese, a traditional iced coffee with almond syrup, is my preferred summer beverage. Resisting the temptation to order just one is challenging, so I often try to sneak a sip from anyone accompanying me. Perfect for cooling down in the afternoon or paired with a pasticciotto for breakfast, this beverage embodies the essence of Puglian summer.

BEVERAGES TO ENJOY IN PUGLIA

In Puglia, the locals frequently indulge in a light wine known as *Negroamaro*. For those who favor a robust, intense red wine boasting black fruit notes and a hint of velvety spiciness, *Primitivo di Manduna* stands out as an exceptional selection. This wine pairs exquisitely with grilled beef, lamb, game, or mature cheese. An alternative choice is the *"Es" Primitivo di Manduria*, characterized by its dense, inky-black color and aromas featuring cedar, dried spices, and balsamic notes. Meanwhile, **"Per Lui"** presents a dark, profound, nearly black wine with a 15% alcohol content crafted entirely from Negroamaro grapes. Opting for organic wine enthusiasts, the *"17" Gioia del Colle DOC Primitivo* proves to be an excellent option. This wine showcases a dense, juicy texture, a enduringly smooth finish with a touch of spice, and a robust 16.5% alcohol content.

BEST PLACES TO DINE & WINE IN PUGLIA

L'Antica Locanda: Located in Noci, this establishment is renowned for its exquisite seasonal cuisine. Chef Pasquale Fatalino is dedicated to preserving the traditional flavors of Valle d'Itria, offering an unyielding commitment to quality amidst the rising tourist influence in Puglia. Indulge in the antipasto misto, featuring a delightful array of salumi, formaggi, olives, and vegetable dishes. The pasta dishes celebrate the local tomatoes and cheeses, and don't forget to leave room for Chef Fatalino's specialty – grilled meat. | **Da Tuccino:** Positioned on the sea just north of Polignano a Mare, this upscale fish restaurant is a tribute to Neptune. Known for serving some of the finest pesce crudo in the Provincia di Bari, Da Tuccino's spaghetti con le cozze is a spectacular highlight. The unique grappa palate cleanser at the end of the meal adds a strangely refreshing touch to the dining experience. | *Address:* Contrada Santa Caterina 69, Polignano a Mare.

La Rotonda: Situated on the litoranea south of Monopoli, It is a charming restaurant-shack offering a picturesque view of the sea. Specializing in ricci di mare (seasonal sea urchins), cozze fritte (fried mussels), grilled octopus, and basic pasta dishes, it provides a delightful dining experience on a patio overlooking the coastline. | *Address:* SS Savelletri-Torre Canne, Fasano. | **L'Aratro:** In Alberobello, where many restaurants cater to mass tourism, L'Aratro stands out. This alternative gem serves meticulously selected cheeses, cured meats, and simple durum wheat pasta dishes. The owner, also a sommelier, takes pride in incorporating Slow Food recognized products into the menu. | *Address:* Via Monte San Michele 27, Alberobello.

Di Cosimo: A Bari landmark renowned for its pizza and u' panzerrott' (pizza dough stuffed with mozzarella and tomato sauce, deep-fried). Whether queuing up for takeout or finding a table in the side room, Di Cosimo offers a satisfying dining experience. | *Address:* Via Modugno Giovanni 31, Bari. | **Lido Bianco:** Perched on a rocky outcropping above a cove with turquoise waters, Lido Bianco is a beautifully situated restaurant. Specializing in crudi (raw shellfish), their antipasto misto di mare is a culinary masterpiece, featuring insalata di mare, smoked salmon with orange zest, shrimp crepes, and more. | *Address*: Via Procaccia 3, Monopoli. | **L'Orecchietta:** This pasta shop and trattoria in Guagnano sells fresh pasta and traditional dishes for takeout, highlighting seasonal produce, local pasta shapes, and hearty meat dishes. | *Address:* Via Vittorio Veneto 49, Guagnano. | **Panifico Fiore:** Known for its excellent bread, Panifico Fiore bakes in the back and serves focaccia topped with tomatoes and olives. The result is a crispy-bottomed flatbread with a spongy interior, offering a delightful blend of sweet and salty flavors. | *Address:* Strada Palazzo di Citta' 38, Bari. | **Farmacia dei Sani:** Deep in Salento's interior, this restaurant offers innovative dishes inspired by the region's ingredients, elevated with modern techniques and creative flavor contrasts. | **La Succursale:** A busy pizzeria near Lecce's university, La Succursale serves thick-rimmed pizzas with craft beer, assorted salads, legume dishes, and cheese plates. | **Le Macàre:** This friendly trattoria presents a survey of Salento's sea and land-based specialties, including roasted octopus, eggplants stuffed with mozzarella, and ragù misto.

WHERE TO SIP COCKTAILS

→ **QUANTO BASTA:** A craft cocktail bar & Salento's first venture into global spirits, offering excellent drinks that blend foreign & domestic flavors. | *Address:* Via Marco Basseo 29, Lecce. | → **CUBI:** Opened in 2017, this craft cocktail bar in southern Salento mixes proper cocktails, providing a contemporary touch to the region's bar scene. | *Address:* Via S. Giuseppe, 12, 73024 Maglie LE, Italy | → **CAFFÈ PARISI:** Nestled in Nardò's historic center, Caffè Parisi offers old-school café culture, a large aperitivo spread & a prime location. | *Address:* Piazza Antonio Salandra 38, Nardò.

WHERE TO INDULGE IN SWEETS & COFFEE

→ **Avio:** Located near the Castello in Lecce, Avio is a coffee shop serving a special blend of local Quarta coffee. The espressini freddi offers a rich summer alternative to classic caffe' espresso. | *Address:* Corner of Via Trinchese and Via XV Luglio, Lecce. | → **Alvino:** Found in Piazza Sant'Oronzo in Lecce, Alvino is a bar and café serving local sweet and savory snacks like pasticciotti & rustici. | *Address:* Piazza Sant'Oronzo 30, Lecce. | → **Bar Cotognata:** Leccese: Renowned for cotognata, Lecce's quince paste, Bar Cotognata offers a range of sweet specialties. | *Address:* Viale Marconi 51 Lecce. | → **PASTICCERIA ASCALONE:** Established in 1740, this family-owned institution in Galatina attracts pasticiotti lovers from across Salento. | *Address:* Via Vittorio Emanuele 17, Galatina. | → **NATALE:** Located around the block from Alvino in Lecce, It is a gelateria serving classic & creative flavors inspired by local specialties. | *Address:* Via Trinchese 7, Lecce. | ↠ **Pasticceria Nobile:** In San Cataldo, Pasticceria Nobile offers hot delightful pasticciotti even in the summer heat. | *Address:* Via Marco Polo 9, San Cataldo | ↠ **Super Mago del Gelo:** A gelateria in Polignano a Mare specializing in granita, Super Mago del Gelo offers slushy fruit ice with unique flavors like gelso nero (black mulberry) & mandorla (almond). | *Address:* Piazza Garibaldi 22, Polignano a Mare.

TOP SEAFOOD DINING SPOTS IN PUGLIA

IL TRAPPETTO: Housed in a converted old mill carved into the rock, this establishment serves delectable dishes such as peppered mussels and fried sea bass fillets. During the summer, diners can enjoy their meal in the Orte of the Court botanical garden, complete with numerous vegetarian options. | *Address:* Via Casale, 168, Vico del Gargano (FG). Tel. +39 347.9153363. | **LA RIPA:** In the heart of the Vieste Grotto lies "La Ripa," an inn set in a grotto. The menu showcases seafood specialties like octopus carpaccio with tomatoes and olives, sautéed clams or mussels, marinated anchovies, and various local pasta dishes, all highlighting the flavors of fresh fish. | *Address:* Via Cimaglia, 16, Vieste (FG). Tel. +39 0884.708048.

BARI'S OCTOPUS DELICACY: Bari, the main city of Puglia, is not to be missed. Near the old city, close to the port, fishermen prepare a traditional octopus dish known as "polpo rizzato" every afternoon. This dish involves a unique process where octopuses are curled up by being repeatedly beaten until they become crunchy, served alongside a popular local beer, Peroni.

SATISFY YOUR SEAFOOD CRAVINGS IN CASTRO AND GALLIPOLI: Picture this: You've just explored the sea caves or returned from a paddle boat tour in the small coastal village of Castro. Hungry and still in your swimwear, head to *Porto Vecchio*, a tiny friggitoria near the beach, for freshly made fried calamari, shrimp, and a bottle of fresh white wine to take away. | *Address:* Via Scalo Delle Barche, 73030 Castro, (LE) – 3245648429.

GALLIPOLI, another must-visit city, offers an unforgettable street seafood experience. At sunset, old fishing boats dock at the Old Port, transforming into small outdoor restaurants serving fresh fish paired with local wine. | **TRICASE PORTO AND SANTA MARIA DI LEUCA:** Venture south to Tricase Porto, a district with 300 inhabitants in the town of Tricase, known for its wooden platform beside the crystalline sea. La Bolina offers a reasonably priced menu, limited seating, and the chance to sample excellent wines from Salento, complemented by appetizers in a cozy sofa area. | *Address:* Lungomare Cristoforo Colombo, Tricase (LE) – 0833 775102. | **OSTERIA TERRA MASCI**, where the Ionian and Adriatic Seas converge. For a seafood treat, visit Osteria Terra Masci, where culinary tradition meets natural beauty amid dry stone walls, green antique boats, and wooden tables beneath a charming pergola. One of the highlights is the spaghetti with monkfish, shrimp, breadcrumbs, and green pepper.

DINING AT A MASSERIA

Masseria are fortified farmhouses scattered throughout the Italian countryside often offering lodging to guests. While some masserie are upscale establishments, others provide a more intimate, rustic experience, allowing guests to dine alongside the family, as was the case at Masseria Ferri.

AT MASSERIA SANT'ANGELO IN CORIGLIANO D'OTRANTO, guests, including hosts Rocco and Ursula, occasionally joined by friends, gathered around a lengthy table on the terrace. Here, a continuous array of dishes was presented—approximately eight antipasti, followed by pasta, cheese, dessert, and fruit. The fare, although straightforward, was delectable, offering an ideal opportunity to sample local specialties. Given that masserie operate as working farms, guests have the chance to taste self-produced wine, cheese, olive oil, and jams, in addition to enjoying vegetables freshly harvested from the garden.

MASSERIA IL FRANTOIO: is among my preferred destinations for both accommodation and dining in Puglia. It is a 500-year-old organic olive farm which offers remarkable eight-course tasting menus featuring nearly all farm-produced ingredients in a magical setting with ancient olive trees & charming flower-filled courtyard,. The tranquility, connection with nature, and rich historical ambiance contribute to its appeal. Owned by the same family for 500 years, the farm was abandoned for two decades until the current owners, Armando and Rosalba, transformed it into one of Italy's first agriturismo establishments in the 1990s. The extensive grounds, featuring thousands of olive trees and various crops, provide a remote feel while being just a 10-minute drive from Ostuni. Masseria Il Frantoio is sure to exceed your expectations with a blissful retreat, relaxation and exceptional dining.

PUGLIA'S FOOD FESTIVAL

Puglia hosts a multitude of small-scale festivals throughout the year, each dedicated to celebrating and showcasing the richness of its culinary offerings. Recognized as one of Europe's premier agricultural hubs, Puglia takes pride in producing significant quantities of Italy's renowned wine, olive oil, fruits, and vegetables. Below is a curated guide to some of the most noteworthy food festivals that unfold annually, presenting an opportunity for indulgence during your Puglia villa holiday.

January: Mid-January marks the Puccia dell'Ampa celebration in Lecce, dedicated to a wood-baked bread filled with pickles or aged ricotta cheese known as a culinary delight. The festivities span a whole weekend, emphasizing the significance of this presumably delectable sandwich.

February: As February draws to a close, the town of Celenza Valfortore hosts the Festa della Pignata (Octopus Festival), an unmissable event considering Puglia's stellar reputation for seafood.

March: Easter in Santa Cesàrea Terme, Lecce, brings forth the 'cuddrura' – a ring-shaped, deep-fried sweet bread available in local bakeries throughout the Easter season.

April: The Festival of San Giorgio in Vieste, amidst religious commemorations, fireworks, parades, and horse racing, pays homage to the 'frittato' – an omelette akin to the Spanish tortilla. Later in the month, the Sagra dei Tarallucci e Vino event in Alberobello celebrates biscuits and wine featuring 'taralli' – traditional ring-shaped biscuits, sweet or savory.

May: Ortranto dedicates a festival to truffles towards the end of May, with numerous food stands lining the historical center of the town. May and June witness the Sagra della Ciliegia Ferrovia festival, celebrating the humble cherry, held in towns like Leverano, Conversano, and Turi.

June: During the first half of June, Brindisi hosts the Negroamaro Wine Festival, dedicated to the Puglian Negroamaro vine, featuring over a hundred and fifty stands showcasing the vine's products. At the end of June, Otranto celebrates San Pietro e Paolo, blending delicious food with Salento folklore.

July: Numerous towns honor the 'frisella' in July, a dried, bagel-shaped bread topped with tomatoes, oil, oregano, and salt. Additionally, the town of

Crispiano hosts a unique festival combining liver, snails, bread, and ice cream as part of its annual festivities.

August: In early August, Zollino celebrates 'sceblasti,' a Greek focaccia dotted with tomatoes, cooked in wood-fired ovens, traditionally meant to be the first bread baked of the day. August also witnesses the Sagra della Polpetta in Felline (meatballs) and the Sannicandro di Bari, paying tribute to the local pasta, orecchiette.

September: Bari celebrates its sausage specialty in September with the 'Sammichele' festival, culminating in a feast paired with mozzarella and red wine.

October: Toward the end of October, the towns of Muro Leccese and Ortelle celebrate roast 'maiale' – pork. Originating as a means to feed local farmworkers, the festival now features specially created dishes in restaurants and market stalls.

COOKING CLASSES: MASTERING PUGLIAN CUISINE

Puglia's culinary style is celebrated for its uncomplicated approach, emphasis on freshness, and utilization of locally sourced, seasonal ingredients. From the handmade orecchiette pasta to the rich olive oil and delectable seafood, the flavors of Puglian cuisine offer a genuine feast for the senses.

Numerous cooking classes are available in Puglia, ranging from brief sessions to in-depth, multi-day programs. When selecting a class, several considerations including your skill level, interests, Budget and where you will be staying in Puglia come into play.

Well-regarded cooking classes in Puglia include: **Puglia Culinary Centre at Castello di Ugento:** This prestigious culinary school provides a range of classes, from brief workshops to extensive 15-week programs. Students learn from skilled chefs and have the chance to explore local markets and producers. | **Veronika's Adventure Authentic Puglian Cooking Class:** Held in a traditional Puglian masseria (farmhouse), this hands-on class teaches participants to prepare classic dishes such as orecchiette pasta, fava bean purée, and pasticciotto (a ricotta-filled pastry). For more options of cooking classes you can choose from, visit: **http://tinyurl.com/Cooking-Classes-in-Puglia**

Regardless of the cooking class you opt for, a memorable and delectable journey into the world of Puglian cuisine awaits you.

CHAPTER 6: PUGLIAN IMMERSIVE EXEPERIENCES

WINE TASTING & TOURS

When it comes to exploring wineries in Puglia, the options are abundant, offering a delightful experience for wine aficionados. Puglia proudly hosts some of Italy's finest wineries, making it a haven for those who appreciate the art of winemaking. Whether you possess a sophisticated palate or simply enjoy the occasional glass of red or white, Puglia promises a journey of exquisite flavors and diverse wine offerings.

Embarking on a tour of the region's premier wineries is one of the best ways to immerse yourself in the rich tapestry of Apulian wine. With an array of choices, it can be challenging to know where to begin. Noteworthy among the best wineries in Puglia are **Cantina di Venosa**, **Cantine Paololeo**, and **Leone de Castris**. These establishments are renowned for their outstanding wines, picturesque landscapes, and knowledgeable staff. During your tour, indulge in a variety of wines, from crisp whites to full-bodied reds. The experience extends beyond tasting, allowing you to delve into the winemaking process and the storied history of wine production in Puglia. Some wineries even offer curated food pairings, enhancing the overall tasting experience with cheeses, olives, and cured meats.

For an enriching Puglia experience, a wine tour is a must-do activity. With access to some of the region's finest wineries, your visit is sure to be memorable. So, grab a glass of your preferred Apulian wine, relax, and savor the breathtaking scenery and flavors that define this captivating region. Don't miss the opportunity to explore the best wineries in Puglia and unravel the uniqueness that makes this region truly special.

PUGLIA WINE AREAS

Puglia boasts four primary wine regions, each contributing to the rich oenological landscape:

Salento: The southernmost part of Puglia, characterized by its flat, fertile, and sunny terrain. Representing over half of Puglia's DOC wine regions, Salento is known for wines such as Negroamaro, Primitivo, and Malvasia Nera. | **DOC Primitivo di Manduria Area:** Situated east of Taranto on the Salento peninsula, this area is distinct and separate from Salento. Renowned for producing some of Puglia's top Primitivo wines, characterized by density, darkness, and fruitiness. | **Gioia del Colle:** North of Salento and in proximity to Bari, this region experiences more moderate temperatures. The Primitivo wines here tend to be slightly more acidic and restrained than those of Manduria. The area is recognized for blending Primitivo with other red varieties like Montepulciano, Negroamaro, or Malvasia Nera. | **Castel del Monte DOC Area:** Located further north in central Puglia, this vast wine area derives its name from the 19th-century fortress built by Emperor Frederick II. Notable for wines based on the local Nero di Troia variety, known for elegant floral aromas and robust, tannic structures. The Castel del Monte area also explores other varieties like Aglianico and Bombino Nero.

BEST WINERIES IN PUGLIA

Carvinea Winery: Situated near Carovigno in the upper Salento countryside, Carvinea cultivates Primitivo, Negroamaro, Montepulciano, and Aglianico. | **Polvanera Winery:** Founded in 2003 north of Gioia del Colle, Polvanera boasts approximately 62 hectares of vineyards, with 60% dedicated to Primitivo and the rest to various native red and white varieties—all certified organic. | **Chiaromonte Winery:** Established in 1826 in the Gioia del Colle DOC area, Chiaromonte specializes in wines centered around Primitivo. All vineyards of the company are certified organic, garnering awards and positive reviews for their initiatives. | **I Pastini Winery:** Founded in 1996 in Valle d'Itria near Martina Franca, I Pastini utilizes ancient viticultural traditions alongside modern winemaking techniques. Managed by the Carparelli family, the winery focuses on recovering and enhancing native vines such as Verdeca, Bianco d'Alessano, and Minutolo. | **Gianfranco Fino Winery:** Established in 2004, Gianfranco Fino started with a small vineyard in the Manduria region. Over the years, the winery expanded to cover 37 acres, including ancient-growing vineyards, receiving accolades such as the Winemaker of the Year award from Gambero Rosso. | **Rivera Winery:** Recognized as an example for quality wine production in Puglia, Rivera emphasizes the potential of the Castel del Monte DOC area. Apart from Nero di Troia, the winery cultivates Bombino Nero, Montepulciano, and Aglianico. | **Due Palme Winery:** Founded in 1989 in Cellino San Marco, Due Palme emerged from the merger of three large wine cooperatives. As one of the largest cooperative wineries in Puglia, it has around 400 producers and offers a broad portfolio, ranging from dry red and white wines to sweet and sparkling wines. | **Tormaresca Winery (Marchesi Antinori):** Established at the end of the 1990s, Tormaresca is part of the expansion initiative by Marchesi Antinori. It comprises two estates—one in Salento DOC and the other in Castel del Monte, cultivating both traditional native varieties and international ones like Cabernet Sauvignon, Merlot, and Chardonnay. | **Viglione Winery:** Located near Santeramo in Colle, Viglione focuses on Primitivo wines while also cultivating traditional native varieties.

OLIVE OIL TOURS AND TASTINGS

Amid its diverse attractions, one standout gem is the golden elixir – Olive Oil, famously hailed as Puglia's liquid gold. Olive oil in Puglia transcends mere culinary use; it embodies a way of life and serves as the lifeblood pumping vitality into Puglia's culture, economy, and tourism. Often overlooked by tourists, Puglia stands as a global leader in Olive Oil production.

Puglia's Olive Oil Production Data: Contributes 40% to Italy's olive oil production | Comprises 60% of the rest of Italy's olive oil production | **The Olive Oil Making Process:** Embarking on the epic Puglia olive oil journey commences in the region's expansive olive groves, gracing the landscape from Bari beach to the storied Trulli Alberobello. Harvesting is typically done by hand or with small rakes to preserve the superior quality of olives. Puglia boasts different olive varieties, contributing to the diverse range of Puglia olive oil, including Coratina, Ogliarola, Leccino, and Cellina di Nardò.

MUST-VISIT OLIVE OIL FARMS & MILLS IN PUGLIA

Masseria Brancati – Located near Ostuni, offering an olive oil tour amidst ancient olive trees. | **Antico Frantoio Muraglia** – Renowned for traditional granite millstones.

OLIVE OIL TASTING IN PUGLIA

Beyond mill visits, an olive oil tasting tour tantalizes taste buds. ***Consider these tips:*** Color doesn't dictate quality; tastes can range from peppery and grassy to nutty or fruity. | Engage your sense of smell; warmer oil releases more aromas.

PAIRING OLIVE OIL WITH PUGLIA'S REGIONAL CUISINE

Following an olive oil tasting, explore culinary pairings integral to Puglia's gastronomy: ***Focaccia*** – Infused with olive oil | ***Taralli*** – Unleavened dough rings complemented by olive oil dip | ***Friselle*** – Twice-baked bread rounds, drizzled with olive oil

CYCLING

The fusion of Puglia and cycling is gaining popularity among numerous tourists who opt to spend their vacations in the versatile heel of Italy. Stretching over 400 km, Puglia, adorned with remarkable Masseria-farmhouses, alongside the nearby Basilicata, is now a premier destination for national, European, and international cycling holidays, akin to Tuscany and its agriturismo.

WHY PUGLIA IS A CYCLING DESTINATION

Puglia has emerged as a renowned destination for cyclists, drawing attention for various reasons. The geographical makeup, featuring both flat and hilly terrain, coupled with the diverse landscapes, contributes to its allure. Puglia offers an array of attractions, including delectable cuisine, architecturally rich towns, a leisurely lifestyle, and over 800 km of coastline, showcasing rocky cliffs, crags, and expansive sandy shores.

CHOOSING CYCLING ROUTES IN PUGLIA

While Puglia lacks dedicated bike paths, the abundance of country roads transforms into veritable cycle routes, flanked by countless olive trees providing shade and enhancing the overall experience. Selecting the most picturesque bike paths to connect captivating sites and towns such as Lecce, Matera, Cisternino, Martina Franca, Alberobello, Ostuni, Gallipoli, Leuca, and Otranto is a key consideration for cycling in Pugia.

EXPLORING KEY STOPS ON CYCLING ROUTES

Lecce: For cyclists touring Salento, Lecce serves as a logical starting and ending point for a captivating bike tour in the southeastern tip of Italy. | **Matera:** This unique city, recognized as a UNESCO heritage site and European Capital of Culture, is best explored on foot due to its ancient Sassi. Matera is historically and geographically linked to Puglia, providing cyclists with diverse routes to the Alta Murgia or the hills of the Itrìa Valley.

CYCLING THE ITRIA VALLEY

Encompassing Locorotondo, Cisternino, and Martina Franca, the Itria Valley, a karstic depression, showcases the iconic trulli and is an essential stop for cyclists exploring Puglia. Alberobello, the trulli capital, and Ostuni, located on the border between the valley and the Salento plain, are integral parts of cycling tours.

Cisternino: Fondly referred to as the "Kasbah" of the valley, Cisternino offers a unique culinary experience with small restaurants called Fornelli, once butcher shops transformed into charming eateries. | **Martina Franca:** Martina Franca provides cyclists with an authentic experience and a chance to savor local specialties. | **Alberobello:** Known as the capital of Trulli, Alberobello is a must-visit destination for cyclists. Staying overnight in a trullo, a traditional dry stone hut with a conical roof, offers an immersive experience. | **Ostuni:** A cycling tour here provides a fascinating journey through history and olive oil production.

CYCLING IN SALENTO

Salento, famed for its clear sea and stunning marinas like Otranto, Castro, and Salve, is a primary attraction for cycling in Puglia. Starting from Lecce, cyclists can explore the coastal roads, visiting picturesque towns and enjoying the captivating beauty of the Ionian and Adriatic seas.

Gallipoli: Historically known as Kale Polis, Gallipoli's historic center, situated on an island, offers cyclists breathtaking views of the Ionian Sea. A cycling tour along the scenic road on the walls provides a unique perspective. | **Leuca:** Reaching the most extreme point of Italy's heel is achievable through the Ionian coast or the scenic coastal road from Otranto. Leuca, with its Monumental Fountain and Devil Cave, is a fascinating destination for cyclists. | **Otranto:** As the most eastern town of Italy, Otranto is a cycling hotspot with its Byzantine church, Romanesque Cathedral, and the stunning Tree of Life mosaic. Nearby attractions include the Alimini Lakes, offering a diverse landscape for cyclists to explore.

Cycling through the sun-kissed lands of Puglia, with the sea as a constant backdrop, offers a unique and enriching experience. To make the most of beautiful Puglia, consider booking a cycling tour that will cover the charming white villages of the Itria Valley down to the Salento coasts is with tailored itineraries and shorter cycling options that ensures cyclists of all levels can revel in the beauty, history, and culture of this captivating region. Get ready to pedal and explore the wonders of Puglia!

HIKING

Porto Selvaggio: Embark on a captivating journey starting from Torre Uluzzo (Nardo), unfolding an extraordinary route through a wild and untamed landscape that promises an unforgettable experience. | **Sentiero Vecchio del Ciolo (Gagliano del Capo):** Discover a breathtaking view along one of the most romantic hiking routes in Salento. This path is ideal for those who appreciate the allure of untouched nature. | **Riserva Naturale del Bosco delle Pianelle:** Delight in a remarkable hiking adventure in the Valle D'Itria region, meandering through holm-oak trees and encountering wild animals amidst a beautiful backdrop. | **Sant'Isidoro: Palude del Capitano:** Choose to traverse this path either on foot or by bike, located north of Porto Selvaggio. It forms part of a nature reserve, showcasing the beauty of its surroundings. | **San Giovanni Rotondo:** Valle dell'Inferno: Embark on one of the most captivating rocky environments in the Gargano area. This challenging trekking route unfolds in a stunning karst valley of unparalleled beauty. | **Castro: Parco delle Querce:** Nestled in an area surrounded by dry stone walls high above the sea, Parco delle Querce offers a remarkable hiking experience. | *Colli di Ostuni:* Indulge in a hike featuring an extraordinary view along hilly paths that guide you from Cisternino to Ostuni. | *Riserva Marina di Torre Guaceto:* Immerse yourself in the protected marine area of rare beauty, enjoying the picturesque landscape during a rewarding hiking experience. | **Parco di Punta Pizzo in Salento:** Explore the coastline of Parco di Punta Pizzo, featuring a captivating combination of beaches and Mediterranean scrub, making it one of the top trekking destinations in Puglia. | **Gravina di Laterza:** Considered one of the largest canyons in Europe, the Gravina of Laterza is a natural wonder that demands your attention. This canyon is a must-see in the realm of the natural world.

WATERSPORTS

Puglia stands out as a haven for water sports enthusiasts with its extensive coastline, crystal-clear waters, and reliable winds, Puglia provides a diverse range of activities suitable for various skill levels.

Sailing: Discover the enchanting coastline and secluded coves aboard a sailboat or catamaran. Whether opting for a self-rental or a guided tour, the experience promises to be memorable. | **Windsurfing and Kitesurfing:** The Salento peninsula, situated in the southern part of Puglia, is renowned for windsurfing and kitesurfing. Its consistent winds and shallow waters make it an ideal destination for both beginners and seasoned riders. | **Stand-up Paddleboarding (SUP):** Explore the coastline at your own pace with SUP, relishing the scenic beauty. Delve into yoga SUP or embark on a SUP tour to uncover hidden caves and grottoes. | **Scuba Diving and Snorkeling:** Dive into the rich underwater world of the Adriatic Sea, adorned with vibrant coral reefs, shipwrecks, and marine life. Scuba diving and snorkeling trips offer a glimpse into the depths of this captivating realm. | **Kayaking:** Navigate the coastline, traverse mangroves, or reach secluded beaches via kayaking. It provides a splendid way to stay active while basking in the tranquility of the natural surroundings. | *When considering water sports in Puglia, keep the following factors in mind: Consider these factors for water sports in Puglia:* **Time of Year:** Optimal conditions for windsurfing and kitesurfing are from spring to autumn, while summer is ideal for other water sports. | **Location:** Puglia's coastline has diverse beaches, each with unique conditions. Some areas are better for specific water sports, so choose accordingly. | **Skill Level:** Puglia accommodates all skill levels, from beginners to experts. Choose activities aligning with your experience for a safe and enjoyable time.

HORSEBACK RIDING

Puglia's captivating landscapes and picturesque coastline provide an ideal setting for horse riding enthusiasts. Riding through olive groves, vineyards, and along the coastline offers a unique way to discover the natural charm of the region. For both seasoned riders and beginners, there are numerous riding stables that cater to various skill levels, providing not only riding experiences but also lessons and training for those looking to enhance their abilities.

A favored horse riding destination in Puglia is the ***Parco Naturale Regionale Costa Otranto – Santa Maria di Leuca e Bosco di Tricase***. This natural park, with its diverse terrain of forests, hills, and coastline, serves as a paradise for riders.

Another sought-after location is ***Centro Equestre Parco di Mare***, near Cisternino, offering lessons and excursions that range from leisurely rides through olive groves to more challenging routes along the coast.

Horse riding in Puglia extends beyond appreciating the scenery; it is an opportunity to immerse oneself in local culture and traditions.

Many stables and schools provide insights into the region's history and cuisine, often including meals and wine tastings as part of the riding experience. Whether you're an adept rider or a novice, exploring Puglia on horseback is a wonderful way to connect with the region's breathtaking landscapes, engage with local culture, and craft enduring memories. To identify farms with riding school in Puglia, visit: *http://tinyurl.com/apulia-horse-riding*

PUGLIAN FOLK MUSIC AND DANCE

Delve into the essence of Pulgia, and you'll uncover a lively tradition of folk music and dance that will make you tap your feet, eager to join in. Taking center stage are the **Pizzica** and its counterpart, the *Tarantella*. These high-energy dances are synonymous with Puglia, especially the Salento peninsula in the south. The music incorporates tambourines, fiddles, and accordion, creating a rhythmic beat that compels your body to sway.

There are two Varieties of Pizzica: ***Pizzica Tarantata***: Often considered the "exorcism" dance, with dynamic, spinning movements believed to cure those bitten by the *tarantula spider* (though its historical accuracy is debated). Look for it during festivals like *La Notte della Taranta in August*, a month-long celebration featuring concerts and dancing in towns across *Grecìa Salentina*. | ***Pizzica d'Amore:*** This milder version, also known as the *Pizzicarella*, is a courtship dance where men showcase rhythmic footwork and playful gestures to impress the ladies. Witness it in towns like *Galatina* and *Cutrofiano* during their summer festivals.

While the Pizzica takes the spotlight, Puglia offers other musical and dance treasures including: **Tamburello**: Admire the skill of tambourine players in traditional ensembles, particularly in Gargano and Salento. | ***Canto a tenore:*** This polyphonic singing tradition from Sardinia has found a home in Salento, creating a unique choral experience. | ***Folk songs:*** Each town has its own collection of songs, often sung in dialect, reflecting local stories and traditions.

EXPERIENCING THE MUSIC AND DANCE: *Festivals*: Immerse yourself in the festive ambiance of local events like the *Festa del Redentore in Fasano* or the *Sagra del Tarocco in Francolise*, where music and dance play a central role in the celebrations. | ***Live performances:*** Seek out traditional music nights in piazzas, restaurants, or dedicated venues like "*le pizziche*" in Salento. | ***Dance lessons:*** Embrace the opportunity to learn the steps yourself! Many towns offer workshops where you can grasp the basic moves of the Pizzica. If you are interested in taking a pizzica dance lesson, visit: ***http://tinyurl.com/Pizzicia-Dance-lesson***

PUGLIA FESTIVALS AND EVENTS CALENDAR

Explore the vibrant festivals and events happening throughout Puglia, regardless of your location in the region. This comprehensive calendar covers winter, spring, summer, autumn, and the festive Christmas season.

WINTER EVENTS IN PUGLIA
January - February

Sacra Rappresentazione dei Magi: Witness a live portrayal of the Holy Nativity Scenes in Monopoli during January. | **Il Carnevale di Putignano**: Experience one of the world's longest and oldest carnivals in Putignano, lasting up to two months with parades, floats, and various events. | **I Falò di San Giuseppe:** Celebrate Father's Day on March 19th with bonfires in towns across Puglia, blending pagan and Christian traditions.

SPRING EVENTS AND FESTIVALS
March - May

La Festa di San Nicola: Commemorate the arrival of San Nicola's relics in Bari with a grand procession, attracting pilgrims from around the world. | **La Festa di San Cataldo:** Celebrate San Cataldo, the patron saint of Taranto, with events including a rowing competition, street food festival, and fireworks. | **Buongiorno Ceramica:** Explore the rich traditions of Italian ceramics during a nationwide event in Laterza and Grottaglie.

PUGLIA EVENTS IN SUMMER
June - August

La Scamiciata: Witness a historical re-enactment of the victory over the Turks in Fasano during June. | **La Notte di San Giovanni:** Enjoy music and tradition during the magical summer nights in Bitetto, Putignano, and Ostuni in June. | **San Pietro e Paolo:** Experience the seaside town of Otranto during the festival celebrating its local food and Salento folklore on June 28th-29th. | **Danza delle Tarantole:** Participate in processions and dances honoring archaic divinities in Galatina on June 29th. | **Locus Jazz Festival:** Attend a popular jazz festival featuring international performers in Bari, Locorotondo, and Fasano. | Fasano Music Festival: Enjoy concerts in archaeological sites around Fasano during three weekends in July. | **Alberobello Light Festival:** Witness the illumination of Alberobello's trulli town center with star images, celebrating Van Gogh's 125th anniversary in the last week of July. | *Locomotive Jazz Festival:* Experience jazz concerts in various venues around Salento in July or August. | *La Festa di Santa Domenica:* Visit Scorrano for a vibrant celebration of its Patron Saint with illuminations, fireworks, and festivities around July 6th. | *Festival della Valle d'Itria*: Attend the 48th classical music and opera festival in Martina Franca during July and August. | *Otranto Jazz Festival:* Enjoy three days of jazz concerts at Otranto Castle, usually on the third weekend of July. | *La Festa di Santa Cristina:* Join the rowing regatta and other events celebrating the town's Patron Saint in Gallipoli from July 23rd to 25th. | *Mercatino del Gusto:* Experience an open-air food market in Maglie during August. | *Corteo Storico di Federico II e Torneo dei Rioni:* Celebrate Holy Roman Emperor Stupor Mundi with a historical parade in Oria in August. | *La Festa dei Martiri Idruntini:* Commemorate the martyrs with solemnity, processions, and a stunning firework display in Otranto from August 13th to 15th. | *Sagra di Ferragosto:* Enjoy a music festival and concerts featuring pizzica dancers in San Vito dei Normanni on August 15th.

La Festa della Madonna di Leuca: Witness the procession of the Madonna of Leuca followed by fireworks in Santa Maria di Leuca on August 15th. | *Sagra Pirotecnica della Valle d'Itria:* Attend a pyrotechnics competition during the 5-day celebration of Locorotondo's patron saint, San Rocco, in August. | *La Notte della Taranta:* Experience one of Italy's biggest festivals, celebrating Pizzica Pizzica in the towns of Grecia Salentina in August. | *Mareviglioso:* Celebrate the sea's bounty in Polignano a Mare at the end of August. | *Fiera di Sant'Oronzo:* Join lively music events, food stalls, and fireworks in Lecce from August 24th to 26th. | *La Cavalcata di Sant'Oronzo:* Witness the parade of the saint's statue with knights on horseback in Ostuni from August 25th to 27th.

AUTUMN EVENTS IN PUGLIA
September - November

Festa te lu Mieru - Wine Festival: Experience a popular wine festival in Carpignano Salentino during September, filled with shows, music, folk dances, and, of course, wine.

CHRISTMAS IN PUGLIA

Start the Christmas season early in Puglia, with festivities beginning on

November 22nd. Explore the tradition of making pettole and creating presepi, witness town bands playing Christmas carols, and indulge in festive feasts featuring Puglian specialties. The charming old town centers come alive with Christmas lights and decorations, creating a magical atmosphere across the region.

CHAPTER 7: SHOPPING & SOUVENIRS

TOP 5 SOUVENIRS TO TAKE HOME FROM PUGLIA

When visiting Puglia, the charming heel of Italy, don't miss the opportunity to take home some authentic souvenirs. Whether you're exploring for a weekend or enjoying an extended stay in one of our luxurious holiday villas, Puglia offers a rich selection of gifts and mementos to cherish your memories.

1. Exquisite Embroidery: Indulge in luxury embroidery, a prestigious gift deeply rooted in Puglia's culture and history. Dating back to the tradition of Corredo matrimoniale, where brides received hand-embroidered linens from their families, this art form continues to thrive with modern influences. Whether for a special occasion or to adorn your home with authentic Puglian craftsmanship, refined embroidery makes a timeless keepsake.

2. Fine Puglian Wine: Treat your loved ones (or yourself) to a bottle of exquisite Puglian wine, a delightful reminder of your time in this renowned wine region. Explore local wineries through an unforgettable wine tour, sampling prestigious grape varieties and learning ancient winemaking techniques under the guidance of professional sommeliers. With autochthonous grapes like Negroamaro and Primitivo, Puglia offers a diverse selection of bold and flavorful wines to suit every palate.

3. Ceramic Treasures from Grottaglie: Discover the rich tradition of ceramic craftsmanship in Grottaglie, known for its high-quality pottery adorned with the DOC seal. Take a leisurely stroll through the ceramic district, where artisans create intricate works of art, from knights on horseback to whimsical whistles and symbolic Pumi figures. Visit renowned studios like Cocci D'Autore to admire masterpieces and perhaps even participate in a ceramic class to create your own unique souvenir.

4. Extra Virgin Olive Oil: Experience the "green gold" of Puglia with a bottle of premium Extra Virgin Olive Oil, a staple of the Mediterranean diet and a symbol of the region's culinary heritage. Puglia boasts vast olive tree plantations, contributing to its picturesque landscape and producing some

of Italy's finest olive oil. Share the gift of health and flavor with your friends and family, or join in the annual olive harvesting for a hands-on experience during your villa stay.

<u>5. Papier-Mâché Artistry:</u> Immerse yourself in the whimsical world of papier-mâché, a beloved art form in Puglia known as *cartapesta*. Encounter masterpieces throughout the region, from intricate statues to vibrant masks showcased in festivals and souvenir shops. Opt for a unique souvenir by participating in a papier-mâché workshop with acclaimed artist Claudio Riso in Lecce, where you can create your own personalized masterpiece to treasure the memories of your Puglian adventure.

Indulge in these top Puglia souvenirs to capture the essence of this enchanting region and share its beauty with your loved ones back home.

BEST PLACES FOR SHOPPING IN PUGLIA

Puglia, with its diverse landscapes and rich cultural heritage, is not only an ideal destination for a villa holiday but also offers fantastic shopping experiences. From authentic souvenirs to delectable local specialties, explore the bustling markets and unique shops in these Puglian towns and cities.

GALLIPOLI: UNEARTH HIDDEN TREASURES

Gallipoli is a treasure trove for shoppers, especially at its outdoor markets. The town hosts a captivating antique market on the first Sunday of each month, where you can discover a plethora of hidden gems. Spend an entire day navigating this lively market, where bargaining is not only common but also encouraged. Take a leisurely stroll along the Ionian Sea, and after your exploration, treat yourself to the freshness of the local fish market.

BARI: BLEND OF TERMINAL MARKETS & FASHION BOUTIQUES

As Puglia's third-largest city, Bari is a shopping haven offering a diverse range of experiences. Fashion enthusiasts will be delighted by the numerous boutiques showcasing the latest trends and designer items, including brands like Dolce & Gabbana and Oscar de la Renta.

Bari boasts several weekly markets and daily Terminal markets. Two noteworthy markets to explore during your Puglia holiday are **_Mercato Coperto Santa Scolastica_** and **_Mercato San Nicola_**. Immerse yourself in the local lifestyle, shop for fresh produce, grocery items, and savor the renowned "**_Focaccia Barese_**."

ANDRIA: SWEET INDULGENCE

For those with a sweet tooth, Andria is a must-visit destination. The **_Museo del Confetto Mucci Giovanni_**, a museum and shop, unveils the art of crafting "confetti" or sweets. Experience a delightful blend of confectionery and Italian culture for a memorable day out. The tempting samples may entice you to stock up on confetti to bring home.

LECCE: PAPIER-MÂCHÉ CAPITAL

In the city of Lecce, known for its luxury holiday experiences, papier-mâché goods take center stage, representing a longstanding tradition and a symbol of the region. Visit special workshops to peruse the creations of skilled artists, ranging from religious icons to contemporary designs. Not only can you purchase these artistic pieces as souvenirs, but you also have the opportunity to learn the craft and create your own valuable works.

CHAPTER 8: PRACTICAL INFORMATION

VISA REQUIREMENTS

The visa requirements for a visit to Puglia, Italy, are contingent upon your nationality and the duration of your intended stay. For citizens of Schengen Area countries, there is no need for a visa to enter Italy for stays of up to 90 days within a 6-month period. A valid passport or identity card suffices for entry. However, citizens of non-Schengen Area countries may require a visa based on their nationality and the length of their stay. To determine the specific visa requirements for your nationality, consult the Italian Ministry of Foreign Affairs website on *https://www.esteri.it/en/ministero*

For non-Schengen Area citizens, general visa prerequisites include a valid passport with at least 3 months validity beyond the planned stay, a completed visa application form, two recent passport-sized photographs, proof of travel insurance with a minimum coverage of €30,000 for medical expenses, and evidence of sufficient funds to cover the stay (e.g., bank statements, travel bookings). Stays exceeding 90 days may necessitate additional documentation, such as proof of accommodation and a return ticket. Specific visa types, such as short-stay (up to 90 days), long-stay (beyond 90 days), transit, study, and work visas, have their own distinct requirements. It is crucial to initiate the visa application well in advance of the trip, considering varying processing times. Some additional recommendations for a Puglia visa application include ensuring all necessary documents are prepared, meticulously filling out the application form, submitting the application to the Italian embassy or consulate in your home country, paying the application fee, and being ready for an interview if required.

CURRENCY AND BANKING

The official currency is the Euro (€). While cards are widely accepted, it's advisable to carry some cash for smaller purchases and rural areas. ATMs are readily available in major towns and cities. Major credit cards are widely accepted, but beware of potential foreign transaction fees.

LANGUAGE AND COMMUNICATION

Italian is the official language. English is spoken in tourist areas, but learning basic Italian phrases is beneficial. Italians use expressive gestures; a friendly demeanor with open body language is appreciated.

HEALTH AND SAFETY TIPS

Consult your doctor for recommended vaccinations, especially if venturing outside tourist areas. | Public healthcare is good, but having travel insurance is advisable. | Bring necessary medications. | Protect yourself from the sun with sunscreen, sunglasses, and a hat, particularly during the peak summer months. | Exercise caution against pickpocketing in crowded areas. | In case of emergencies, dial 112.

ETIQUETTE AND CULTURAL NORMS

Italians generally dress smartly, especially in cities. Casual attire is acceptable in tourist areas, but modesty is advised in religious sites.

Greetings involve a handshake and eye contact, with cheek kisses exchanged in close circles. Dining is a leisurely affair in Italy, where tipping is not expected but appreciated for exceptional service. Most people in Puglia are Catholic, so respect religious sites and dress modestly when visiting. Be aware of afternoon siestas, as some shops and businesses may close during that time. Smoking is prohibited indoors in public places, with designated outdoor areas available.

60 BASIC USEFUL ITALIAN PHRASES AND VOCABULARY

GREETINGS AND ESSENTIALS

Hello: *Ciao* (informal) /chao/, *Buongiorno* /bwohn-johr-no/ (good morning), *Buonasera* /bwoh-nah-seh-rah/ (good evening)
Goodbye: *Ciao* (informal) /chao/, *Arriveder*ci /ah-ree-veh-dehr-chee/ (formal) | **Yes: Sì** /see | **No: N**o /no | **Please:** Per favore /pehr fah-voh-reh | **Thank you**: Grazie /grahts-ee-eh | **You're welcome:** Prego /preh-goh | **Excuse me: Sc**usi /skoo-zee/ (formal) | **I'm sorry**: Mi dispiace /mee dee-spyah-cheh | **Do you speak English?**: Parli inglese? /pahr-lee een-gleh-zeh | **I don't understand:** Non capisco /non kah-pee-skoh | **How much does this cost?:** Quanto costa questo? /kwahn-toh koh-stah kweh-stoh

GETTING AROUND

Where is the bathroom?: *Dov'è il bagno?* /doh-veh eel bahn-yoh | **Can I have the bill, please?:** *Posso avere il conto, per favore?* /pohs-soh ah-veh-reh eel kohn-toh, pehr fah-voh-reh | **Help!:** *Aiuto!* /ah-yoo-toh | **Call the police:** *Chiamate la polizia!* /kyah-mah-teh lah poh-lee-tsyah

NUMBERS

Uno (one): /oo-no | **Due (two)**: /dweh | **Tre (three)**: /treh/ | **Quattro (four)**: /kwah-troh | **Cinque (five)**: /cheen-kweh | **Sei (six)**: /say/ | **Sette (seven)**: /set-teh | **Otto (eight)**: /oht-toh | **Nove (nine)**: /noh-veh | **Dieci (ten)**: /dee-eh-chee/

FOOD AND DRINK

I would like to order...: *Vorrei ordinare...* /vohr-ray ohr-dee-nah-reh | **Menu:** *Menu* /meh-noo | **Water:** *Acqua* /ah-kwah | **Wine:** *Vino* /vee-no | **Beer:** *Birra* /beer-rah | **Coffee:** *Caffè* /kahf-feh | **Pizza:** *Pizza* /peet-sah | **Pasta:** *Pasta* /pahs-tah | **Bread:** *Pane* /pah-neh | **Cheese:** *Formaggio* /for-mah-djoh | **Meat:** *Carne* /kahr-neh | **Fish:** *Pesce* /peh-she | **Fruit:** *Frutta* /froo-tah | **Vegetables:** *Verdure* /vehr-doo-reh | **Delicious:** *Delizioso!* /deh-lee-tsyoh-so/

PLACES

Hotel: *Albergo* /ahl-behr-goh | **Restaurant:** *Ristorante* /ree-stoh-rahn-teh | **Shop:** *Negozio* /neh-goh-tsyoh | **Bank:** *Banca* /bahn-kah | **ATM:** *Bancomat* /bahn-koh-maht | **Hospital:** *Ospedale* /oh-speh-dah-leh | **Train station:** *Stazione ferroviaria* /stah-tsyoh-neh fehr-roh-vyah-ree-ah | **Bus stop:** *Fermata* *dell'autobus* /fehr-mah-tah del aw-toh-boos | **Beach:** *Spiaggia* /spyah-jah | **Church:** *Chiesa* /kyeh-zah | **Museum:** *Museo* /moo-zeh-oh/

CULTURE

Thank you very much: *Grazie mille!* /grahts-ee-eh mee-leh | **It was a pleasure to meet you:** *È stato un piacere conoscerti!* /eh stah-toh oon pyah-cheh-reh koh-noh-shehr-tee | **I love Puglia!:** *Adoro la Puglia!* /ah-doh-roh lah poo-lyah | **Beautiful:** *Bello* /beh-lo/ (masculine), **Bella** */beh-lah/* (feminine) | **Good:** *Buono* /bwoh-no/ (masculine), **Buona** */bwoh-nah/* (feminine) | **Interesting:** *Interessante* /een-teh-res-sahn-teh | **Fun:** *Divertente* /dee-ver-ten-teh/

PACKING TIPS

Preparing for your trip to Puglia can pose a challenge, depending on the season and your planned activities. Here are some general recommendations to assist you:

ESSENTIALS

Comfortable footwear: Given Puglia's enchanting towns with cobblestone streets and historical sites, comfortable walking shoes are essential for a day-long exploration. | **Crossbody bag:** Keep your belongings secure and within reach while you navigate through the charming locales. | **Sunscreen and hat:** Shield yourself from the strong Puglian sun by packing sunscreen and a hat. | **Reusable water bottle:** Stay hydrated, especially during warmer months, and contribute to environmental sustainability by carrying a reusable water bottle. | **Travel adapter:** If you're visiting from outside Europe, ensure you have a travel adapter to charge your electronic devices. | **Converter plug:** For visitors from outside Italy, a converter plug may be necessary to use your electronics.

CLOTHING

Light and breathable fabrics: Pack clothing made from light and breathable materials such as cotton and linen, suitable for Puglia's warm climate. | **Layers:** Bring a light sweater or jacket for cooler evenings, particularly during spring and fall. | **Swimsuit:** If beach time is on your agenda, don't forget to pack a swimsuit. | **Long Pants:** For visits to religious sites, it's important to have long pants to cover your knees and shoulders. | **Scarf:** A versatile accessory, a scarf can serve as a blanket, sarong, or a cover for your shoulders when entering churches.

Additional items: Umbrella | First-aid kit | This Guidebook | Italian phrasebook

USEFUL CONTACTS

- Medical Emergency Service: 118

- Police / Polizia: 113

- Carabinieri (Local Police Assistance): 112

- Fire Department: 115

- ACI Car Breakdown Service: 116

- Financial police / Guardia di Finanza: 117

- Forestry & Environmental Emergency: 1515

- Forestry & Environment Vigilance: 800-865065

- Coastguard – Sea Recovery: 1530

- Local Tourism Authority: 080.5589745

- National Motorway Authority: 892525

- National Railway Authority: 892021

It is also a good idea to save the phone number of your hotel or accommodation provider in case you need to contact them for assistance.

BOOKS TO READ BEFORE VISITING PUGLIA

Head Over Heel: Seduced by Southern Italy by Chris Harrison: This hilarious and captivating memoir tells the story of Harrison's decision to leave his life in Australia and move to a small village in Puglia. It's a great way to get a feel for the laid-back lifestyle and friendly people of the region. | **Stories from Puglia: Two Californians in Southern Italy by Mark Tedesco:** This book follows two Californians as they experience the culture and traditions of Puglia. It's a mix of personal anecdotes, historical information, and practical tips for travelers. | **La Puglia: In the Heart of Italy by Carol King:** This beautiful book is filled with stunning photography and insightful text that explores the history, culture, and food of Puglia. It's a great way to get a comprehensive overview of the region. | **By the Ionian Sea: Rambles in Southern Italy by George Gissing:** This classic travelogue was first published in 1901 and offers a fascinating glimpse into Puglia at the turn of the 20th century. It's a bit more challenging to find than some of the other books on this list, but it's worth seeking out if you're interested in history. | **Puglia: The Land of Apulia by Corrado Alvaro:** This book is a love letter to Puglia, written by one of Italy's most celebrated authors. It's a beautiful and moving read that will make you want to book your trip immediately.

In addition to these books, you might also want to consider reading a few novels set in Puglia. This can be a great way to get a feel for the region's atmosphere and culture. Here are a few suggestions:

- The Flight of the Falcon by Daphne du Maurier
- Casa Rossa by Francesca Marciano
- Involuntary Witness by Gianrico Carofiglio

MOVIES TO WATCH BEFORE EXPLORING APULIA

LaCapaGira (1999): Set in Bari, the film delves into the activities of a small group of Apulian criminals involved in smuggling cigarettes and drugs. Viewers are treated to glimpses of iconic locations such as the seafront, Corso Vittorio Emanuele, and the narrow streets of Bari Vecchia. | **Pinocchio (2019):** While the story begins in Tuscany, key scenes unfold in Apulia, including the Blue Fairy's home in a Masseria near Bari, and encounters between Pinocchio and the Cat and the Fox in Ostuni. Other notable locations include Noicàttaro, near Bari, for Fire-Eater's theater, and the sea of Polignano for the natural habitat of the DogFish. | **Stardust (1973):** Bari serves as one of the film's locations, showcasing Bari Vecchia, the seafront, and Teatro Petruzzelli. Additional scenes were shot in the countryside between Martina Franca and Locorotondo. | **The Life Ahead (2020):** Set in Bari, the story revolves around Madame Rosa, a Holocaust survivor and ex-prostitute, who cares for the children of prostitutes, including Momò, an orphan of Senegalese origins. The film captures the beauty of Bari, its harbor, sea, and unique folklore. | **No Time to Die (2021):** Shot in Apulia and Basilicata, the movie showcases the stunning Apulian countryside, including a car pursuit scene filmed near Gravina, near Bari, with an iconic jump off a bridge by James Bond. | **The Girl with the Pistol (1968):** Set in Sicily but filmed in Apulia. Scenes were recorded in Polignano a Mare, Conversano, and Alta Murgia. The plot revolves around the accidental kidnapping of a young Sicilian woman and her pursuer's subsequent escape to the United Kingdom. | **Mio Cognato (2003):** Set predominantly in Bari, especially Bari Vecchia, with additional scenes recorded in Locorotondo. The film captures an iconic scene featuring the Stadio San Nicola illuminated by night lights as the characters stop to relieve themselves.

USEFUL WEBSITES FOR VISITING PUGLIA

Puglia Turismo Website: Explore the official tourism hub for Puglia, providing comprehensive information about the region's attractions, towns, and upcoming events. Visit: *https://www.viaggiareinpuglia.it* | **The Thinking Traveller:** Delve into detailed guides to Puglia, featuring itineraries, hidden gems, and slow travel tips on this comprehensive website. Explore further: *https://www.thethinkingtraveller.com/italy/puglia/all-villas-in-puglia* | **Walks of Italy:** Uncover detailed walking guides to various parts of Puglia, including the Gargano Peninsula and the Salento, with insights from *https://www.utracks.com/Italy/Self-Guided-Walking/Walking-in-Puglia* | **Moovit:** Stay informed with real-time public transport updates for buses, trains, and metros in Puglia using the Moovit app. Explore more: *https://m.moovitapp.com* | **TheFork:** Secure restaurant reservations in Puglia with TheFork, a convenient app for booking tables at various eateries. Find out more: *https://www.thefork.com* | **Google Translate:** Overcome language barriers in Italy with the translation capabilities of Google Translate. Access it here: *https://translate.google.com* | **Puglia Food Tours:** Immerse yourself in the culinary delights of Puglia through guided food tours. Explore options at *https://puglialy.com/puglia-food-wine-tour* | **Puglia Bike Tours:** Discover the picturesque landscapes of Puglia on two wheels with bike tours - *https://ciclismoclassico.com/tours/la-bella-puglia* | **Puglia Cooking Classes:** Enhance your culinary skills with cooking classes in Puglia. Find out more at *https://www.trullidelbosco.com/en/attraction/cooking-class-puglia-alberobello* | **Puglia Wine Tours:** Explore the rich wine culture of Puglia through guided tours. Learn more about wine tasting experiences at *https://www.winetourism.com/wine-tasting-tours-in-puglia*

USEFUL APPS TO EXPLORE PUGLIA

Sherazade: A storytelling app for Android and iOS, Sherazade acts as a digital guide through Salento, narrating tales of love, struggles, daily life, and legends at specific locations. Immersive stories are told by real or imaginary characters, offering a unique travel experience.

Eventi Puglia: Use this app to navigate the vibrant events & festivals, discover local nightlife, filter events based on preferences, and immerse yourself in the authentic colors, flavors, and sounds of the region's cultural scene, especially during the summer. | **AdriaticoIonio:** Solve the Adriatic or Ionian Sea dilemma with this popular app among Salento locals and tourists. It provides real-time images of the seas based on wind direction, aids in choosing local routes, and offers insights into the best beaches and events through user reviews. | **La Puglia è Servita:** An 18-year-old gastronomic handbook app, La Puglia è Servita, is a connoisseur's guide to the best restaurants, pizzerias, trattorias, and local foods in Puglia. | **Wheelmap:** Wheelmap is a German worldwide open-source map app showcasing accessible routes. Especially useful for those with mobility considerations, it provides real-time information on accessible areas, routes, and points of interest globally. | **MyPuglia - Multilanguage Offline Guide:** Overcome internet limitations with MyPuglia, an online and offline map run by locals. Weighing around 20 MB, it ensures seamless navigation without 3G, featuring the "Amerigo" function for personalized activity suggestions based on location, time, and weather conditions. | **Puglia App:** Utilize the official app of Puglia Turismo for information on attractions, events, and transportation - *https://www.regione.puglia.it/web/turismo-e-cultura/app* | **Trenitalia:** Access the Trenitalia app for convenient booking of train tickets with the Italian national train company - *https://www.trenitalia.com/en/purchase/mobile_ticketing.html*

PUGLIAN TOURIST INFORMATION CENTERS

The official tourism website for Apulia, *www.viaggiareinpuglia.it*, offered by the Regional Department for Tourism and Culture, is exceptional to the extent that you might not need a tourist information point during your visit. If you visit any of the listed towns below, consider visiting (I.A.T.) for a map, local event info, or a friendly chat.

BARI PROVINCE: **Alberobello:** Via Monte Nero, 3. Tel +39 080 4322060 | **Andria:** Piazza Catuma, Tel +39 0883 290293 | **Barletta:** Corso Garibaldi 208, Tel +39 0883 531555 | **Noci:** Piazza Plebiscito, Tel +39 080 4978889 | Trani: Piazza Trieste 10, Tel +39 0883 588830

BRINDISI PROVINCE: *Brindisi:* Lungomare Regina Margherita, Tel +39 0831 523072 | *Ceglie Messapica:* Via Giuseppe Elia 16, Tel +39 0831 371003 | *Francavilla Fontana:* Via Municipio 16, Tel +39 0831 811262 | **Fasano:** Piazza Ciaia 10, Tel +39 080 4413086 | *Ostuni:* Corso Mazzini 6, Tel +39 0831 301268

FOGGIA PROVINCE: *Manfredonia*: Piazza del Popolo, Tel +39 0884 581998 | *Margherita di Savoia:* Via Gargano 8, Tel +39 0883 654012 | *San Giovanni Rotondo*: Piazza Europa 104, Tel +39 0882 456240 | *Vieste:* Piazza Kennedy, Tel +39 0884 708806

LECCE PROVINCE: *Lecce:* Via Vittorio Emanuele 24, Tel +39 0832 332463 | *Gallipoli:* Piazza Imbriani 10, Tel +39 0833 262529 | *Otranto:* Piazza Castello, Tel 0836 801436 | *Santa Cesarea Terme:* Via Roma 209, Tel +39 0836 944043

TARANTO PROVINCE: *Martina Franca:* Piazza Roma 37, Tel +39 080 4805702 | *Taranto:* Corso Umberto 113, Tel +39 099 4532392

CHAPTER 9: DETAILED ITINERARY FOR EXPLORING PUGLIA IN 8-DAYS

Instead of attempting to squeeze all the "must-see" places in Puglia into a single itinerary, I've crafted a plan that's practical and ensures you won't spend endless hours driving each day. Realistically, it's impossible to cover every corner of Puglia in just one week. Therefore, this itinerary offers a structured approach to maximize your time and minimize unnecessary driving. I've deliberately omitted locations north of Bari, such as Trani, Andria, Barletta, or the Gargano peninsula, not because they lack charm (they're fantastic!), but because they require significant travel time, which isn't efficient within a week-long timeframe. Most of Puglia's major attractions lie south of Bari, so traveling extensively north only to backtrack south isn't practical. Additionally, the lack of airports closer to the northern areas means starting your journey there would entail considerable additional driving, which isn't ideal for a one-week trip. Each recommended destination in this itinerary includes my favorite sites, top dining spots, and helpful tips for an enhanced experience.

DAY 1 - DISCOVERING BARI & AUTHENTIC PUGLIA VIBES

Bari often escapes the tourist radar. Its remarkable transformations in recent years has howerver make it a fascinating destination. Situated by the sea, Bari boasts a well-preserved historic center, Bari Vecchia, characterized by its labyrinthine streets. You'll encounter delightful culinary offerings, excellent shopping opportunities, and a vibrant nightlife scene. Be prepared for its bustling atmosphere, which might initially overwhelm unaccustomed visitors.

MORNING

Kick off your exploration in Bari Vecchia, immersing yourself in its authentic local life. Begin near the castle **(Castello Svevo)**, where you'll find charming alleyways with elderly women crafting orecchiette, the region's signature pasta resembling "little ears." Wander through the narrow alleys, making sure to visit the **Duomo (San Sabino Cathedral)** and the **Basilica di San Nicola**. Indulge in a traditional snack of Bari-style focaccia from **Panificio Fiore** or **Panificio Santa Rita**. Afterward, take a stroll along the lungomare, the seaside promenade, towards the **Teatro Petruzzelli**, Bari's iconic theater. Don't miss the Fish Market, offering an authentic glimpse into local life and the freshest seafood at reasonable prices.

AFTERNOON

At the market, seize the opportunity to savor "sushi pugliese," featuring raw seafood—a distinctive culinary tradition of the region. Delicacies like raw squid, gambero rosso, raw mussels, and raw octopus await your taste buds. If you're still hungry, grab a quick bite at Mastro Ciccio, renowned for elevating traditional street food into inventive creations. After a late lunch, explore **Via Sparano** and **Via Argiro**, two pedestrianized streets lined with elegant boutiques and designer brands, leading from the Old City to the train station. Now, it's time to unwind and relax at your hotel.

EVENING

For dinner, indulge in a traditional seafood feast at **Ristorante Biancofiore**, my top pick in town. Refer to Part 2 of Chapter 3 for more restaurants & dining in Bari for more culinary recommendations.

DAY 2: BARI TO MATERA

While not technically in Puglia, Matera is within easy reach and offers a captivating journey back in time. Departing from Bari, the landscape transforms as you ascend onto the Murge plateau, culminating in the ancient city of Matera.

MORNING

Embark on your journey to Matera, with a pit stop in *Altamura* along the way. Although Matera is accessible by public transport, the journey via diesel train takes over two hours and isn't available on Sundays. | *Altamura,* about 45 minutes from Bari, beckons with its renowned old bakeries, notably Santa Chiara from the 15th century. Indulge in traditional bread, *focaccia*, and *pasticcio altamurano*—a stuffed focaccia delicacy. | Another local specialty is the *pasticcio altamurano*, a stuffed focaccia filled with baccalà (codfish) or tuna, onion, and olives. | From Altamura, it's a brief 20-minute drive to Matera. Upon arrival, drop off your bags at your hotel, likely situated within one of the city's unique cave dwellings, known as "*sassi*."

AFTERNOON

Start your exploration in the *cittá alta (upper town)*, wandering through its enchanting streets. Matera's charm lies in its labyrinth of staircases, alleyways, churches, and panoramic viewpoints. | **For lunch**, head to *La Latteria*, where you can sample the finest cheeses, local cured meats, and traditional dishes like *crapiata* (legume soup), *fave e cicoria* (mashed fava beans with chicory), or *cruschi* (dried and deep-fried peppers). | **Afterward**, descend to the *Sassi*, Matera's lower district, famous for its cave dwellings. While the area can get crowded between 11 AM and 3 PM, consider returning later in the afternoon or early morning for a quieter experience. Don't miss the iconic *"rupestrian"* churches, such as *Chiesa di Santa Maria di Idris* and *Chiesa di Santa Lucia alla Malve*, though visiting during peak hours may diminish the experience. For a unique perspective, find a scenic viewpoint to admire the *Sassi*, reserving indoor visits for attractions like the *Cripta del Peccato Originale* for tomorrow.

EVENING

In the evening, explore the main square, *Vittorio Veneto*, and stroll along *Via delle Beccherie* and *Corso Vittorio Emanuele*. Via delle Beccherie, despite its name ("street of butchers"), now hosts artisanal craft shops and boutiques leading to the cathedral. Pause at *Piazza del Sedile* for aperitivo, enjoying the lively atmosphere. Corso Vittorio Emanuele offers a leisurely stroll and leads to the picturesque *Piazzetta Pascoli*, offering a splendid view of the illuminated Sassi.

For dinner, indulge in high-end cuisine at **_Baccanti_** or savor a casual meal at **_Oi Mari_** for pizza. Before dinner, treat yourself to a drink with a view at Quarry, boasting a stunning terrace and excellent cocktails.

DAY 3: NATURE TREKKING & RUPESTRIAN CHURCHES IN MATERA

Switch things up today with a gentle hike amidst nature and ancient cave dwellings, followed by a visit to an exceptional Rupestrian Church, a unique gem exclusive to this area.

MORNING

For another glimpse of the **_Sassi_**, aim for an early morning visit to beat the crowds. Consider renting an audio guide for insights, though exploring the churches and dwellings is best with a private guide. Get ready for some outdoor activity as you embark on a **_scenic hike_** from the old town of Matera through the ravine and into the Morgia Materana canyon. While you can hire a guide, this trek is easily manageable on your own. Grab a panino and some water or pack a picnic lunch for the trail. The hike covers a roundtrip of 6 km and takes approximately 2.5 hours. After your hike, retrieve your car and venture slightly out of town to explore the **_Cripta del Peccato Originale_**. Nestled within a cliff overlooking a gulley, this 8th-century church boasts stunning frescoes. Access is via a delightful short hike from the parking area. Note that visits must be arranged in advance due to limited visitor numbers, as the church is located on a private farm.

AFTERNOON

Upon returning to town, unwind at your hotel. As evening approaches, if you're in the mood for an aperitivo and mingling with locals, head to **_L'Antica Credenza_** in Piazza San Francesco, a bustling spot.

EVENING

For dinner tonight, reward yourself with a hearty meal in a charming setting. Set within a cave, **_L'Abbondanza Lucana_** offers a delightful gastronomic journey, showcasing hyperlocal cuisine from the Basilicata region. Don't miss their excellent antipasti selection. Conclude your evening with a nightcap at **_Caffè Tripoli_**. If you find yourself with spare time during your stay in Matera, here are a couple of unconventional activities to consider: **Explore a cistern like La Raccolta delle Acque**, showcasing historical water collection and filtration methods, or visit a putridarium, such as the one found in the **_Chiesa Rupestre di San Pietro Barisano_**—a crypt where bodies were prepared for burial, offering a fascinating glimpse into ancient practices.

DAY 4: MATERA TO LECCE VIA THE VALLE D'ITRIA

Today promises a full day of exploration with a significant amount of driving, so start your day with a hearty breakfast. Your journey will take you through the picturesque hills of the Valle d'Itria, visiting charming villages like Alberobello, Locorotondo, Cisternino, and Ostuni before reaching your final destination, Lecce. Today's itinerary requires a car, but if you prefer an alternative, consider hiring a driver-guide who can chauffeur you from Matera to Lecce, making stops throughout the Valle d'Itria along the way.

MORNING

Start your day by picking up your car and driving to **Alberobello**, renowned for its iconic Trulli houses with stone roofs. The journey takes approximately an hour, and after the initial stretch, you'll re-enter Puglia after about 15 minutes. While Alberobello is charming, it tends to get heavily touristy. Hence, it's best visited before 11 AM, before the influx of tour groups, or after 5 PM when they've departed. The town is divided into two sections by the main street: ***Monti***, the more touristy side with many trulli converted into gift shops, and ***Aia Piccola***, quieter with a few preserved trulli open for exploration.

Take a brief stroll, perhaps enjoy a coffee, then head towards **Locorotondo**. If you're a cycling enthusiast or prefer walking, consider traversing the scenic countryside lanes between Alberobello and Locorotondo. These paths offer picturesque views of well-tended farms, olive groves, and residences, creating a fairytale-like ambiance. Several cycling routes are available, and you can rent bicycles or e-bikes in town. A 15-minute drive south from Alberobello brings you to Locorotondo, a charming hilltop town adorned with whitewashed buildings and cobblestone streets. Noteworthy are the vibrant displays of flowers and plants adorning balconies, a result of a local competition for the most beautiful balcony.

Continue your journey for another 15 minutes to reach the picturesque town of **Cisternino**, whose historic center has been recognized as one of Italy's most charming "**borghi**." Don't miss visiting the ***Chiesa Matrice*** and ***Torre Civica*** before a leisurely stroll down Via Basilioni to ***Vittorio Emanuele square.*** Cisternino is an excellent spot for lunch, famed for its butcher shops that traditionally transitioned into cooking establishments in the evenings. Indulge in ***bombette***, skewers of pork wrapped with cheese and peppers, or venture into the local specialty, gnumnarid, which offers a unique culinary adventure. ***Capocollo***, a local cured meat, is also worth sampling. ***Bére Vecchia*** is a recommended choice for this type of meal. Alternatively, if you prefer to dine in Ostuni, another 25-minute drive away, **_Osteria del Tempo Perso_** offers a fine dining experience.

AFTERNOON

Ostuni, rising majestically from a plain and perched atop a hill overlooking the Adriatic, presents a captivating sight. It's a larger town, so anticipate some traffic upon arrival. Once parked, head to **_Piazza Della Libertá,_** where you'll find the town hall and a statue of **_Sant'Oronzo_**, the patron saint of Lecce and Ostuni. Wander through the old quarter towards the cathedral, exploring the charming alleys along the way. Before departing Ostuni, treat yourself to some of the finest gelato at **_Cremeria La Scala_**, renowned for its freshly made offerings crafted from local ingredients.

EVENING

The journey from Ostuni to Lecce takes about an hour. After a long day of exploration, take some time to relax at your hotel until dinner. If you're in the mood for gourmet cuisine, consider dining at **_Duo_**, **_Primo_**, or **_Tre Rane_**. For a more laid-back atmosphere, **_Doppio Zero_** is a great option. Afterwards, if you still have some energy to spare, head to **_Alvino_** for a refreshing drink.

DAY 5: DISCOVERING BAROQUE LECCE

After yesterday's adventures, take a leisurely day to explore Lecce. With its baroque and rococo architecture, pedestrian-friendly center, elegant boulevards, and numerous squares, Lecce promises a delightful experience.

MORNING

Start your day with a private guided tour after breakfast to gain insight into the city's rich history and abundant art and culture. A 2-hour tour is ideal to cover the highlights and uncover some hidden gems. Spend the late morning and early afternoon immersing yourself in the historic center of Lecce. Here are some notable landmarks to explore:

→**Porta San Biagio, Porta Napoli, and Porta Rudiae:** These beautiful historic gates served as the entrances to the city and are significant architectural features.

→**Piazza Sant'Oronzo:** The main square of Lecce, home to an excavated Roman amphitheater, provides a glimpse into the city's ancient past.

→**The Cathedral and Basilica di Santa Croce:** Marvel at the stunning architecture of these religious landmarks, with the recently restored façade of Basilica di Santa Croce being a highlight.

→**Chiesa di Santa Chiara, Chiesa di San Matteo:** Explore these charming churches, each with its own unique character and history.

→**Castello Carlo V:** Take a detour to visit an exhibit inside this castle, offering insights into Lecce's medieval heritage.

AFTERNOON

When you're ready for lunch, head to *La Cucina di Mamma Elvira* for trendy Pugliese cuisine with innovative twists. Alternatively, if you're looking for a quick bite, *Il Pizzicotto* serves excellent pizza by the kilo. Adjacent to Pizzicotto, you'll find *Mezzo Quinto*, known for its stewed horse meat in a red sauce—a local specialty. Both establishments offer outdoor seating, allowing you to savor your meal while soaking in the atmosphere of *Via Degli Ammirati.*

Later in the afternoon, arrange for a relaxed wine tasting experience at *Crianza*, hosted by Enrico at his stylish enoteca. Consider staying here for dinner to continue indulging in excellent wine and gastronomic delights.

EVENING

For dinner options, **_A'Roma_** offers delectable pasta dishes and Roman cuisine in an inconspicuous location just outside the historic walls. Look for the sign and ring the bell for entry. If you're in the mood for seafood, head to the classy **_Alex_** for a memorable dining experience.

After dinner, unwind at **_Quanto Basta_**, one of Italy's finest bars located in the old city. The vibrant atmosphere, with locals enjoying drinks on the sidewalk and spilling into the narrow streets, sets the perfect scene for a relaxing evening.

During your time in Lecce, be sure to sample a **_rustico_**—a puff pastry filled with mozzarella, béchamel, and a touch of tomato sauce—and a caffe leccese —an espresso served with ice and sweetened, syrupy almond milk. For those with a sweet tooth, don't miss the divine chocolate-covered figs at the **_chocolatier Maglie._**

DAY 6: TRAVELING FROM LEUCA TO OTRANTO

Today's agenda involves reveling in the glorious sunshine as you embark on a coastal journey from Santa Maria di Leuca to Otranto.

MORNING

Commence your day by driving south from Lecce towards **Santa Maria di Leuca**, which marks the southernmost point of Italy and serves as the starting point for a scenic drive to Otranto.

You have two route options available: one that leads inland directly to Leuca, and another that takes you to Gallipoli on the coast before reaching Leuca. **Gallipoli**, a picturesque fishing village boasting delightful beaches and a charming historic center, is worth a visit. However, if you're eager to continue your journey, you can skip this stop. Upon reaching Leuca, where the Ionian Sea meets the Adriatic, take a moment to savor a coffee while soaking in the breathtaking views. Spanning 60 kilometers along Road SP 358, your drive will be adorned with sun-kissed cliffs overlooking the coastline. Along the way, you'll encounter enchanting beach villages like **Tricase**, **Castro**, and **Santa Cesarea Terme**, offering opportunities to pause for a snack and a swim. For thrill-seekers, **Ponte Ciolo**, a 30-meter-high bridge spanning a small cove along your route, presents the chance to witness cliff jumpers in action. Make sure to traverse this route leisurely, making stops in the quaint villages to relish a refreshing dip and marvel at the awe-inspiring vistas. As you approach Otranto, you might catch glimpses of **Albania** across the sea.

It's worth noting that this stretch of coastline is rocky, and sandy beaches are scarce until after Otranto. Most swimming spots here consist of boardwalks or cement jetties extending into the water.

AFTERNOON

Numerous lunch options await you along the route and in Otranto. If hunger strikes earlier, **Taverna del Porto** in Tricase offers delectable fresh seafood. In Otranto, **L'altro baffo** is a recommended dining spot, specializing in seafood, as is customary in this region. For those willing to sacrifice culinary indulgence for a seaside view, *I Villani D'Aragona* offers dining directly by the water.

Following lunch, don't miss the chance to visit the **_Cathedral of Otranto_**, home to a magnificent floor mosaic dating back to the 1100s. The cathedral opens its doors after 3 pm. Within the church, you'll also find the remains of over 800 martyrs who perished during an Ottoman occupation of the city in the late 1400s. From Otranto, you can opt for a swim at a sandy beach near **_Torre dell'Orso_** or head directly back for the 35-minute drive to Lecce.

EVENING

Enjoy your final evening in Lecce, Puglia's most elegant city, before embarking on your journey northward for a few days of seaside relaxation.

DAY 7: COASTAL RELAXATION IN SAVELLETRI

No visit to Puglia would be complete without spending a few days unwinding by the seaside. Today, we'll venture north from Lecce to the Savelletri area renowned for its Masseria-style accommodations, sandy beaches, and tranquil waters. In Savelletri, I recommend booking a stay at a Masseria for your final two nights. These historic fortified farmhouses from the 1800s have been transformed into elegant and sophisticated hotels, nestled amidst olive groves along quiet country roads. Beyond the fishing village of Savelletri, you'll find an array of hotel options catering to various budgets. Notable high-end choices include **_Torre Coccaro_**, **_Torre Maizza_**, and **_Borgo Egnazia_**, while **_La Peschiera_** offers a more intimate and exclusive experience. During the shoulder season, prices tend to be more reasonable compared to the summer peak. Some hotels feature private beach clubs, while others offer complimentary shuttle services to nearby beaches.

MORNING

Embark from Lecce towards Savelletri in the north, passing through Ostuni once more along the way. Upon arriving in Savelletri, check into your chosen hotel and take delight in the picturesque surroundings and inviting pool, or head straight to the beach for a leisurely morning. You can indulge in a beachside lunch with your toes in the sand.

AFTERNOON

Spend the afternoon basking in the sun, as the summer heat makes it less than ideal for exploration. For dinner, most hotels boast excellent restaurants serving fresh local cuisine. Should you desire to venture out, consider dining at a restaurant in **_Monopoli_**, which also offers a charming atmosphere for an evening stroll. Alternatively, explore the port area of Savelletri.

EVENING

Monopoli comes alive in the evening, bustling with activity. As a larger town compared to Savelletri and nearby Polignano, Monopoli boasts a quaint harbor, scenic promenade, and a delightful town center. Be sure to visit the stunning **_Cathedral_** and the **_Grotto Churches_** adorned with exquisite frescoes.

DAY 8: BEACHSIDE LEISURE, CULINARY DELIGHTS & POLIGNANO A MARE

On your final day in Puglia, take it easy with a blend of light sightseeing and relaxation by the sea.

MORNING

Start your day with more beach time, followed by lunch back at your hotel. For a unique culinary experience, consider trying freshly caught local sea urchins at *__Il Principe del Mare__*, located along the coastal road just outside Savelletri. Despite its unassuming appearance with plastic tables on the sand, this establishment offers unbeatable freshness, with the urchins opened and prepared before your eyes.

AFTERNOON

In the afternoon, indulge in an olive oil tasting, cheese making demonstration, or perhaps a pizza/pasta class offered by many hotels. Alternatively, continue soaking up the sun on the beach.

EVENING

In the evening, venture to Polignano a Mare for a delightful visit. Perched atop cliffs, this town offers dramatic vistas and a charming atmosphere, although it lacks major tourist attractions. For a culinary treat, savor a gourmet seafood panini at *__Pescaria__* and indulge in delicious gelato at *__Supermago del Gelo__*. Don't miss the opportunity to enjoy a speciale, an espresso with cream and lemon zest, at a local café. For dinner, *__La Locanda di Felisiano__* is a fantastic choice for seafood on your last night in Puglia. Although slightly challenging to locate, this restaurant offers excellent cuisine, fair prices, and a warm, festive ambiance.

Following a splendid dinner, it's time to bid farewell to Puglia as you prepare to depart for your next destination. Thank you for visiting, and safe travels!

EXPLORE THE GARGANO PENINSULA & THE COAST OF PUGLIA IN 8 DAYS

Embark on a leisurely 8-day journey through Puglia, immersing yourself in nature and exploring captivating landmarks. Commence your adventure in Trani, a charming coastal city conveniently close to Bisceglie, offering an ideal gateway to nearby wonders such as the impressive Castel del Monte, ancient archaeological sites like Canne, and the intriguing Dolmens and Menhir. Your stay in the Gargano promontory promises a blend of untamed lush forests and serene sandy beaches.

HIGHLIGHTS

→Discover Trani & coastal villages from Mattinata to Rodi Garganico.
→Delve into the history of Castel del Monte, an iconic symbol of Apulia. →Embark on scenic hikes in the Gargano National Park or thE Umbra forest.
→Unwind on pristine beaches or venture to the picturesque Tremiti islands. → Enjoy a guided exploration of Castel del Monte's architectural marvels.

DETAILED ITINERARY

Day 1: Arrival In Bari - Drive To Trani

Begin your Puglia adventure with a warm welcome at Bari airport, where your Personal Concierge awaits to assist you in picking up your rental car. A scenic 40-minute drive brings you to Trani, a delightful coastal city offering a perfect base for exploration.

Day 2: Free Day In Trani

Take advantage of a leisurely day in Trani to immerse yourself in its rich history, from the magnificent **Cathedral of S. Nicola Pellegrino** to the imposing **Castle built by Frederick II**. Explore nearby attractions such as **Barletta** and **Canne**, steeped in ancient lore, or marvel at the enigmatic **Dolmens** and **Menhirs** dotting the landscape.

Day 3: Alta Murgia National Park & Castel Del Monte

Embark on a journey to **Alta Murgia National Park**, where the striking landscape sets the stage for the awe-inspiring **Castel del Monte**. Dive into the castle's secrets with an English-speaking guide before exploring the charming town of **Altamura** and savoring its renowned **Pane di Altamura**.

Day 4: Alberobello & Castellana Grotte

Discover the UNESCO World Heritage Trulli district in Alberobello, with its unique cone-shaped dwellings, before venturing underground to explore the mesmerizing

Castellana Caves.

Day 5: Free Day In Vieste
Indulge in the beauty of Vieste, the Pearl of Gargano, with its breathtaking coastline and historic landmarks like the **_Swabian Castle_** and the **_Cathedral of the Assumption_**. Wander through the city's labyrinthine streets and soak in its Mediterranean charm.

Day 6: Gargano National Park & The Umbra Forest
Explore the diverse landscapes of Gargano, characterized by lush pine forests and dramatic cliffs. Venture into the **_Umbra Forest_**, a haven of ancient oaks and wildlife, and discover prehistoric treasures like the **_Paglicci Cave_**.

Day 7: Explore The Gargano Coast & Tremiti Islands
Embark on a scenic drive along the Gargano coast, visiting charming villages like **_Vico del Gargano_** and **_Monte Sant'Angelo_**. Alternatively, unwind on the pristine beaches of **_Mattinata_** or embark on a day trip to the idyllic **_Tremiti Islands._**

Day 8: Farewell To Apulia!
Conclude your journey with fond memories as you bid farewell to Apulia, returning your rental car at the airport before departing for your next adventure. Safe travels!

BONUS CHAPTER

OFF THE BEATEN PATH: SECRET GEMS & HIDDEN TREASURES

Among Puglia lesser-known but remarkable destinations lies **_Grecia Salentina_**, often referred to as the _Greece of Salento_. Throughout history, Southern Italy has been home to numerous Greek settlements, collectively known as **_Magna Graecia_**. These settlements span across various regions, including Calabria, Basilicata, Sicily, and notably, Puglia. Situated at the southern tip of Puglia, **_Grecia Salentina_** encompasses eleven towns: Sternatia, Melpignano, Martignano, Calimera, Carpignano Salentino, Corigliano d'Otranto, Castrignano dei Greci, Martano, Soleto, Zollino, and Cutrofiano.

In many of these towns, locals still speak Griko, a dialect influenced by both Modern Greek and Italian. While not typically considered a top destination in Puglia, exploring the picturesque towns and villages of Grecia Salentina offers a journey through time, showcasing the coexistence of two distinct cultures over centuries.

CASAMASSIMA, BARI

For those seeking unique experiences in Puglia, a visit to Casamassima, a small village in the province of Bari and part of the Authentic Villages of Italy, is highly recommended. This charming medieval village revolves around an 8th-century Norman tower, which evolved into a residential "castle." Casamassima's distinctiveness lies in the color of its houses, painted blue. Legend has it that in the 17th century, the duke who acquired Casamassima made a vow to the Madonna of Constantinople to shield the village from a plague epidemic. In gratitude, the duke had the houses painted blue, reminiscent of the Madonna's cloak. Referred to as the "Blue Village," Casamassima's unique aesthetic has drawn comparisons to Chefchaouen, Morocco, due to its blue-hued buildings. The village's main attraction is its historic center, characterized by narrow alleys, blue-painted houses, quaint courtyards, and flower-adorned balconies.

CANTINE POLVANERA, BARI

Puglia's favorable climate and extended growing season create ideal conditions for grape cultivation, particularly for indigenous varieties like Primitivo, Negroamaro, and Nero di Troia. Visiting a winery is a fantastic way to experience Puglia, and Cantine Polvanera, a small family-run vineyard near Gioia del Colle, offers an authentic experience. Cantine Polvanera focuses on producing high-quality wines from indigenous grapes and welcomes visitors to tour their cellars and sample their wines. They offer a range of wines, including white, red, rose, and orange varieties. In addition to wine tastings, visitors can enjoy light lunches or wine pairings with local products amidst the vineyard's serene surroundings.

GROTTAGLIE, TARANTO

Grottaglie is a cultural shopping haven in Puglia, renowned for its exquisite ceramics. With a longstanding tradition dating back to ancient times, the town boasts a rich history of pottery production. Grottaglie's landmarks, including the **Church of San Francesco d'Assisi**, feature stunning ceramic displays. For a deeper understanding of Grottaglie's ceramic heritage, the ***Museo della Ceramica*** showcases remarkable artworks. The town is dotted with artisanal ceramics shops, where visitors can browse various styles and even witness the crafting process firsthand.Gr ottaglie offers a unique opportunity to purchase authentic ceramics directly from the artisans, potentially acquiring future family heirlooms.

PORTO CESAREO, LECCE

Porto Cesareo, nestled in the Salento Peninsula, is a hidden gem renowned for its pristine beaches and rich history. The town boasts some of Puglia's most beautiful beaches, such as ***Spiaggia Grande*** and ***Torre Lapillo***, ideal for swimming, snorkeling, and relaxation. Beyond its beaches, Porto Cesareo's historical center, with ancient ruins, museums, and churches, offers a glimpse into its storied past.

Visitors can also explore the nearby ***Isola dei Conigli***, a nature reserve inhabited by a colony of wild rabbits. Peak season is during the summer months, so planning accommodations and activities in advance is advisable, as English may not be widely spoken in the area.

NOCI, BARI

Noci, a hidden gem in Puglia, offers a retreat for those seeking countryside tranquility and authentic Italian cuisine. Founded in the Middle Ages, Noci's narrow streets, whitewashed buildings, and picturesque piazzas evoke a sense of timeless charm. The town's history is evident in its architectural landmarks, including the **Church of San Domenico** and ***megalithic dolmens.*** Noci is renowned for its local delicacies, particularly *orecchiette pasta* and indigenous wines like ***Primitivo and Negroamaro***. Wine festivals are a highlight in Noci, offering opportunities to indulge in regional flavors and celebrations.

SPECCHIA, LEECE

Specchia, nestled in the province of Lecce, is an authentic Italian village ideal for exploring the Salento region. Surrounded by ancient olive trees and situated at a slight elevation, Specchia offers easy access to beautiful beaches and tourist attractions. Named among Italy's Most Beautiful Villages, Specchia enchants visitors with its medieval charm and picturesque main square, **_Piazza del Popolo_**. The village is renowned for its exceptional gelato, adding to the allure of its vibrant local atmosphere.

GIOVINAZZO, BARI

Giovinazzo, a serene coastal town, captivates visitors with its tranquil ambiance and rich history. Nestled along the sea, the town boasts charming architecture, cobbled streets, and enticing restaurants. Less crowded than neighboring towns, Giovinazzo exudes charm and authenticity, offering a quintessential Italian experience. Accessible by road and rail, Giovinazzo is a must-visit for those seeking peaceful surroundings and sumptuous scenery.

SANTA MARIA AL BAGNO BEACH IN LECCE

Located on the Ionian side of Lecce, near Gallipoli, Santa Maria Al Bagno is an ancient fishing village boasting one of Puglia's finest beaches, Spiaggia di Santa Maria Al Bagno, nestled in the town center. With its azure waters and cliff-surrounded coastline adorned with quaint old houses, this hidden gem is a picturesque destination worth exploring.

TORRE GUACETO IN BRINDISI

Contrary to typical scenic beach towns, Torre Guaceto stands out as one of Puglia's top beaches owing to its status as a nature reserve. Situated in the northern province of Brindisi, it offers expansive stretches of pristine white sands and tranquil, crystal-clear waters—a haven for families seeking a day of swimming and snorkeling amidst a backdrop of protected marine life. For those who prefer unspoiled natural beauty and quieter beaches, Torre Guaceto is a must-visit.

PORTO GHIACCIOLO BEACH IN MONOPOLI, BARI

Nestled within Monopoli, Porto Ghiacciolo Beach is a secluded cove, perfect for unwinding and enjoying the tranquility. Often frequented by locals, it offers a serene setting for swimming, sunbathing, and indulging in the local cuisine at nearby restaurants and cafes—a quintessential Italian summer experience away from the crowds.

BITONTO NEAR BARI

Bitonto, a small town near Bari in Puglia, offers a glimpse into the region's rich history and architectural heritage, notably showcased in its 11th and 12th-century cathedral, Duomo di Bitonto. Despite its lack of tourist amenities, Bitonto's authenticity and untouched charm appeal to those seeking an off-the-beaten-path experience, immersing themselves in the local way of life devoid of commercialization.

ORIA IN BRINDISI

Tucked away in the dry lowlands of Salento within the province of Brindisi, Oria remains a hidden gem amidst neighboring tourist hubs like Lecce and Locorotondo. Perched atop a hill, this charming village offers an authentic glimpse into Puglia's past, with remnants of its once-thriving Jewish community. With its historic castle and cathedral, Oria provides a serene retreat away from tourist crowds, ideal for those craving an authentic and tranquil experience.

GROTTE DI CASTELLANA IN BARI

A marvel of nature, Grotte di Castellana offers a unique and captivating experience in Puglia. Spanning 3 kilometers in length and 70 meters in depth, these caves showcase intricate formations and vibrant colors, making it a fascinating destination for exploration. Whether visited during the day or illuminated at night, Grotte di Castellana promises an unforgettable adventure, especially for families with children eager to delve into its wonders.

SCAN THIS QR CODE TO EXPLORE PUGLIA HIDDEN GEMS ON THE MAP

TOP 10 FAMILY-FRIENDLY ACTIVITIES IN PUGLIA

Puglia provides a plethora of engaging experiences for families with children. With its lengthy coastline, breathtaking beaches, intriguing historical landmarks, and delectable cuisine, Puglia offers an ideal setting for a memorable family getaway. Whether you seek sun-soaked beach days, cultural explorations, or culinary adventures, Puglia caters to all interests. In this article, we'll highlight the top 10 child-friendly activities in Puglia, ranging from wandering through picturesque towns to savoring local delicacies and basking on the sunny shores of the Adriatic and Ionian Seas.

1. Explore Alberobello: A UNESCO World Heritage Site renowned for its iconic trulli houses with cone-shaped roofs, Alberobello captivates children with its fairy-tale-like ambiance and enchanting narrow streets.

2. Discover Castellana Caves: Delve into the mesmerizing underground world of the Castellana Caves, offering thrilling adventures for kids amidst intricate karst formations and customizable tour options suitable for all ages.

3. Embark on a Zoosafari Tour: Experience the excitement of a wildlife park near Fasano, featuring a captivating combination of a drive-through safari and an amusement park with opportunities to feed animals and observe them up close.

4. Enjoy a Day at Sandy Apulian Beaches: Relax on Puglia's pristine sandy beaches, perfect for families with designated areas equipped with games and amenities for children, such as Torre Guaceto, a nature reserve offering guided tours and marine exploration activities.

5. Take a Boat Tour for Dolphin Watching: Set sail in the northern Ionian Sea with the Jonian Dolphin Conservation for a chance to observe dolphins in their natural habitat, providing an educational and unforgettable experience for kids.

6. Participate in Fishing Tourism: Engage in responsible tourism activities with Pugliavventura's Fishing Tourism program, allowing children to learn about marine environments and traditional fishing practices aboard a fishing boat.

7. Experience Adventure at Indiana Park: Immerse yourself in an exhilarating adventure at Indiana Park, an adrenaline-fueled adventure park nestled in a scenic oak forest, offering thrilling acrobatic courses suitable for all ages.

8. Visit the Dinosaur Park: Delight children with a visit to the Dinosaur Park in Castellana Grotte, showcasing life-size dinosaur replicas based on fossils discovered worldwide, providing an educational and exciting experience.

9. Go Horseback Riding: Discover the beauty of Puglia on horseback with numerous riding schools offering scenic countryside rides, carriage tours, and beachside adventures suitable for both beginners and experienced riders.

10. Spend a Day at Aquapark Egnazia: Enjoy a splashing good time at Aquapark Egnazia, one of southern Italy's largest water parks, featuring water games, pools, and endless fun for children of all ages.

TOP PUGLIAN ROMANTIC EXPERIENCES

The picturesque countryside, quaint historic villages, rich cultural traditions, and idyllic seaside destinations of Puglia make it an ideal location to fulfill your romantic dreams. Increasingly favored by couples from around the globe, a Puglia honeymoon promises to be a magical beginning to a lifetime of happiness together. Immerse yourselves in the breathtaking natural beauty of Puglia, where enchanting landscapes await. From the renowned "masserie" of Salento with their ancient olive groves to the iconic "Trulli" in Valle d'Itria, Puglia offers a perfect backdrop for romantic moments, whether you prefer a rustic or luxurious setting. Whether you choose to spend your evenings watching the sunset on the beach or embark on a day-long adventure exploring charming towns, Puglia's diverse landscape sets the stage for romance. Here are the 10 best romantic experiences not to be missed during your Puglia honeymoon.

1. DINE IN A CAVE AT GROTTA PALAZZESE RESTAURANT
Indulge in a candlelit gourmet dinner at Grotta Palazzese Restaurant, nestled within a limestone cave in Polignano a Mare. With its mystical ambiance and panoramic views of the Adriatic Sea, this renowned restaurant offers an unforgettable dining experience.

2. WANDER AMONG THE TRULLI OF ALBEROBELLO
Explore the enchanting town of Alberobello, famous for its unique Trulli houses. Lose yourselves in the narrow streets of the Rione Monti district, where clusters of Trulli create a fairy-tale atmosphere, especially magical after dark.

3. STAY IN ROMANTIC HOTELS
Experience the romance of Puglia's Valle d'Itria by staying in a luxury Trullo resort or an elegant masseria. Whether you prefer the rustic charm of a Trullo or the refined ambiance of a luxury hotel like Masseria Torre Maizza or Hotel Don Ferrante, Puglia offers accommodations to suit every romantic taste.

4. SWIM IN THE POETRY CAVE
Discover the breathtaking Poetry Cave, a natural seawater swimming pool near Roca Vecchia in Salento. With its crystal-clear waters and captivating scenery, this hidden gem is perfect for a romantic escape.

5. EXPLORE THE TREMITI ISLANDS
Escape to the secluded paradise of the Tremiti Islands, where azure seas and rocky coasts create a romantic backdrop for your adventures. Explore historic landmarks, stroll along nature trails, or snorkel in the pristine waters together.

6. TAKE A ROMANTIC ROAD TRIP
Embark on a romantic road trip through the scenic Itria Valley, where ancient olive trees, vineyards, and panoramic vistas await. Drive from town to town in a vintage car, sampling regional delights and admiring UNESCO heritage sites along the way.

7. CHARTER A YACHT FOR A VIP EXPERIENCE

Treat yourselves to a VIP experience by chartering a luxury yacht and exploring the picturesque coastline of Puglia. Whether you opt for a romantic dinner cruise or a private day trip, sailing the azure waters of the Adriatic Sea is sure to create lasting memories.

8. EXPERIENCE A ROMANTIC GETAWAY IN TRANI

Spend a romantic day exploring the historic city of Trani, with its Romanesque Cathedral and charming old town. Wander through narrow streets, visit medieval churches, and savor a romantic dinner overlooking the sea.

9. RELAX IN APULIA SPAS

Indulge in pampering treatments and unwind together at one of Apulia's luxurious spas. From indoor pools to steam rooms, these spas offer a variety of services to relax and rejuvenate body and soul.

10. EXPLORE THE ITRIA VALLEY'S WHITE VILLAGES

Discover the charming white villages of the Itria Valley, where whitewashed walls and cobblestone streets create a romantic ambiance. Explore Locorotondo, Cisternino, and Ostuni hand in hand, taking in the panoramic views and vibrant culture.

ROMANTIC HOTELS IN PUGLIA (RECOMMENDATION)

Luxury Retreat: Masseria Torre Maizza 5*, Savelletri Di Fasano
Nestled within a sprawling estate with panoramic views of the glistening Adriatic Sea, Masseria Torre Maizza offers a luxurious escape steeped in rustic Italian charm. Set amidst ancient olive groves and fragrant orange trees, this exquisite hotel occupies a meticulously restored 18th-century watchtower, once sought after by pilgrims and monks for its sanctuary-like ambiance. While its historic roots evoke a sense of tranquility, Masseria Torre Maizza also excels in curating unique and unforgettable experiences for guests. From horseback riding to wine-tasting at local wineries, and gourmet bicycle tours to nearby mozzarella farms and olive oil estates, every moment promises to be memorable.

Mid-Range Gem: Hotel Don Ferrante 5*, Monopoli
Discover the allure of Hotel Don Ferrante, nestled within the charming confines of Monopoli Old Town, where an ancient fortress meets the serene sea. This captivating boutique hotel, boasting only 10 rooms, offers an intimate retreat perfect for romantic getaways. From the moment you awaken to the gentle sea breeze to the soothing lullaby of the calm waves as you drift to sleep, Hotel Don Ferrante envelops you in an enchanting ambiance. Unwind, relax, and savor every moment, as you ponder whether life could possibly be more blissful.

Budget-Friendly Retreat: Abate Masseria Resort, Noci
Step into the charming world of Abate Masseria Resort, a delightful retreat nestled within an ancient ploughman's residence dating back to the 17th century. Once an agricultural hub and a place of worship for local farmers, this quaint hotel offers a unique blend of traditional Puglian architecture and modern comforts. Surrounded by lush forests and olive groves, Abate Masseria Resort provides a serene backdrop for a romantic escape. Immerse yourself in the tranquility of nature and create cherished memories amidst the rustic charm of this hidden gem.

CONCLUSION

Puglia stands as an unparalleled destination brimming with history, natural beauty, culinary delights, and immersive experiences waiting to be explored. From the charming towns of the Gargano Peninsula to the picturesque landscapes of Terra di Bari, the enchanting allure of the Itria Valley, and the sun-kissed shores of Salento, every corner of Puglia offers a unique and unforgettable adventure.

Whether you seek cultural enrichment, gastronomic indulgence, or simply the joy of discovering hidden gems, Puglia exceeds expectations at every turn. As you navigate its winding streets, savor its delectable cuisine, and immerse yourself in its rich traditions, you'll find yourself captivated by the timeless allure of this enchanting region.

With careful planning, an open heart, and a spirit of adventure, your journey through Puglia promises to be nothing short of extraordinary. So pack your bags, embrace the warmth of Puglian hospitality, and embark on a journey that will leave you with cherished memories to last a lifetime. Grazie e arrivederci, until we meet in the heart of Puglia's splendor.

Printed in Great Britain
by Amazon